HARVEY PENICK

HARVEY PENICK

*The Life and Wisdom of the Man
Who Wrote the Book on Golf*

◆

Kevin Robbins

Houghton Mifflin Harcourt
BOSTON   NEW YORK
2016

For information about permission to reproduce selections from this book,
write to trade.permissions@hmhco.com or to Permissions, Houghton Mifflin Harcourt
Publishing Company, 3 Park Avenue, 19th Floor, New York, New York 10016.

www.hmhco.com

Library of Congress Cataloging-in-Publication Data
Names: Robbins, Kevin.
Title: Harvey Penick : the life and wisdom of the man
who wrote the book on golf / Kevin Robbins.
Description: Boston : Houghton Mifflin Harcourt, [2016]
Includes bibliographical references and index.
Identifiers: LCCN 2015037555 | ISBN 9780544148499 (hardcover)
ISBN 9780544149076 (ebook)
Subjects: LCSH: Penick, Harvey. | Golf coaches — United States — Biography.
Classification: LCC GV964.P44 R64 2016 | DDC 796.352092 — dc23
LC record available at http://lccn.loc.gov/2015037555

Book design by Chloe Foster

Printed in the United States of America
DOC 10 9 8 7 6 5 4 3 2 1

Excerpts from Harvey Penick's correspondence are courtesy of the Harvey and
Tinsley Penick Collection, Stark Center, University of Texas.

For Suzy

What is it about Harvey that the world fell in love with? I think it was his spirit. He was always wisely powerful, always positive. Harvey spoke in simple words, and if you listened, sooner or later you understood.

— BUD SHRAKE, at the funeral for Harvey Penick, April 5, 1995

Contents

Introduction

ON A STICKY Texas morning in the late summer of 2013, the only son of Harvey Morrison Penick settled into a heavy wooden chair and prepared to trace the arc of time. He sat less than two miles from where his father once had an epiphany, then thought to buy a cheap notebook, fetch a ballpoint pen, and sit down to write.

Tinsley Penick unraveled a button-and-clasp archival box that September morning with long, curved fingers. They were the fingers of a golfer, just like those of his dad, and those of the many champions who absorbed their swingcraft from Harvey's short, infrequent, yet potent words. At seventy-five, Tinsley resembled his late father in sharp silhouette: tall, lean, brittle, abrupt joints, a frame bent at the hips in a posture of modest supplication. But he most evoked Harvey in the length of his face, which carried the same narrow nose and crisp, gentle, topaz eyes that had seemed to parse the movement of a golf swing at the level of an atom.

"Let me get my glasses," Tinsley said.

There was no sound but his airy voice that morning in the H.J. Lutcher Stark Center for Physical Culture and Sports, a gallery space and research facility on the fifth floor of Darrell K Royal–Texas Memorial Stadium in Austin. The box he prepared to open held the notebook that his father maintained for more than half of the twentieth century. No one knows precisely when Harvey began recording his notes, but it was certainly sometime in the early 1930s, more than a decade after he became, at the age of eighteen, the first Texas-born golf professional. No one knows when he wrote his last note either.

Yet millions of people around the world now know the essence of those words left in dainty strokes of ink. They are some of the most famous observations about golf in the history of the ancient game. They're the ideas that became *Harvey Penick's Little Red Book* and four subsequent titles — not counting a twentieth-anniversary edition of the original published the year Tinsley met with me on the campus of the University of Texas to page through the 6,365 words in the Scribbletex notebook together for the first time.

This project began, in a circular way, on Christmas Day 1992. I wasn't much of a golfer then. But I did hope to become one, and that connected me to Harvey and his book.

My maternal grandmother, a kindly hairdresser named Lola Martin who played golf to an excessive handicap but found high joy in the random and wicked vagaries of the game, left the *Little Red Book* for me in bright wrapping paper under her hand-cut Christmas tree in Raytown, a suburb of Kansas City, Missouri. It's been with me through my many moves from city to city, from shelf to shelf, and finally to Texas.

Texas is where I did become the player I hoped to be. It's where I met Tom Kite and Ben Crenshaw and Tinsley Penick and the hundreds of other golfers who populate the sprawling tree of influence that Harvey left when he died quietly in his home as the sun set one April evening in 1995. I wish my grandmother could see me now, writing the early words of the first biography of Harvey. The last time I saw her, she was in a nursing home, where she had been for a long time, rendered infirm by a series of strokes. When she became so frail that my mother summoned the family home to Missouri, the grandchildren took turns sitting at her bedside overnight so our grandmother would not be alone. It was my night to sit when she died, with my hand resting on her arm.

"From Grandma Martin," she had written inside the cover of my *Little Red Book.* The book became my bellwether, not only because my grandmother had given it to me, but because, to me and millions like me, it felt like a sacred text, close to holy for anyone who wants to play in the fewest swings and divine the richest pleasures of the game. I've read those 175 pages so often that the spine of the book has begun to disintegrate, and now it's as delicate as an old rubber band. I can tell which of the seventy-nine tiny chapters — call them lessons if you wish — resonated most with me in 1992. I marked them with an X in red ink on the table of contents. The most important ones got two.

"All of these things in here I've heard many, many times," Tinsley said as he followed his father's words with his fingernail. We were halfway through the notebook, and I'd been watching for about an hour as Tinsley traced the blue-lined pages. Years after Harvey's death, the Penick family donated to the Stark Center the many cardboard boxes of newspaper clippings, interview transcripts, magazine stories, photographs, relics, books, albums, audio recordings, and videotapes they had collected about Harvey. The family had curated the life of a man who rarely left the tight radius enveloping the home where he was born, the four other houses he owned, the three Austin Country Club locations where he taught, and the plot where he is buried under a wide Texas live oak, marked by a modest stone where people leave golf balls for the caretakers to collect. But the boxes in the Stark Center validate a monumental existence: Harvey's reach in golf crossed continents and generations, and it is hard to imagine the birth of golf in the American Southwest taking place without him.

Tinsley and I talked some, but mostly we just read together in silence, as people do with priceless texts in museums. We paused at a page near the back, where Harvey had noted in the light lead of a pencil an observation that his pupil Kathy Whitworth, who won a record eighty-eight times on the LPGA Tour, had once shared with the *Dallas Morning News.*

"Harvey was to me what Merlin was to King Arthur," the shaky cursive read.

This is a story about a Merlin and his vast court of King Arthurs.

· · ·

Tinsley introduced himself to me at the door of his house in early 2005. He had invited me to his house in the hills of northwest Austin, where he lived in retirement with his cheerful wife, Betty Ann, to tell me about Harvey. We sat in the bright sunlight of their living room and talked for a story I was preparing to mark the tenth anniversary of his father's death, which was a solemn occasion in Austin, the city that still loved him and always will.

I told Tinsley about my grandmother. I told him about the marks in my *Little Red Book.* I revealed to him that I thought his father meant as much to modern golf as carbon means to the universe, because I'd already written this line, even before the first interview: "In death, Penick lives."

My editors at the *Austin American-Statesman* evidently agreed with that rather sweeping assertion. The line ran above the fold on April 5, 2005, on the front page.

We didn't know it at the time, but Tinsley and I were having the earliest conversations for this biography, the first comprehensive treatment of Harvey's life beyond the anecdotes that he and Bud Shrake sprinkled like cane sugar inside the four books they wrote together.

Harvey lived for ninety years. He was born when only two golf courses existed in Texas. It was an era of hickory shafts, sand greens, and plucky little caddies like Harvey, who fell under the spell of golf as an eight-year-old boy carrying a handful of clubs for a quarter at a ragged little country club with a tree that provided members with a good place to tether their mounts. By the time of his death, a week before a graceful Masters Tournament whose outcome will forever defy reason and logic, Harvey had seen hickory evolve into steel and graphite. Over the course of almost eighty years, he had witnessed a parade of great American players, from Francis Ouimet and his stunning victory at the 1913 U.S. Open to Bobby Jones and Walter Hagen, from Jack Nicklaus to Tiger Woods, from Betsy Rawls to Mickey Wright and Kathy Whitworth, from Byron Nelson and Ben Hogan to Ben Crenshaw and Tom Kite. Many of them had been his pupils. That made them his friends.

He chose a quiet, uncomplicated, and uncluttered existence, even when he was a famous and wealthy author whose name readers saw in the *New York Times*. "It didn't take much for him to be happy," Crenshaw told me in the spring of 2014. "He had a wonderful job that he loved. He had a lot of fulfillment, helping people." Harvey spent most of his life in close proximity to a creaking two-story house on Cedar Street in central Austin, near the northern edge of the University of Texas campus, where his parents raised him and his four brothers. Three Penick boys caddied at Austin Country Club. Harvey was the youngest. The other two left the club, but Harvey never did. Even after he retired as the club's head professional in 1971, he remained for more than twenty years as the starter at the first tee and the most respected instructor in Texas. He never left teaching. "Harvey knows as much about the basics of golf as any man in the world," the great Byron Nelson once remarked. Harvey never stopped learning. He never quit watching with those topaz Penick eyes. When people wonder where Harvey learned his covenants of golf, the answer is clear. He saw them.

Harvey lived a singular and, some would say, one-dimensional life. He took his family on one vacation, to the Texas coast in 1946. There is one picture of that occasion. Everything else he did, he did in the service of golf. He spent almost every day of the week at the country club, first as a caddie, then as a shop assistant, then as a head professional, then as a starter — for seventy years a teacher, for his entire life a disciple.

Harvey followed the paths of his Scottish forebears, men who rose from the caddie yard to become the earliest golf professionals in America. He was, in the exquisite words of the incomparable Herbert Warren Wind, a "fine example of the old American pro, the homebred who had spent all of his life in the game, gathering knowledge as a stone gathers lichen." In the early 1900s, Americans such as Harvey came to the golf profession by learning to shave hickory shafts, file the beveled edges of irons at a workbench, and bind the whipping around crude ferrules where the heads and shafts met, by watching a lot of golf, both good and bad, and by playing it. No one that far back went to school to study golf. No one took tests or studied merchandising or agronomy or business. Instead, they went outside to practice and teach and think. The education of a golf professional in those years came from watching and doing.

And writing. Harvey wrote down many notes about the game. He jotted them on pieces of paper that he stored in his desk, and when the volume reached a level of impending chaos, he drove to the store and purchased a bound Scribbletex notebook, 9⅛ inches tall by 5¾ inches wide, manufactured in Texas by Southwest Tablet of Dallas, with fifty sheets, ruled on both sides in blue. It was the kind of notebook a student might buy for English class. The cover was red.

Harvey tabbed his pages under sections: *swing, lie, turn,* and the like. He wrote in blue, black, and green ink, and sometimes with a number 2 pencil. He did not write down ideas. He did not write down theories. What he did write down were truths. Harvey filled his Scribbletex with cold, unadorned proof: drills and images and aphorisms that he believed because he had seen them work, time and time again. They were neither fanciful nor complex. They were the earliest whispers of what would become the most popular and best-selling sports book of all time.

When he finished an entry, Harvey would store the notebook in his heavy wooden rolltop desk, in view of no one but his son, and not then until many years after he'd begun writing in it. It was his personal effect, and it might have remained no more than that but for a windy day in 1991 when Harvey—eighty-seven years old, frail, diminished, exhausted, and acutely aware of his own mortality—listened to his conscience.

"One morning last spring I was sitting in my golf cart under the trees on the grass near the veranda at Austin Country Club," Harvey wrote in the opening chapter of the *Little Red Book,* published in 1992.

> I was with my nurse, Penny, a patient young woman who drives us in my golf cart a few blocks from home on days when I feel well enough for the journey. I don't stay more than an hour or two on each visit,

and I don't go more than three or four times a week because I don't want the members to think of me as a ghost that refuses to go away. I don't want to cut into the teaching time of any of our fine club professionals, either. I can see Jackson Bradley out teaching on the practice line, and there are moments when I might want to make suggestions, but I don't do it. However, I can't refuse to help when my old friend Tommy Kite, the leading money winner in the history of the game, walks over to my cart and asks if I will watch him putt for a while. Tommy asks almost shyly, as if afraid I might not feel strong enough. His request makes my heart leap with joy.

Harvey reflected a great deal as an older man. He had the time for contemplation now that he was no longer required to sustain the schedule he once kept.

I spend nights staring at the ceiling, thinking of what I have seen Tommy [Kite] doing in tournaments on television, and praying that he will come see me. If Tommy wants, I will break my rule that I never visit the club on weekends, and will have Penny drive me to the putting green to meet with Tommy on Saturday and Sunday morning, as well as on Thursday and Friday. I know it exasperates Penny that I would rather watch Tommy putt than eat the lunch she has to force on me.

Bud Shrake, a novelist, screenwriter, and former *Sports Illustrated* reporter who lived in the hills near Austin Country Club, was sitting with Harvey in a golf cart one spring afternoon in '91. A shiny Texas grackle hopped through the branches above. Squirrels skittered through the Saint Augustine grass. Harvey wondered: Had he been selfish? Was it wrong to hoard this knowledge of his? Had he been granted these eighty-seven years of life, more than seventy-eight of them in the company of golf, so that he would pass along what he had learned?

Yes, he decided. Yes, he had.

"I want to show you something that nobody except Tinsley has ever read," Harvey told Shrake. He handed him the Scribbletex. "Would you get it into shape to be published?"

The two of them met every Saturday morning for months. Shrake recorded their visits on cassette tapes, audio archives that capture the voice and spirit of a man who spoke about golf and life in the same sentence. Their interactions were brief. Harvey was getting weaker. But he was committed to the *Little Red Book*. Writing it and the other books gave him reason to live. He survived until his friends came to tell him, on the Sunday afternoon before the 1995 Masters, about a bronze statue of Harvey and Kite unveiled that afternoon near the veranda at his club. He died knowing they thought it was perfect.

Harvey was buried in an old cemetery in Austin, just blocks from the original Austin Country Club, where his life's work had begun in 1912. On the morning of his funeral, passersby on Loop 360 could glance to the east of Pennybacker Bridge, which spanned Lake Austin, and notice that the flags at the club hung at half-stick.

Ten years later, Shrake and I talked about that day for the story I was preparing for the *Austin American-Statesman*. He said, "More than anyone I have ever known, Harvey lived his life by the Golden Rule. That quality may be at the bottom of what has attracted the world to him."

The books Shrake wrote with Harvey hint at that life. They reflect on the players who learned under Harvey: Kite and Crenshaw; Whitworth and Rawls and Betsy Cullen; Davis Love Jr., who played for Harvey at the University of Texas, and his son Davis Love III; Wright and the Sandras, Palmer and Haynie; amateurs Ed White, who won an NCAA Championship under Harvey at Texas, and the incomparable but doomed Morris Williams Jr., who nearly won a national championship himself and surely would have captured many professional titles had he lived long enough.

Harvey's books endure as meditative and personal testimonies about encounters with greatness, about the rise of golf in Texas before Texas became the important golf state it is now, about what changes and what remains the same, and about the meaning of friendship. The books sketch a life richly lived, but their scraps of anecdote leave spaces in that life. This book is an attempt to fill in those spaces.

I remember my last visit in 2005 with Shrake, who was trying to explain to me the undertaking he embraced that morning when Harvey summoned him to his cart under the trees.

"It was like a sacred obligation," Shrake said.

So this is for me.

KEVIN ROBBINS

PART I

THE YARD

Chapter One

IN THE DINING ROOM named for him at Austin Country Club, among the artifacts on the latte walls and the awards and the letters from U.S. presidents (two) and winners of major championships (many more), there is no evidence that Harvey Penick ever had a childhood. The pictures are all of a man. The man is on a golf course, holding a golf club, wearing golf clothes, talking to a golfer, or, in the case of a portrait that hangs between two glass cases of mementos, pondering a life in golf. On a piece of old paper, the handwriting of a man notes the principles of a proper golf grip and the essence of ball position. The earliest picture of Harvey appears to have been made when he was in his late teens. He already was a full-time head golf professional.

Over there is a framed letter from Bobby Jones, typed on January 6, 1960. On the far wall, a blue-ink note from Kathy Whitworth was signed in 1997 with a salutation of love. Pictures of Patty Berg and Betty Hicks and Mickey Wright, each of them addressed to Harvey, are arranged near a piece of White House stationery bearing a message of gratitude from President George H. W. Bush to Harvey; at the other end of the room, President Bill Clinton's letter of condolence to Harvey's wife Helen is propped up in an inexpensive frame under a woolen newsboy cap. There are pictures of golf teams, pictures of men who won the Masters Tournament, and pictures of men who won the U.S. Open Championship sitting with Harvey and smiling. There are black-and-white photographs that are turning yellow. There are medals and proclamations and certificates from events such as the 1942 Hale American National Open. There are so many references here to the man Harvey Penick and his place in the sport that it's easy to overlook the eight-year-old boy who wondered, in the year 1912, what to do now.

The bustling city of Austin had paved the street a block over from the Penick household on Cedar Street, where the quiet, twig-thin boy lived with his parents and older brothers. Cedar Street, like the rest of Harvey's orbit back then, was bald Texas dirt scraped by wind—less a street than a path with wagon ruts and hoofprints. It was short enough that the entire length could be viewed from the porch of the Penick house, broad enough that the milk cow could be walked in the morning with the wagons chittering from Seekatz Meat Market with sacks of flank, and far enough from Congress Avenue that no one heard the streetcars hissing. The Penick family of Austin lived a long way from the city center in 1913. From his bedroom window upstairs, Harvey could peel open the cotton curtains, look out over the tops of the live oaks, and see the end of everywhere.

North.

Harvey was eight years old that summer, and he had heard fanciful stories about Fort Worth and Dallas, about the stockyards and the bank buildings and the clothiers for men who favored seersucker in the summer and merino wool in winter. A lot of boys Harvey knew at Pease Elementary School carried reasonable hopes of growing a fortune in Texas. A lot of money was made and spent up there, two hundred miles away, in the two cities that most defined the state. But Harvey never cared much for money.

East.

New wealth could also be found in Houston and the surrounding towns that seemed to float on oil and oil money. Four years before Harvey was born, the Lucas No. 1 well coughed up a fury of mud, gas, and black syrup: Spindletop, near Beaumont, ripped the young and still-developing state from its agrarian roots and thrust it into the soon-booming age of big energy. Many of Harvey's friends yearned to one day buy a morning ticket for the interurban rail down at the union depot at Congress and Cypress, settle in for the daylong ride to the bulging oil camps, arrive that evening for a supper of Gulf catch, and wake to hard, dirty work and the promise of certain prosperity. But that sounded to Harvey like such an unhappy way to live.

South.

Beyond San Antonio, cowboys tended cattle on vast swaths of fertile land in the Rio Grande Valley. All the children in Austin knew of King Ranch. It was the biggest and the best ranch in the entire West. If an ambitious young stowaway from Manhattan could survive oppressive drought and grow a 15,000-acre Mexican land-grant purchase into a livestock empire of more than 146,000 acres — Richard King and his partners even created the first American breed of beef cattle within its fences — then a boy from dusty Cedar Street could rustle a few such animals for an honest wage. But Harvey never had the wandering spirit of a cowboy.

West.

West was the desert. West was six hundred miles of prickly pear cactus and mesquite trees and blinding sun through no clouds all the way to El Paso on the edge of Mexico. West was the ragged Davis Mountains and the yawning Big Bend to be explored; deep and dry canyons to cross on the way; cold springs to swim; frontiers to conquer; and factual and imagined rigors that Harvey and his friends read about in their schoolbooks. There lay the romance of the American West. West was rugged. West was hostile. Some of Harvey's adventurous classmates were eager to confront the sands of the Chihuahuan Desert. They might not stop until they got to California. Maybe the Pacific.

Harvey knew he wasn't built for that. So he stood at his window and stared out.

He wondered what he would be, what he would do, where he would go. But he also understood that as a boy of eight in a family of seven, he needed to be useful and, when possible, out from underfoot. He knew sacrifice at a young age. His older brother Tom, tougher than Harvey and gritty, had taken an interesting job a short walk from Cedar Street at a place the gentlemen called Austin Country Club, which had a curious hub of recreation called a golf course, the only one in town. Tom Penick was something called a caddie. Harvey knew nothing about caddies or golf or gentlemen, but he knew the work paid in coins, because his brother dumped out his pockets at night and Harvey saw them on the chest of drawers. Money. Tom had money. He also had stories of playing a game that gave people fits of frustration and, when the ball flew just right, a dizzy kind of joy.

Fourteen years earlier, the gentlemen strode in their stiff collars and black coats along Congress Avenue. The first paved road in the capital city of Texas, it was still unimproved in 1899. Some in the group passed the limestone facade of the Hancock Opera House, owned by the mayor. John Philip Sousa and Lillian Russell performed there when they toured this far south and west.

Some walked south from the university, along the Austin Electric Railway Line and past the smudged windows of the Raatz Department Store. Blocks away, the *Ben Hur* steamboat churned into port on the Colorado River, known then as Lake McDonald. A Model A sputtered. Horses clopped through the silt. Wagons rattled through ruts. The men in their business attire monitored their pocket watches that November afternoon in Austin. The time neared 4:30.

They gathered on bustling Sixth Street, shook hands outside the opulent Driskill Hotel, stepped inside the columned lobby with marble floors, and swung open the tall and consequential doors of Austin golf.

Lewis Hancock, the son of a former member of the Texas House of Representatives and the prosperous owner of the opera house, had invited seventy-five acquaintances to the important meeting that day. Twenty-five of them came. It was a Monday, November 13, nearly two decades since Hancock had graduated magna cum laude from the law school at Harvard, where he met friends from the East who traveled widely. Some of them had returned from as far away as Scotland, where, they reported, they had seen the most interesting sight: grown men occupied with balls and sticks on the windswept pastureland of the coasts, called *links*. Hancock was intrigued. His Harvard friends told him the Scots called it *golf.*

Hancock opened his opera house after law school and became a banker in Austin. He mingled with a privileged demographic in the capital of Texas, where a wobbly state government and the sixteen-year-old University of Texas attracted families of imagination, energy, and means. Austin was still a modest town on the edge of the American frontier, registering fewer than 22,000 residents on the eve of the twentieth century. It offered croquet fields, baseball diamonds, a racehorse track, and a fledgling UT football team with an eight-game season and a brewing rivalry with the Fightin' Aggies of Texas A&M a hundred hard miles away in College Station. But it had nowhere to play golf.

Few places in Texas did. Only Dallas and the port city of Galveston had golf courses by that time, one course apiece. But the game was spreading fast. In 1896, when the Dallas Golf and Country Club was established, barely eighty courses existed in the forty-five United States of America. Four years later, there were 982.

The Dallas Golf and Country Club opened with a crude set of holes and rumpled sand greens, which preceded the Tom Bendelow–designed creation that would follow nine years later. The course in Galveston was noteworthy only because it was on the brink of obliteration: in September 1900, less than a year from the afternoon when Hancock gaveled his meeting to order, a hurricane would bury the teeming island in angry Gulf waters, drown more than six thousand people, and erase any suggestion that a golf stroke had ever been executed there.

By the time Hancock finished his invitation list, the Apple Tree Gang of transplanted Scots was in its twelfth year of cursing bad bounces, rimmed putts, badly sliced niblicks, and forever-lost balls on the Yonkers orchard that became the Saint Andrews Golf Club, the oldest continuously existing course in the nation. Other manifestations of the game had come and gone. Early forms had even been tendered as near to Austin as San Antonio, seventy miles to the south, where a British statesman and House of Commons member named John Cumming Macdona fashioned nine temporary golf holes in 1887 on the parade ground at Fort Sam Houston. He tied bandanas to sticks, plunged them into the earth, and showed the early Texans how to take dead aim with a gutta-percha ball. The spectators were amused but uninspired to salvage the curious course from the pounding of U.S. Infantry boots. The Macdona course vanished before the divots grew back.

Back in Austin, Hancock sensed an opportunity to bring golf to his people. Smitten with its possibilities, he made a list of possible participants, men with sound sporting instincts and a predilection for adventure. He requested a meeting room at the Driskill, the finest hotel in the city, and waited to address a room full of enthusiasts clamoring, as he was, for the creation of a formal club.

That day he welcomed men such as William H. Bell, the director of the Austin National Bank, and David A. McFall, a judge and newspaper editor. Also in attendance were Robert West, an attorney; David Franklin Houston, a professor and the future president of the university; James Clever, a physician; Richard Corner, the owner of a bookstore; Colonel C. L. Test, a Rough Rider and expert marksman; and Joseph Thorburn, a cotton merchant. Professors of botany, education, Latin, oratory, philosophy, and political science rounded out the attendance that November afternoon, when the rise of a humble but transcendent golf professional named Harvey Penick became possible.

The gathering at the Driskill decided that afternoon to form the blandly named Austin Golf Club, with "goods, chattels, rights, credits, and assets" of $150. All twenty-five men agreed heartily to join. The body elected officers, who stipulated in the articles of incorporation that the club "support and maintain a golf club and promote innocent sports." The chairman appointed a committee to secure property, which presented its own set of complications. What kind of land was best for an inland golf course? Should there be water? Trees? Dunes? No one knew. No one there had ever created a golf club. But no one cared enough to bother with small concerns. They were exuberant.

Golf was coming to Austin. The club established a $5 initiation fee, monthly dues of $1, and, after some discussion, a lower fee schedule for women. Austin Golf Club would welcome enthusiasts regardless of which water closet they used.

None of the charter members realized yet what a critical decision that was.

The committee assigned to find land nominated an area north of the city center, "just east of the University, the eastern part of Hyde Park, and the land outside of Hyde Park, and to the east of said park," the *Austin Daily Statesman* noted the next day. "This latter named location, known as the Euck league, was considered the most appropriate, as it was not so public as the other places, and was considered more favorable, as to surroundings." In 1899 that seemed to satisfy the few requirements of early golf in Central Texas.

The officers proposed to lease the one-hundred-acre parcel for five years. It sat far enough from the bustling city—with its streetcars, carriages, saloons, and general stores—to evoke a sense of sanctuary. A large mesquite tree above a small dale offered suitable accommodation for the tethering of a horse and the hanging of a coat, with room for the construction of a clubhouse, should the club determine the need. The limestone bed of Waller Creek tumbled gently through its western third. A subtle crease in the land afforded the chance to negotiate the game on intriguing slopes, but most of the property was flat, simplifying construction demands for the mules and plows tasked with leveling the fairways, such as they were. Also, because the course sat high and exposed in a place vulnerable to a scraping springtime wind from the southeast, nature would play an invisible role, as it did on the sandy linksland courses on the far side of the Atlantic Ocean, the ones Hancock had heard so much about in Harvard Yard.

Houston, the professor and committee chairman, wrote: "It is open and free from trees, is of sufficient extent for any number of holes, is so sloped that the course may begin and end near the same spot, and is reasonably accessible. The owners or their agents have been seen and say that no objection will be made to using the land for golf." Neighborhoods were buffered from the property by surrounding roads, many with no formal names yet. Soon, boys who lived close to the club would walk those roads every afternoon, kicking dust, waiting for a chance to earn a quarter, which seemed like a fortune for the modest assignment of carrying four or five hickory-shafted golf clubs for a couple of hours and poking the grass for errant balls.

Ten blocks away, Daniel and Mollie Penick were raising their five sons in a two-story house on Cedar Street, where their youngest boy, Harvey, looked out from his window and wondered about his world.

The Penicks were new to Austin. Their three oldest sons — Fred, Roger, and Tom — were born near Houston, in Waller County, where Daniel Penick and six of his siblings settled in 1891 after migrating by covered wagon from the Rocky River region of south-central North Carolina. One of twelve siblings, Daniel Penick was named for his grandfather, a Presbyterian minister on the Piedmont plateau. He was two weeks from turning twenty-two when he married Mollie Miller, a native Texan who never vacated her home state. The couple gave their fourth boy, born shortly after they moved from Waller County to Austin, the family name of Tinsley. Their fifth, Harvey, arrived on the twenty-third day of October in 1904.

By that time, the new members of Austin Golf Club were staging handicaps and competing for medals. The nine-hole course only vaguely resembled the ancient links at Carnoustie or Muirfield or Royal Troon: the Texans employed long-handled scythes to open their walking paths in the high grass, mules dragged cedar logs across crusty imperfections to smooth the fairways, and someone sank tomato tins in the ground and judged them to be suitable holes. The members adored it.

The Connerly brothers, born in Alabama and educated at the University of Texas, demonstrated the highest aptitude on the sticky, oily sand greens at the club. In 1904 Bob Connerly became the first Texan to qualify for the national amateur, contested that year at Baltusrol. No one else could manage to finish a nine-hole round in Austin in fewer than a hundred swings. Bob Connerly could break 90.

But the members of Austin Golf Club had causes for joy that had nothing to do with scores. The original clubhouse opened on a Friday evening in June 1901, giving members the option of storing their clubs in formal lockers and imbibing after play in a designated lounging room. The single-story building, built on a slight rise, included a wraparound balcony "built on the style of the old southern home veranda," according to the following day's *Austin Daily Statesman*, which customarily cheered any suggestion of progress at the club. The newspaper called the addition "one of the handsomest little club houses to be found anywhere in the sunny south land" and also noted that the course itself was "considered amongst the best to be secured anywhere."

The article concluded: "The Austin golfers are in a position to rear back on their dignity and reputation and announce to the world that they are the real thing."

Austin continued to grow, providing a stream of potential club members. The population of the city rose to more than 25,000 in 1905, by which time Austin Golf Club was thriving. The staff organized New Year's oyster roasts for the members, whose numbers had reached more than seventy, and afternoon teas for Easter. The membership formed a travel team that competed in home-and-home matches against squads from Waco, Galveston, and San Antonio. Mixed foursomes, made up of men and women members, played friendlies on Wednesday afternoons. The local newspapers posted scores and brief stories about every event at the course and new clubhouse. Austin Golf Club was five years old and permanent.

Meanwhile, ten blocks east of the festivities, Daniel and Mollie Penick had no time for a pastime like golf. Daniel worked nights as an engineer with the city water utility. Mollie had five rambunctious sons to feed and clothe and get to school before the bell. They had the cow to milk in the yard out back, two small barns to fill with alfalfa hay for the family mules, and church to attend on Sunday mornings. Golf was not an option for the modest Penicks of Cedar Street.

But having a way to chase the boys out of the house to earn money was appealing, which is why Daniel and Mollie allowed Tom to walk over to the golf club near Hyde Park and ask whether caddies were needed. They were.

Tom decided that his younger brother, meek as he was, might make a good caddie given his attention to detail, his natural politeness in the company of elders, and his inclination to not speak unless spoken to. Tom told Harvey he'd like to teach him the proper way to carry a handful of hickory clubs and trace the arc of a shot so no ball got lost in the high grass. It was a lot of fun, Tom told his brother. He was even learning to play himself.

Harvey nodded. He almost always was agreeable, especially when there were good times to be had or money to be earned for candy or the cinema. He walked up to Thirty-Eighth Street. He wheeled to the right. His shoes kicked clouds of dust on the seven-block walk that morning in the middle of Texas. He arrived at what looked to his topaz eyes like a puzzle.

He was charmed instantly by the odd happenings in the open meadows of the golf club. He watched men in white cotton shirts and bowler hats hurl wooden-shafted tools — like garden hoes, with smaller blades on the end — at the tiniest ball he had ever seen. The motion of the game amused Harvey. It also intrigued him like nothing in his life ever had. He felt oddly drawn to this place. He felt connected to the ground and the wind and the sun and the trees, as well as the strongest sense that he had been summoned. He had no explanation for it. He found no reason to need one.

Harvey tugged at the trousers draping his thin legs. He marched toward the caddie shack, where Tom had said to meet him.

Harvey never again had to stand at his second-floor bedroom window looking for answers. Now he knew right where he was supposed to be.

Decades later, as he lay near death in his home surrounded by reminders of how much he had meant to the game, Harvey tried to articulate his connection to golf for his fourth book project. "I feel God in the trees and grass and flowers, in the rabbits and the birds and the squirrels, in the sky and water," he wrote. "I feel that I am home." He knew it the moment he arrived at the golf club to have a look around.

But young Harvey didn't know everything. He couldn't predict the sacrifices required by the game to which he had just blindly tethered his life. There would be groggy mornings before dawn, opening the shop for the club members who liked to play in the cool summer dew, and tired evenings after dusk, waiting for the players fitting in late rounds after work. There would be no time for the family he would have: the patient and committed wife who found companionship with friends in her husband's absence and the son and daughter whose later memories of their father would amount to fond recollections of his arrival home after they went to bed. Harvey would make a point of getting home in time to recite prayers with them before they went to sleep. He would do his best to go to church with his family, but Sundays would be busy at the club, with all the lawyers and merchants and university professors hoping to play one more round before the workweek. Harvey would try to see his kids after school, but it would never be for long. He would have lessons to give, a shop to keep, clubs to bind. There would be little time for more in the life of a golf pioneer in Texas.

When he was eight years old and certain that he had found the reason for his life, Harvey didn't know about the time it would take and the toll it would exact.

Tom Penick was five years older than Harvey. Among the Penick boys, he was the roughest, with a surly side. He was scrappy enough to handle himself in the caddie yard, which could be a traumatizing place for the cowardly or weak. Games of dice, poker, and craps filled the empty spaces between jobs. Fistfights erupted. Boys came home with shiners under their eyes and scrapes on their knuckles. But Tom got steady work and found no trouble.

Harvey and his brother Tinsley were nearest in age — less than two years apart — and in spirit. They were quiet, mindful, respectful lads who accepted their places in a family of five boys. They were too young in 1912 to carry golf clubs with their brother, but they wanted to work. They wanted to be outside. They also were curious: why were so many people in Austin swept away by a game involving sticks and balls?

The first recorded competition staged at the club occurred in 1910. The final match of the state amateur competition that year aligned the Connerly brothers, Bob and Fred; Bob won. It was the third of his four consecutive Texas amateur titles.

The first golf competition in Texas had been held in 1903, when forty-four men flailed through two rounds at the Dallas Golf and Country Club. The Texas Golf Association organized three years later in Houston. "PLAYERS ORGANIZE: A Texas Golf Association Has Been Formed," shouted a headline in the *Houston Chronicle*. The group formalized rules, established competitions, and created a sense of community for the trickle of golf professionals arriving from points east. A decade before the emergence of the Professional Golfers' Association (PGA) of America, the TGA was emblematic of the hasty evolution of golf across the nation as the sport expanded from the local club level to include state associations.

The lineage of the profession of golf in Texas began two thousand miles from Austin. The first year-round professional at Austin Golf Club was Willie Maguire, who summered at Wollaston Golf Club near Boston and, thirty years later, would be elected a vice president of the PGA of America. Maguire was part of the typical migration of golf professionals during the era—feisty and unmannered men introduced to the game in the harsh caste system of the caddie yard. Most of them arrived from Boston, Chicago, New York, Philadelphia, and New Jersey. Their clubs went dormant for the cold winters of the Northeast, so these restless professionals went south, literally following the warmth of the sun.

Harvey turned eight years old in the fall of 1912. Austin Country Club was a busy place, and there were bags available for everyone. The membership had reached its imposed cap of three hundred, and club officials had voted to buy the land, rename their club Austin Country

Club, and expand the course to eighteen holes. Progress moved at a brisk clip. The country club reflected the community around it: Harvey's hometown was asserting itself as the center of politics, education, and culture in Texas.

On those rare days when he went downtown with his family or friends, Harvey saw a city rising around his golf dreams. Buildings of three and four stories lined the streets. Impressive houses of worship — notably the Tenth Street Methodist Church and the Saint Mary Cathedral — towered in the developing cityscape. Scarbrough's Department Store had erected the first skyscraper on Sixth Street in Austin three years before. It was only eight stories tall, but to the eyes of an eight-year-old boy who lived on a dirt path, it touched the constellations.

Three railroads hurtled passengers in every direction. Congress Avenue had been paved from the Colorado River north to the sunset-pink granite walls of the Renaissance Revival–style Texas Capitol, twelve blocks in all. Trolleys hustled citizens up and down the bustling thoroughfares. Harvey stayed near his parents on their trips into the city, which even President Theodore Roosevelt had visited. He didn't want to get lost.

Pedestrians on Congress strolled past the Majestic Theater, the Lammes Candies store, the Maverick Café, and Tom Smith's grocery, where the many customers' leather-soled shoes had rubbed concave grooves into the plank floor. On weekends, while Harvey carried golf clubs for 25¢ a round, his friends escaped to see picture shows at the Queen Theater, where a man with a monkey sold peanuts and popcorn, or Skinny Pryor's Cactus Theater between Eighth and Ninth Streets, where a cranky cattle drover named Bill Blocker sat in the front row and critiqued the manner in which movie stars handled their horses on the screen. The movies, filmed in a new place called Hollywood in California, cost a nickel to see. But Skinny Pryor let the nickel-less children inside for nothing if no adults were around to see.

Harvey and the other caddies at Austin Country Club read with amazement about the 1913 U.S. Open, held at The Country Club in

Brookline, Massachusetts. They learned that Francis Ouimet, a twenty-year-old former caddie at The Country Club and reigning champion of the Massachusetts Amateur, had won in a playoff in a soggy Boston rain. Ouimet shot 72, one stroke over par, to beat two titans, Harry Vardon and Ted Ray, the great but aging British champions who were on an exhibition tour of the eastern states. The victory sealed the popularity of golf in the United States. Everyone wanted to be Francis Ouimet. Especially Harvey.

His parents allowed him to caddie after school and on weekends. Harvey coasted through his classes, not bothering to do more than was necessary to achieve average marks, then threw his entire energy and attention into golf. He earned regular bags at the club. He was a model caddie. Naturally stoic and eager to serve, Harvey instinctively knew the value of silence to a player deep in concentration.

Besides, he was far too busy trying to memorize the variables that produced the best shots. Harvey wanted more out of golf than a bag to carry for a quarter. He had read about Francis Ouimet in the sports pages of the Austin newspapers and wanted to understand how Ouimet seemed to command the destiny of a ball. Harvey watched the way the good players at his club held the club in their fingers, not in their palms. He studied the parabola of their swings. He noticed how they trapped the ball at impact, how every swing found its bottom in just the right place. He paid careful attention to the sound of a good shot. He would always remember that *whoosh*. Nothing made him feel quite so alive.

Harvey also learned the practical skills of his occupation. He taught himself to manipulate a tool called a shiper, a long pole attached to a flat piece of wood wrapped in cloth, the bottom of which smoothed a player's line on the crust of the sand greens. He remembered to keep pace with the members so they never had to wait for their clubs, and they rewarded him with occasional permission to attempt a full swing with their spoons or to roll putts on the greens he had shiped so well. Harvey practiced his own swing when time allowed. Between loops, he and the other caddies took turns swiping at blades of grass in the yard behind the shop. He imagined himself swinging a weed cutter.

Harvey learned to practice with purpose. With school and work and his chores at home, he found limited room in his life for practice, so he made sure his practice meant something. Every swing, every move, mattered. He instinctively understood that practice without deliberate concentration — on a drill, on a target, on a blade of grass at the bottom of a few swings in the caddie yard before a job — was just another way of wasting time. He was beginning to understand the difference between practice and play. He also was starting to appreciate the role of teaching. "Some players learn quicker with lots of practice and less frequent actual play," he reminisced many years later. "My own thought is that the young golfers who develop the fastest are those who get sound teaching from the beginning. They practice a reasonable amount and play every chance they get." In other words, they threw themselves at the game. No one understood that commitment like Harvey did.

Harvey tried hard to do a good job at the club. The effort came naturally to him, and he loved the work. He thrilled at noticing how different shots rose and fell in different winds and different temperatures, how certain actions produced specific aerial results. His impressionable mind became an inventory of cause and effect. He thought at night about what he had seen that afternoon and tried to make sense of patterns. He wanted to simplify a complicated riddle. He wanted answers, not mysteries.

Harvey spent as much time as he could around Willie Maguire, the head professional, who preached to members the trinity of grip, stance, and alignment of the body. Harvey trusted everything he saw Maguire teach. It seemed so clear to him. When it was time for him to carry clubs, Harvey remembered the words and lessons of his early mentor, and he paid close attention to the fidelity between what Maguire taught and what he saw a member do — or not do — in the course of a round. Harvey's grasp of the game broadened through his constant and repetitive exposure to the infinite interactions of intent, action, and the causal relationships between the conditions of the environment and the force imparted on the ball. He was acquiring the subtle secrets of golf through saturation. He thought about golf all of the time.

As his reputation grew as an able and dedicated caddie and the better players at the club sought his services, Harvey was often in the presence of the best the game had to offer at that time and place. His bearing as a caddie reflected the traits of a champion player: alert, composed, focused, attentive, patient. And so very driven. He taught himself the coordinates of the sand greens like a cartographer mapping a desert. He studied the seasonal direction of the Central Texas winds. He embraced the vagaries of luck, both good and bad. Harvey possessed a rare trait in golf: he accepted the uncontrollable forces — wind, rain, an invisible depression in a putting line, a bad bounce off of a rut in the middle of a fairway, the presence of tension and fear and submission and rage in the players. Other men cursed such external (and internal) forces, but Harvey learned at an early age that they were as much a part of golf as the hickory shaft. The more he watched golf, the more inclined he became to welcome its unpredictability. A bad shot didn't anger him. He never swore. The most profane word anyone ever heard Harvey say was not even a word at all. *Shuckits,* Harvey would mutter. Sometimes, when he lost a ball in the weeds or missed a putt he should have made, Harvey stood silent for a moment, one foot crossed in front of the other, his thin frame resting on a cleek. *Shuckits.* Then he'd turn to observe the next play in his group. That was the important matter: to watch. Harvey was a watcher. He was, quite unintentionally, teaching himself to become the teacher the world had never seen.

Maguire left Austin in 1914, Harvey's second year as a caddie, to become the head professional at Houston Country Club. Maguire was replaced by a man named J. M. Watson, whose appointment ended a few months later when William R. McKenzie arrived from Atlanta; McKenzie was then replaced in quick succession by George Dow and, later, Carl Baker. Harvey found something in each of them to remember. The club, meanwhile, launched an expansion that more than doubled the size of the property, from thirty to seventy acres, and added nine holes. "An eighteen-hole golf course is gradually being brought up to standard," noted the *Austin Daily Statesman*. "The ground is adapted to the making of a splendid golf course." The club now had tennis courts, a billiard room, lockers, and showers.

Harvey felt like a part of something. He had a place. As the country club thrived, he considered himself an essential, if small, part of the enterprise. At night, as he lay fighting sleep, Harvey replayed scenes from the day in his mind. He began to see patterns and themes, which kept him awake even longer. He had noticed that the better players, for example, took more time over shots before they swung their clubs. They seemed to be in a trance. He had noticed that poorer players struggled with their grip on the handle of the club, while the elite players seemed simply to place their fingers over the shaft, like a tongue in a groove. He thought about conviction. He thought about little truths that were becoming apparent to him. "Indecision spoils more shots than people realize," he concluded. "Never doubt your club selection. Once your mind is made up, hit it with confidence. The same rule applies to reading greens. Don't be wishy-washy. The difference in distance between clubs is only about ten yards, but a missed shot can be the difference between a birdie and a bogey."

The clarity that came to him at night assured Harvey that he had made the correct choice for his life, even though it meant missing out on so many other opportunities. The club made him feel needed. He liked to feel needed. He began to think he might stay forever.

So much of golf appealed to Harvey. He loved to be in the out-of-doors. He loved to exert his body. He loved to fill his time in ways that involved no reading, writing, or arithmetic more complex than adding nine digits on an Austin Country Club scorecard. But most of all, Harvey loved an enigma.

Harvey was on a never-ending quest on a golf course. The golf swing and the flight it produced fascinated him like chipping for fossils in the limestone along Waller Creek, fishing for bass in Lake McDonald, or reading in the *Austin American* about Ty Cobb fascinated his friends. Harvey even enjoyed the solitary pleasure of collecting practice balls for members such as Lewis Hancock, who later engaged him as a caddie, but not without concerns that Harvey consumed too much candy. "It's all right to eat that candy while we go along," Hancock told him. "Just see that it stays in your mouth and doesn't get on my clubs."

When he was twelve, Harvey was elevated to shop assistant. That meant more work, more time spent at the club, but he embraced the new job in the way his friends at school flocked to explore the outer edges of the booming town and the newly discovered swimming holes on the Colorado River. The other boys invited Harvey along, but he declined. His life as a shop assistant left no room for exploring or swimming. He had clubs to wipe, bags to carry, balls to watch, and swings to study as if he were an anthropologist just now encountering a new civilization.

Harvey apprenticed under McKenzie, Dow, the former World War I infantryman Baker, and, finally, an Englishman named Jim Smith, whose instruction reminded Harvey of Willie Maguire. The promotion to shop assistant made Harvey a professional — one of the youngest in the nation. It also made him one of a new generation of American golf professionals whose ascension from the caddie yard reflected the path the early professionals from Scotland and England had cleared the century before. But even more important, Harvey's promotion made him the first native-born golf professional in the state. He became, before his thirteenth birthday, one of the founding fathers of Texas golf.

Harvey took pride in his new position. He worked even harder to understand the mechanics of the swing — and especially the golfer's mind, which was no small accomplishment for a boy whose formal education would end at high school commencement. His authority grew. Even at such an early age, Harvey was beginning to parse the complicated mechanics of golf movements into simple, digestible fragments of wisdom. His identity took shape. "A golf pro is like a cook," he would say later. "He mixes it up — a little salt here, a little pepper there, where it's needed." The recipes were clear to him as a young man.

Harvey graduated in 1923 in a class of 150 seniors at Austin High School, the only high school in the city. The *Comet*, the school annual, had a tradition of projecting the vocations of the outgoing students. The editors determined that Albert Buss would be an auctioneer and Frances Campbell a debutante. A young woman named Marguerite Cortissoz would become an organ grinder, the yearbook noted, and Evelyn Heath would be a dairy maid. Harold Knape was destined to be a motor cop, Clydine Rountree a burglar, and Nolen Young a champion pugilist. The long, tanned, and serious face of Harvey Penick appeared on page 17. He, the *Comet* predicted, would work in golf. It was perhaps the least far-fetched prediction of the year.

"Harve" was his nickname in 1923. He was also known as "Sarazen's Rival." He wore a muted coat and tie, his wavy hair piled high and shining, for his class portrait. His pale eyes seemed lost in contemplation. He might have been wondering how many golf bags he would carry or how many clubs he could grind that afternoon at the country club after the school bell rang. He might have been calculating the consequence of an open clubface at impact on an uphill lie in a right-to-left wind to a canted green a couple of hundred yards away.

He might have been preoccupied by an impending assignment to caddie for someone important. Harvey often drew the enviable task of carrying clubs for visiting dignitaries, such as the time in the winter of 1922 when he caddied for the long-driving Englishman Jim Barnes, the current U.S. Open champion. Barnes and the reigning British Open winner, Jock Hutchison, were conducting a ten-thousand-mile exhibition-match tour of the Northern Hemisphere, which included seven other stops in Texas at $500 an engagement. They played that drizzly February day with Austin Country Club head professional Carl Baker and two local amateurs. Spectators paid a dollar to attend. The touring professionals made the only birdies in the match — and then only one apiece. No evidence exists that the gallery regretted the commitment of either their time in the rain or the money they spent to be there. The city of Austin was mad about golf.

Or Harvey might have been thinking, while sitting for his picture at Austin High, about an emergent flaw that had invaded his own swing. But probably not. "Harvey Penick is said to be the champion golfer of

Austin," Ruby Elkins wrote in the class history section of the *Comet*. She was premature. But she was also prescient.

Austin High School sponsored teams in football, baseball, tennis, and track, but not golf. The football team won six games that year and lost two. The Hypatian and Sapphonian Literary Societies thrived, well beyond the purview of Harvey, and the Sons of Erin Debating Club practiced the art of persuasive rhetoric. The choral group featured three hundred voices. Harvey's was not one of them. All he strove for after class each day was the school's permission to leave early so he could join his brothers at the club. Those familiar dirt roads in his neighborhood led him there every afternoon.

The debut in 1922 of a new professional golf tournament in San Antonio kindled Harvey's enthusiasm for the game even more. A newspaper editor in the mission city south of Austin cajoled city officials and the proprietors of three San Antonio hotels into raising $5,000 in prize money for the Texas Open, the first stroke-play tournament in the state and the forerunner of the winter circuit later associated with the PGA Tour. The organizers selected Brackenridge Park, the first municipal course in Texas, as the host site. It helped that John Bredemus was the head professional there. An eccentric, Ivy League–educated player and budding golf-course architect, Bredemus knew how to encourage the best players of the time to commit to the new tournament. It was hardly a difficult task. The purse was among the highest offered anywhere. The field for the first Texas Open included Maguire, the former professional at Austin Country Club, as well as Leo Diegel, Harry Cooper, and an elfin twenty-year-old club professional and former caddie named Gene Sarazen. Sarazen lost the Texas Open to Bob McDonald, but would win the U.S. Open and the PGA Championship that summer. Bredemus, meanwhile, began a friendship with Harvey that lasted the remainder of his life. Harvey admired Bredemus's skill, of course. But what he really liked about Bredemus was the man's singular concentration on anything involving golf. Harvey felt a kinship with that.

The second Texas Open in 1923 drew an even better list of commitments. Walter Hagen, Joe Kirkwood, Jack Burke Sr., and Tommy Armour — four of the most important men in Harvey's gathering circle of golf mentors — competed for a record purse of $7,000 for three days in January. Hagen won the first-place prize of $1,500. He beat a lot of fine players and broke Clarence Mangham's eighteen-hole course record by a stroke. The flamboyant Hagen had curried favor with professional golfers when his admittance to the Inverness Club in Toledo at the 1920 U.S. Open effectively disintegrated the informal rule against allowing golf professionals in golf clubhouses. Before then, golfers who played for money were seen as ungentlemanly second-class citizens, and American golf clubs refused to let them inside their doors at tournaments. Most players complied meekly, but not Hagen. He boldly strode into the Inverness clubhouse at that U.S. Open in implicit protest. Officials at Inverness offered no resistance, and so began the era of the professional golfer as celebrity.

Three years later, at the Texas Open, Hagen beat a very good field of such men that included a slender and unsure young player out of Austin. Harvey finished well behind the leaders that week at the second Texas Open. But he accomplished something: he made his debut as a professional at the age of seventeen. The tournament in San Antonio made it pretty obvious to Harvey that his career as a player would be limited, but the opportunities it presented to absorb golf knowledge were limitless.

For instance, as he watched the great players at San Antonio, he began to see what they had in common. "Psychologically," he later told a writer for a golf magazine, "the drive is the most important shot in golf. But the three-foot putt is important, too. You can make up for a missed drive with a three-foot putt. But miss the putt and you walk to the next hole knowing you've lost a stroke." Harvey even began seeing golf in ways that, however curious or odd they seemed to others, held insightful truths. He told the golf magazine, for example, that "good rounds don't impress me. Too often a good round is a good putter. A putter covers a lot of sins." Harvey's signature clarity was emerging as a teenage shop assistant thrust into a Texas golf community literally finding its identity every new morning.

Harvey returned to Austin after the Texas Open to a palette of possibility. He had played in competition with the best golfers of his day. The experience left him emboldened.

It seemed he had the world right in front of him. Austin Country Club had swelled to nearly four hundred members. Some of them were on the faculty at the University of Texas, founded forty years earlier. Harvey never gave much serious thought to college in the fall of 1923. Many of his friends enrolled at UT, though, and they were freshmen when oil was discovered in the middle of two million acres of UT-owned land in West Texas. The output from the Santa Rita No. 1 generously endowed the university with the resource-rich push it needed to begin its slow climb to prosperity — an ascent Harvey would join soon enough.

In 1923 the athletic council at the University of Texas was ten years old. The group had been formed "to see that all sports are conducted in an honorable and beneficial manner," according to the June 2, 1913, letter that effectively became the charter for Texas sports. The council also was charged with affirming that sports "are cultivated as will make it suitable for each student to find suitable exercise." Its third and final duty was "to raise and disburse, in a businesslike manner, the funds necessary to maintain athletics."

By 1923, Texas had seven sports: football, baseball, basketball, track, cross-country, tennis, and wrestling. The 1922 Longhorns went 7-2 in football under retiring coach Berry Whitaker. They beat Oklahoma soundly, but lost to Alabama and Texas A&M. The baseball team won the Southwest Conference. The basketball team finished in second, but ended the season with an 18–12 victory over A&M. There were no varsity sports for women, but the Texas coed sports division sponsored teams in baseball, basketball, swimming, tennis, hockey, archery, and dancing. There was no golf for students of either sex.

The university demonstrated an abiding commitment to athletics. It started construction on Memorial Stadium, funded by five hundred UT student workers who raised pledges of $15,000 in a six-day campus drive. H.J. Lutcher Stark, a member of the board of regents, contributed an additional $15,000. The city generated $150,000 in contributions, matched by donations from alumni in other areas of the state. Twenty-seven dedicated trains brought visitors to the dedication on Thanksgiving 1924, when former governor Pat Neff gave the address and Texas gave Texas A&M a 7–0 loss in the first meeting of the two rivals in the new stadium.

In that era, young men in Austin bought trousers and shirts at the Walter Wilcox clothier. Those who could afford a suit made by Hart Schaffner & Marx shopped at Stebbins & James. After school, the students at Austin High bought Whitman's candy at Renfro's, a fountain on Congress Avenue, and hand-turned ice cream at the Meyer Creamery on West Sixth. The Goldsmith Sporting Goods Company traded in "baseball and football outfits" for the boys who represented the Maroons on the grass fields of play. There was plenty to do and see and buy in the capital city of Texas when Harvey was a new graduate of Austin High.

But Harvey seemed to be interested in nothing but golf. His parents hardly knew what to make of the way golf consumed their son. They had neither the time nor the inclination to play the game themselves, so they viewed it with curiosity. But they also were happy to see Harvey so drawn to something. They might have dreamed that he would become an engineer or a banker or a merchant — professions that were nothing like golf — but it was obvious that golf was keeping Harvey engaged and interested. Their son wanted to know how to shave hickory shafts. He sought to master the proper way to grind the leading edges of wrought-iron niblicks. He concerned himself with basic agronomy and learned to care for soil and grass to hone his course-maintenance techniques. He taught himself to weed. Using a basic weed cutter, swinging it back and forth, he realized how similar the action was to a sound golf swing. Harvey tucked away the image and returned to his self-enforced studies.

His education accelerated with every trip he made to the country club to carry a bag and, when he was finished, to think. He experimented with creative ways to nourish grass, such as spreading bat guana (easy to find in Austin) over distressed sprigs. He tried to remember anything that worked — in the caddie yard, on the golf course, with the golf swing, with growing healthy grass in a hot and dry climate like Austin's. Details consumed him.

One day, he thought, he might write down all of these ideas. There were too many to remember. And he wanted to remember them all.

Meanwhile, that spring, Joe Byrne, the chairman of the Austin Country Club greens committee and the chief justice of the Texas Supreme Court, composed a memo on government letterhead to the membership of the club. "It is raining continuously, and the grass and weeds are making a rapid growth," he wrote. The club needed a tractor. Byrne had eyed a Roseman model with a hauling bed that "was being used by the following clubs in Texas: San Antonio, Galveston, Houston and Brook Hollow of Dallas, and giving satisfaction." The cost: $1,400. The purchase would mean a onetime dues increase of $20. Byrne requested $5 upon reply and the balance payable in three installments. He also included news of a development in the golf shop.

Jim Smith, the head professional, had submitted his resignation, effective May 1. When Harvey found out, he plotted at once his plan to succeed Smith. To him, it was a bit like joining the U.S. Army or applying to one of those colleges he'd heard about. The smart kids and the future soldiers knew what they wanted to do next. So did Harvey. His time had arrived. "His assistant, Harvey Penick, has made application for the position," Byrne wrote in a postscript at the bottom of his memo. There was one stipulation. The club would have to hold the position open for a month. Harvey was ready to start right away, but his exasperated parents were making him wait until he graduated from high school.

The membership merrily concurred. Harvey skimmed through the last weeks of his formal education on a cloud. While his classmates planned for summer camps, baseball games, family vacations to the coast, and lots of afternoons at Meyer Creamery and Deep Eddy, "Sarazen's Rival" could barely wait to open the club on the morning of his first day in charge of golf operations at the bustling Austin Country Club. He was eighteen years old.

Chapter Two

WHEN HARVEY REPORTED for his first lesson as head professional in the summer of 1923, he paused to take quick stock of his good luck. He remembered his anxious first day as a caddie. His older brother Tom had taken good care of him, watching for bullies, making sure little Harvey got agreeable members, allowing his younger brother enough independence to experience inconsequential mistakes, exposing him to older caddies who knew what they were doing. Harvey marveled at how much he had learned while carrying golf clubs.

He also thought about the head professionals who had come before him. He privately thanked them for being patient with him and answering his innocent questions. Harvey recalled with fondness the members who had helped him along the way, men such as Lewis Hancock, who allowed Harvey to fetch his balls so long as he kept his fingers, tacky with the residue of candy from Lammes, away from the grips of his clubs. The memory of Hancock made Harvey sad. Hancock had died in his bed of heart disease in 1920. Harvey still could picture the flags at the Capitol flying at half-mast and the somber resolution that city council member Harry Haynes read into the minutes: "His days began and ended in the city he loved and served." Harvey thought about the bronzed plaque that hung over the fireplace at the club. IN MEMORY OF LEWIS HANCOCK, read the engraving, FOUNDER OF THE AUSTIN COUNTRY CLUB, 1899.

Harvey thought also about the golf course there before him on his first morning as head professional. It was twice as big as it had been when he arrived as a scrawny and shy caddie from Cedar Street, but now that he had spent nearly a decade of his life there, it seemed intimate and personal and important to his spirit, like chapel almost. Nine holes had become eighteen. The first hole now played over the intersection of East Forty-First and Red River Streets. Harvey knew the course would soon require grass greens, like the other good clubs in Texas. But those were big plans, and Harvey needed to start small. He turned to his first scheduled lesson, with a man named Franz Fiser.

Harvey watched Fiser take a few swings. With ideas echoing through his head, he said nothing at first. He inventoried the images in his memory of the best golf swings he had seen and concentrated on what he remembered most about them. What were the common themes? What worked? Harvey remained silent. He wanted to make sure he made no mistakes in his first actual lesson as the head professional. But he also knew Fiser expected some kind of return on his $2 investment—the initial fee Harvey charged, if he charged at all. He finally summoned the courage to speak. "Keep your left arm a little straighter," Harvey said, in almost a whisper. Fiser did. His shots pierced the air with authority. Fiser was thrilled. Harvey was relieved.

The office for the golf professional at Austin Country Club was small, dank, and cramped. Harvey loved everything about it. He sometimes stood in the middle of the room and absorbed its perfection—the sweet-smelling hickory blanks stacked about, waiting to be converted into shafts, and the iron heads with the beautiful names that Harvey liked, smiling at the sound of a Scottish word wrapped in a Western drawl. *Niblick,* Harvey would say to himself. *Mashie. Jigger.* He inhaled the scent of the grass blades and the mud that carpeted the floor. Outside, a mule-drawn seed sprinkler with rust-coated wagon wheels awaited duty near the caddie yard, where boys who reminded Harvey of himself not so long ago now looked at him as he once regarded Francis Ouimet.

Ouimet visited Austin on January 4, 1924, and played an informal round at the club. More than ten years removed from his epic victory as an amateur at the U.S. Open, he installed Harvey as his caddie that day for his first experience with the curious sand greens. Harvey embraced every moment of their round. He studied every detail of Ouimet's attack on the golf ball. He appreciated that he was in the presence of a particular kind of greatness that he might never witness again.

Ouimet played that day with Bob Connerly, one of the two brothers who were the most highly skilled club members. Connerly putted better than Ouimet, naturally. "As the ball rolled on the greens it gathered particles of oil," Ouimet later noted.

The U.S. Open champion didn't know much about Texas. The oil kept "the sand from blowing away," he was informed.

Harvey shiped admirably for Ouimet and formed a mental inventory of his many impressions. Harvey admired Ouimet's singular commitment to every shot. His conception of sound fundamentals, which began to form as he watched the good club players and continued to develop from his experiences at the Texas Open, was taking shape in his mind. He knew he would soon have to document his thoughts. He would make time soon for that.

A sportswriter named Lloyd Gregory came to the club shortly after Ouimet returned to Boston. He filed a column on January 12 that celebrated the evolution of Austin Country Club through its fifteen years of existence. "The growth and popularity of golf in this city is nothing less than astounding," Gregory wrote in the *Austin Evening Statesman,* one of two dailies in the city. "Despite a bite in the air, the country club course was crowded Saturday afternoon . . . and this afternoon, barring a tornado, a steady stream of enthusiasts will play."

A few miles away, Austin High School added golf as a sport in the fall of 1924, likely at the behest of Harvey. The new team fielded eight players, including Philip George, who later became an assistant to Harvey at Austin Country Club; his brother Felix, a future professional at a municipal course; and Don Malarkey and Tony Butler, who also would become golf professionals.

The 1924 *Comet* yearbook published a picture of the upstart squad. The caption noted:

> Austin High School, in starting a golf team this year, has originated a high school sport in Texas that is fast becoming popular in the Eastern states and will soon take a recognized place over the country. Austin has the credit of having the first golf team in Texas high schools. The ability to do this has been due to the courtesy of the Country Club, which, unlike most country clubs, has been willing to turn over its links on Saturdays to the High School team.

Golf in Texas continued to grow around Harvey. His appointment as head professional had coincided with the incorporation of River Oaks Country Club in Houston, which commissioned the Scottish-born course architect Donald Ross to shape eighteen holes along Buffalo Bayou on a two-hundred-acre dairy farm known as Four Mile Place. The original three hundred members paid $100 each to join River Oaks, which later factored into Harvey's life and legacy as much as any place outside of Austin.

The club hired Jack Burke Sr. as its first golf professional. Burke hailed from Philadelphia, caddied at Philadelphia Country Club, learned the trade of club-making as a boy, and became an assistant professional, like Harvey, before his eighteenth birthday. By the time he was summoned to River Oaks, Burke had taught golf at Hershey Country Club, Aronimink Golf Club in suburban Philadelphia, Hyperion Golf Club in Des Moines, Iowa, two clubs — Rockford Golf Club and the Wheaton Club — near Chicago, and the Town and Country Club in St. Paul, Minnesota. He'd made a name as a player too. Burke finished second in the 1920 U.S. Open, a shot behind Ted Ray of the Isle of Jersey at the Inverness Club in Toledo, Ohio. He'd beaten the young amateur Bobby Jones, who made his U.S. Open debut that year, as well as many of the great professionals of the time, including Walter Hagen, Jim Barnes, and Harry Vardon.

Like Harvey and many other professionals of the era, Burke toggled between playing tournament golf and teaching the swing to beginners. Cold weather limited the amount of time he could spend earning an income in the clubs up north, so Burke sought winter assignments in warmer-weather states such as Texas. The founders of River Oaks came to him while he was working in a seasonal teaching position at Glen Garden Country Club in Fort Worth and offered him a monthly salary of $300 and concessions from the club-polishing service. Accepting the offer, Jack and his wife, Quo Vadis Quayle, arrived in Houston in 1924 with their one-year-old son, Jack Jr.

Like Harvey, Jack Burke Sr. found himself in the right place at the right time. The arrival of River Oaks — joining clubs in Austin, Houston, San Antonio, Dallas, and Fort Worth — would secure the state's future prominence in the game, and River Oaks would become an important hub for Texas golf.

Burke was a golf professional who straddled two worlds. He divided his time between playing and teaching, winning the Texas PGA Championship five times while developing instructional innovations that influenced the generations after him. Burke designed the aluminum-alloy Blue Goose putter with Tracy Parks, an inventor and friend. Together they created a rubber grip woven with strands of fabric, inspired by the construction of the inside wall of a tire that ruptured on the Burke family car. Both inventions endured. The putter used the gently curved hosel called a *gooseneck*. The cord grip still helps millions of golfers play in the rain.

Burke also bequeathed to golf a lasting set of principles. As Harvey would soon do, he took copious notes from his observations of skilled players and beginners alike on the practice range. He kept his notes in his office at River Oaks, where a Houston amateur named Robert McKinney found them one day while waiting for a storm to clear. McKinney found the notes mesmerizing. He published them in a book he modestly titled *Tips on the Game of Golf, from Jack Burke Sr.* In the spirit of the early teachers from Scotland, Burke's mandates worked because they were simple. Harvey knew when he met Burke that he had found his muse.

Harvey befriended Burke soon after the opening of River Oaks. The two were part of a small but seminal group of Texas-based golf professionals whose livelihoods depended on promoting the sport. Soon after purchasing a lot in the tony River Oaks neighborhood for $3,000 and building a 3,400-square-foot house on Brentwood Drive, Burke would invite Harvey and other fellow professionals to Houston for spontaneous weekend retreats. The group often included Jack Grout, the touring and teaching professional Jimmy Demaret, Henry Picard, Tod Menefee of San Antonio Country Club, and Johnny Dawson, the decorated California amateur. Golf equipment salesmen occasionally joined the gatherings. Everyone at Burke's gatherings shared the same interest, and no one who cared deeply about the direction of golf in Texas was denied an invitation.

"They wanted to know how to play," Jack Burke Jr., the son the Burkes brought with them to Houston, recalled in the fall of 2012. "And they particularly wanted to know how to teach."

The younger Burke remembered listening to the men debate methods, theories, and tactics to impart wisdom. "They didn't talk in academic terms," Burke Jr. said. "They told stories." Burke Sr. had played with the titans of the game; he divined their secrets from paying attention, as Harvey had been doing in Austin. Burke was happy to share the knowledge he'd accumulated at the championships he had played throughout the United States.

"It's a simple game and it should be taught simply," Jack Burke Sr. often reminded his colleagues. "There's a swing in everybody. You've just got to get it out of him."

Harvey listened intently. He trusted the elder Burke and considered him a mentor. Even after the men finished their discussions and were snacking on syrup-coated biscuits, convened around a table for games of pitch, Harvey continued to interrogate his peers.

"He wanted to find the answers," Burke Jr. said. When he did, he committed them to memory.

Back at home, Austin Country Club began to draw attention from outside the city. Harry Cooper—later nicknamed "Lighthorse Harry" by sportswriter Damon Runyon for his fast play at the Los Angeles Open—played an exhibition at the club in the summer of 1924 with Harvey, John Bredemus, and Dan Kenny, a founding member of PGA of Canada. The Lions Club of Austin invited Bill Mehlhorn and Leo Diegel to see the new public course it had built with $1,100 worth of retired municipal bonds, which were burned in celebration on the first tee.

In the fall of 1925, the Australian trick-shot specialist Joe Kirkwood, a man Harvey admired as much as anyone in his life, arrived at the club for an exhibition with Bredemus, now a professional at San Antonio Country Club, and Harvey himself. The spectators who had procured tickets to the event watched Kirkwood shoot 71 that morning to beat Harvey, who shot 73. Kirkwood entertained the gallery with a display of shots hit from different objects, shots hit in different directions, shots hit with different curvatures, shots hit with different implements, and shots hit that no one had ever imagined. Harvey and Kirkwood played as partners in the afternoon and won their match against Bredemus and Tom Lally, the pro from San Antonio.

Harvey loved his work. He found singular joy in rising each morning to immerse himself in the game, the grounds, and the people who played there. His understanding of the swing increased with every lesson he gave. His fascination with instruction fit his temperament: he had an abiding instinct for watching closely, listening intently, thinking discreetly, speaking only when something needed to be said, remaining silent when no solution seemed clear. Harvey endeavored to simplify. He cared nothing for ornamental excess.

Harvey grew immensely under Burke's caring tutelage. He also read as much as he could find about Stewart Maiden, the golf professional from Carnoustie, Scotland, who taught Bobby Jones and Glenna Collett Vare at East Lake in Atlanta. "A man may teach one kid who becomes great," Harvey said. "But two like that is no accident. The best teacher is like the best golfer: He's the one who makes the fewest mistakes."

Harvey drove to Houston as often as possible to sit with Burke and his other peers. Between his lessons and other duties at the club, he kept his swing sharp, and he created a club championship to encourage sportsmanship and competition. He was happy to learn that Texas A&M University in College Station had suggested that the Southwest Conference formally adopt men's golf as an official sport. Southern Methodist and Rice Universities agreed to participate, "and if the support of one more school can be gained, it is very likely that a conference golf tournament will be held in the southwest this year," read an item in the November 25 issue of the *Austin Evening Statesman*. The University of Texas became that school. The conference scheduled its first championship for May 1926 at Houston Country Club. Five of the eventual eight charter schools, including Texas, committed to being there.

The city of Austin christened its own city golf championship in February 1925. More than one hundred players, including many club members who prepared under Harvey, entered the thirty-six-hole competition, which would be won by Billy Drake, a student at Austin High. Tinsley Penick, Harvey's older brother, finished seven shots behind. He edged closer a year later. Tony Butler, who played on the first Austin High School golf team that Harvey helped to create, beat Tinsley in the final match at Lions, the new municipal course in West Austin. The two daily newspapers published scores for the city to see.

They had something else to write about in the winter of 1927: Walter Hagen had roared into town.

The stylish and garrulous player had won eight major championships, including the PGA Championship the summer before, and he was stopping in Austin on his way to San Antonio for the Texas Open. He played Austin Country Club with Edwin Juelg, the reigning Texas PGA champion, and Harvey and Tinsley, who had won the club championship in 1926. Harvey shot 71. Juelg finished the round at 76. Tinsley Penick, rattled in the presence of one of the best players in the game, shot 79. Hagen whistled and hummed his way around in sixty-eight swings, tying the course record. That summer, he won his fifth PGA Championship at Cedar Crest in Dallas.

Hagen later told a sportswriter that he thought Austin Country Club was trickier than Willow Springs, the new venue for the Texas Open. Hagen always found something positive to say about a new golf course, but Harvey still took pride in the remark. He also took an important lesson from the day he played with Hagen.

Harvey scored well, but he topped a shot early in the round. He then topped another. On a walk between shots, Hagen looked over at Harvey and said, "You want a word of advice?"

"Sure," Harvey replied.

Hagen said he thought that Harvey was trying too hard to keep his head still. He wanted to see more freedom in his swing. Hagen said a fluid swing includes a lateral shift with the turn away from the ball. "This gets your weight onto your right foot and your head well behind the ball," Hagen explained, "so you can put power into your blow."

Harvey said nothing. He tried to picture the idea in his imagination.

"It's like throwing a punch," Hagen said.

That night it occurred to Harvey that his entire frame of reference in golf revolved around experiences like that. He learned to play golf, he would say many times in his life, by trial and error. He copied what he liked. He ignored what seemed too complicated. He listened to players and teachers who went about their work in ways different from his own. "They made me think," he said. Now, at the age of twenty-two, Harvey was building a foundation. He was beginning to understand who he was and who he would be.

Harvey taught a free head for the rest of his life. But the advice from Hagen was a mere note in Harvey's curated volume of wisdom. He knew how to find, keep, and share what he saw as the tested truths of golf. It made sense to keep a free head, for instance, and when tested, it worked.

Over the decades many people would ask Harvey who taught him to play and to teach the game so thoroughly. They expected a name. Maybe two. But Harvey's answer never wavered: "Everybody."

· · ·

Golf in the United States was assuming a new level of organization and interest. The Professional Golfers' Association of America had formed in April 1916, nearly three months after a lunch involving club professionals and elite amateurs at the Taplow Club in the Wanamaker department store in New York City. Presidents played. William McKinley famously tried golf, found the frustration insufferable, and lost interest. William Howard Taft and Woodrow Wilson could barely break 100, but they shared the enthusiasm that many shamelessly inept Americans had for the game. The number of golf courses in the country rose from 2,000 in 1923 to 3,500 in 1925, to 5,800 five years later. Nearly two million Americans played at least one round of golf a year.

Events at Austin Country Club reflected the national enthusiasm. The Texas Golf Association staged its annual championship there in 1928, an event of such significance that newspapers from as far away as Houston dispatched reporters to chronicle the rounds and draw sketches of the players. The tournament was flighted, meaning that players were assigned to groups based on their qualifying scores. Harvey's brother Tinsley, a former club champion, represented the best hope for the host venue, which included thirty-five other members as contestants. Tinsley lost in the quarterfinals.

Harvey worked every day. He gave lessons most of the time, given Austin's three hundred days a year of sunshine. He even taught if it rained, if the pupil had that kind of commitment, which some did. Between lessons, Harvey kept a modestly stocked shop, merchandising golf balls and the occasional mashie or spoon, and he liked to grind irons on his bench, sharpening the leading edge for players who took shallow divots, softening the bounce for those who dug. The work literally shaped him. Harvey was a slight man—thin as a mesquite branch, never more than 130 pounds in trousers and belt—but his forearms rippled with lean muscle. He told pupils he got strong by wrestling the rust from the cold steel of the golf clubs he cared for like heirlooms.

Harvey went to church when he could. He sometimes had a void in his lesson sheet that allowed him to attend Sunday services at Hyde Park Christian Church, where his mother was a "pillar." One Sunday morning he noticed a petite young woman with dark hair and aqua eyes singing in the choir. He stared at her from afar and said nothing — as if he were watching a golf swing. As a kid, Harvey had taken an ordinary interest in girls. But his commitment to golf always came before silly distractions such as crushes or actual dates. Something else was happening now. He locked on this girl with the eyes and the voice. He asked after her when the service ended. Someone told him her name was Helen Holmes. She was the daughter of the new pastor.

Holmes was a student that summer at the University of Texas, a few blocks south of Hyde Park. She walked to classes, and Harvey spotted her one morning. He sensed an opportunity. He pulled his green Nash roadster alongside and asked her if she wanted a ride. Holmes liked the car. She also liked the white cap and plus-fours Harvey wore, though she had no idea why a man would be dressed that way in Texas. Holmes knew nothing about golf. She appreciated, however, golf fashion. Nonetheless, she declined the offer.

But Harvey persisted and eventually won her over. They were married two days after Christmas Day 1928 in East Texas, where her father had been called to minister at a new church. Harvey brought his wife home to Austin, took her to the Texas Open, and brought her to the club. One night a member invited them to dinner there. Helen Penick wore her wedding dress. The dining room reminded her of an English hunting lodge, with "hardwood floors and a beamed ceiling." She noticed the slot machine in an alcove.

Sometime later she was summoned back to the club, beyond her husband's purview. The member who had taken them to dinner presented her with a check for $100 and a set of hand-painted dishes. Helen Penick knew that her husband was regarded as much more than a nameless employee who administered lessons, tilled fairways, and hunched over the grinding wheel on his bench in the shop downstairs. It's unclear if Helen also understood what Harvey's career would mean for their marriage. She would not see him often. She frequently would not see him on weekends. She would share him with the club and the players who became his family of a different kind.

Tom Penick, who had introduced his youngest brother to golf as a caddie, was the head professional at Lions, the first municipal course in Austin and one of the oldest in Texas. Penick took the job in 1928, four years after the local Lions Club commissioned the project on 141 acres of land, including some in a floodplain, near the stretch of the Colorado River known as Lake McDonald. Lions was the second golf course in the city after the Austin Country Club course. It offered curious sports men and women lacking the wherewithal — or perhaps sufficient interest — to play private golf a chance to experiment with hickory shafts and mesh-patterned Dunlop balls and discover what all of the excitement was about. The city even upstaged Austin Country Club: the municipal course installed putting greens of natural grass. A year later Harvey convinced the membership to vacate the sticky sand greens — and his beloved shipe — for good.

Harvey spent much of his discretionary time at Lions. His brother had been appointed the first golf coach at the University of Texas when golf became a varsity sport in 1927, and Harvey liked to watch the young collegians when he could. The Penick brothers consulted on the unfamiliar task of supervising a varsity college golf team. They worked closely together on all matters of golf, from the caddie yard at the club to the construction of Lions. With Harvey's help, Tom Penick organized a program that would give rise in their lifetimes to national champions.

The first UT golf team was little more than a thrown-together, self-sustaining group of students with no identity beyond a shared zeal for the game. The Longhorns had no team uniforms, no team bags, no team vehicle, and no team home. Tom Penick allowed the members to practice and play at Lions as often as they liked, but he was busy running the popular municipal golf course. He could do little more for the team than secure tee times for team qualifying and make sure the players knew where the tournaments were and how to get there. He was less a coach than a secretary.

His tenure as the Texas coach lasted four years. When he gave it up, the university asked Harvey to succeed his brother. Harvey wondered how he could assume the responsibility, given his obligations to the club, to the Texas section of the PGA, and to his own playing schedule, which he considered important because watching the great players he played with was one of the ways he became a better teacher. But Harvey knew the university needed him. He accepted the job after the 1930 season.

Tom remained the head professional at Lions. Harvey sent his players there to play one another for 20¢ pecan pies, but he also invited them to the club, which had given him permission to use the course. Harvey's new responsibilities limited the amount of time he could devote to playing tournaments, and his game suffered.

He and Tom entered the 1931 Harlingen Open in the Rio Grande Valley on the South Texas coast, where touring and teaching professionals competed in one round of medal play at the municipal golf course. The field of sixty-five included many of Tom and Harvey's acquaintances: Jack Grout, Mike Turnesa, Denny Shute, Tony Butler, Ray Mangrum, Ralph Plummer, Al Espinosa, Jimmy Demaret, Harry Cooper, and Craig Wood, who later won the 1941 Masters and U.S. Open. Harvey was delighted to learn that he would be sharing the 1:05 P.M. starting time with his dear friend John Bredemus.

Bredemus was a marginal player but a prolific course architect, and his enterprising spirit left an indelible imprint on golf in Texas. Born in Michigan and educated at Ivy League schools as a civil engineer, Bredemus designed dozens of courses in Texas, including Memorial Park in Houston and, with Perry Maxwell, Colonial Country Club in Fort Worth. Bredemus had helped to organize the first Texas Open in 1922, when he was a professional at Brackenridge Park. He later designed the municipal golf course at Memorial Park, "practically in downtown Houston," Harvey wrote years later, "yet [it] is a beautiful, pastoral setting with tall trees and is circled by a jogging path that Bredemus insisted on putting there, rather than the road through the course that some of the city planners wanted." Harvey thought Memorial Park was as good a golf course as Colonial.

The designer of that course traveled the Southwest with a bag of books, a handful of golf clubs, and a sack of checkers and a checkerboard. Bredemus had been an athlete at Dartmouth and Princeton. Harvey respected Bredemus. Others in the emerging Texas golf scene thought him mercurial and aloof, a man who refused to enter a private clubhouse because he never felt like he belonged, but Harvey accepted his idiosyncrasies and sought his counsel throughout their lives. Harvey wrote many years later in a letter to a friend that he considered Bredemus a "fine architect, smart man . . . a straight shooter who gave his best with what he started with." When the club announced in early 1924 that it planned to add nine holes and convert to grass greens — the latter decision no doubt reached under pressure from the debut of the new municipal course in West Austin — Harvey recommended Bredemus for the work. They remained close until 1946, when Bredemus died in Big Spring, Texas. He was buried there under a flat, unremarkable stone etched only with his name and the seal of the Texas PGA.

Harvey knew Bredemus could barely break 75 on his best day, but he was glad to be paired with him in Harlingen the morning of February 7, 1931. As he scanned the rest of the pairings for the tournament, he noticed another name he held in equally high regard: Horton Smith, the magnificent "Missouri Rover" from the Ozark Mountains, who had the purest putting stroke Harvey had ever seen.

Smith joined the tour from Springfield Country Club, where he was a lanky assistant professional with wavy blond hair. He had attended classes at Southwest Missouri State Teachers College before settling on a career in tournament golf. Smith won his first title, the Oklahoma Open, in 1928. A year later, he seized eight more tournaments and earned his nickname: he would travel great distances by car, train, and, when necessary, boat to compete. Harvey admired Smith and considered him a friend. Later in his career, when he became primarily a teacher, Smith taught an amateur from Fort Worth, John Grace, who later befriended Harvey. Grace told Harvey that Smith suggested devoting 90 percent of practice to the vital pitch and chip shots around the green.

"Your short game will help your long game in every way," Smith told Grace. "But your long game won't help your short game at all." Harvey particularly liked a putting drill that Smith used — stroking balls with his right hand exclusively, until he'd developed a keen sense of motion, line, and pace. Harvey recommended it to his pupils for the rest of his career.

The drill failed, however, to deliver Smith to victory at the Harlingen Open in February 1931. A friendly pairing with Bredemus was no help to Harvey either. Wood won that Saturday afternoon in the Rio Grande Valley, the sixth of his eventual twenty-one titles deemed official by the PGA Tour. The players scattered — some of them went on to the next tournament, some of them went home. The Woods and the Smiths and the Demarets chased the purses; the teachers, like Harvey, simply absorbed new ideas to convert into lessons.

But Harvey returned to Austin with more on his mind than how and what to teach to his members.

He had a golf team to prepare at the University of Texas, with no firm idea what that meant. He had helped many fine players get better at the club, but most of them had learned golf from the ground up from Harvey. Now he was meeting accomplished players from other parts of the state who had learned other ideas from other teachers. Harvey was unsure how to handle the inconsistencies between what he believed and what his university players had been taught. Though his personality naturally kept him away from confrontation — he shunned conflict as much as possible — that trait in fact would help him become one of the most successful coaches in the history of college golf.

Harvey had few critics in his life. His kind, disarming disposition earned him loyal friends and admirers, not adversaries, and people were drawn to his warmth. Not surprisingly, his relationships with his players stopped well short of being dominant. "If there's one thing against Harvey, it's that he doesn't motivate players," said an unidentified touring professional quoted in an April 1971 magazine story. "He's so gentle, so mild, that he's not forceful. He doesn't take hold of a guy, shake him and say, 'You're going to win this match.' He doesn't teach competitiveness. He's not aggressive." Harvey's record as the head coach at Texas proved, however, that aggression and force were irrelevant to success. His embrace of learning from other teachers — through the players they sent to him at Texas — would be one of his greatest decisions.

Harvey was twenty-six years old on his first day as a college golf coach in the Southwest Conference. He had no scholarships to award because the NCAA had a rule stipulating that golf scholarships were equal to compensation, and compensation made a professional out of a player. Harvey had the authority to do what he wanted with his team within those codified limits. He had no interest in meddling with his players, however, unless they directly asked for his help or when he noticed a new player hitting his tee shots on par-3 holes from the bare earth. "Bobby Jones did that until he got really great," Harvey would tell him. "Then he always used a tee."

Students who wanted to qualify for his teams typically were commendable junior players from clubs in Dallas, Fort Worth, Houston, San Antonio, or smaller towns in the state. By the time Harvey met them, they already had been trained by proficient club professionals Harvey either knew already or would know soon. He studied their techniques. He paid attention to their mannerisms. He knew, as a part-time college golf coach in the early 1930s, that what he needed was a system. He was beginning to parse the golf swing in ways he could never have predicted. His players learned a great deal from Harvey, but the arrangement was reciprocal: Harvey was learning just as much from them.

One day in Austin, Harvey decided it was time to catalog his ideas. He stopped at a store, scanned the shelves, and found just what he'd come to buy.

Harvey held the notebook for a moment. It felt perfect in his hands: fifty pages, narrow-ruled, with a crimson-red cover made by the Southwest Tablet Company of Dallas. He bought it without a second thought. Sometime later he opened the Scribbletex that would become, in seventy years, one of the most important relics in the history of American golf. He produced a pen. *Most of my knowledge came from other pros,* Harvey wrote in his tiny, precise cursive. *Coaching: Boys had pros from everywhere.*

The hour was getting late. Harvey had lessons to give, a shop to run, a course to care for, a golf team to supervise, a wife to go home to, and more to discover about the game of golf. He closed the crimson-red cover, opened his desk, and placed the Scribbletex inside.

His book had begun.

Chapter Three

HARVEY PLANNED QUALIFYING rounds as the first-year coach of the Texas Longhorns. Rather than select the team himself, a prospect that made him uneasy, he wanted the players to earn their spots on the squad. Harvey strove for the positive. He avoided using the word *don't* in his lessons, for example, preferring to nudge his students with phrases such as "Let's try this," or, "How about this?" or, "What if we tried that?" Picking players seemed untenable. Golf was a meritocracy. Harvey would rather let numbers on the scorecard — the only measure of golf that mattered — dictate the composition of the team.

Four players earned spots in 1931. Dick Gregg, Lane McAfee, Fred Gross, and Jack Tinnin qualified at Lions Municipal to represent Texas in the Southwest Conference. They won head-to-head matches that season against Baylor, Rice, and Texas Christian University, and they tied with Texas A&M and Southern Methodist. They made their new coach proud, but Harvey took no credit. He praised the foundations their teachers at home had given them and their hard work on the range.

Texas finished a distant third in the conference tournament in Dallas. SMU won both the team and individual titles. Gregg and Tinnin played in the NCAA national tournament at Olympia Fields near Chicago, but neither qualified for match play.

Still, the *Cactus* yearbook saw promise in the new Texas golf coach.

"Coach Harvey Penick deserves much credit for the development of the team," it noted, under a team picture that included Harvey. He wore dark, pleated trousers, a dark V-necked sweater, and a tie. His wavy hair, dark and full, shone in the sun. He held a golf club in his left hand. He looked like he could be a senior letterman — one with wrinkles raking his forehead — on the squad.

"With veteran material to work with," the *Cactus* concluded, "he will put formidable teams in the field in '32 and '33."

It was a forgettable year altogether for Texas sports. The football team won six games and lost four, including a 35–7 dismantling by Harvard and a 7–6 season-ending loss to Texas A&M. The basketball team finished in the middle of the Southwest Conference. Baseball ended a game out of first place, won by Texas A&M. Only the tennis team, under head coach D. A. Penick, captured a conference trophy that year.

Daniel Allen Penick was a distant cousin to Harvey. A man of letters born in North Carolina, he had been a Texan since 1882. He was, unlike Harvey, deeply educated in the formal sense. He earned undergraduate and graduate degrees at Texas, taught English and Latin at a high school in East Texas, and became a professor of classical languages at UT after finishing his doctorate in Greek, Latin, and Sanskrit at Johns Hopkins University. He became president of the Southwest Conference the year Harvey became the head professional at Austin Country Club. He was the only tennis coach Texas had ever known.

D. A. Penick's tennis team and the other UT teams were established programs with savvy, veteran coaches. Harvey had never had a golf team of his own. He coached by instinct, from a position of reserve that came naturally to him. But he appreciated priorities, and his lay foremost with the club that employed him. He gave what time he could to the team, but he refused to compromise his duties in the shop and on the practice range at Austin Country Club.

His coaching style struck some as peculiar. He sometimes hid in bushes at home matches at Lions, surveilling his unsuspecting players between the branches and leaves. His instruction to them was brief before competition. "Take dead aim," Harvey advised in his thin, wafer-like voice.

He gave them all a new golf ball, then walked away.

He almost never traveled for tournaments outside Austin. He would miss too many days at the country club if he did, and the country club was his home even more than his actual home. Harvey was sure that his presence at tournaments would make his players nervous. "When they go out on the course, I have already taught them all they know. After that they are on their own." Besides, he reasoned, if they weren't ready to compete on the day of the tournament, no amount of sidelines coaching would help them.

The sensibilities he brought to coaching found their way into the Scribbletex. Harvey favored economy and frugality in his written words as much as he did in his golf lessons. He thought that big words, and especially lots of them, only confused a player. The game seemed complicated enough, especially to people inclined to be analytical. Through watching thousands of players, Harvey sought to simplify the actions involved in a sound golf swing to an elemental level. He wanted to know what worked universally. When he found it, he tumbled it through the finely positioned filters of his mind, until only a precious residue remained. That residue was truth. Nothing went into the Scribbletex until it was truth as he reckoned it.

Listen for swish to see if pupil [is] hitting too soon or too late, he wrote.

Jimmy Demaret came up from Houston today and sure shot up our golf course. He had 28-32-60. I talked to him afterward and he's working on the theory that the elbows should stay together in the swing. He doesn't mean tight together, or in to the body. He just tries to keep them the same distance apart throughout his swing.

Trouble with most of the men players I've seen here at the club (and I suppose all clubs are about alike) is that they try to use tournament players' techniques instead of just making the next step which is right for them.

A pupil doesn't start [the] serious business of making corrections until he's beyond the beginning stage. By then he should have (if I've taught him at all well) a clear picture of what controls the flight of the ball, the path of the club and the angle of the club at impact.

The worst trouble pupils have is that they try to think of the thousand-and-one things they hear.

Confidence is the result of a good swing and of good shots. Confidence never has been very much of a cause.

His ideas seemed primitive to some. Analytical players came to him in search of point-by-point explanations of why things worked the way they did. They often left disappointed. When trying to think of the simplest image possible to share with players struggling with tempo or the initiation of the swing, Harvey advised them to imagine swinging a bucket of water without spilling it. When he wanted someone to stay through the swing at impact instead of straightening his knees or trying to scoop the ball into play, Harvey suggested clipping the top of the tee, regardless of whether there actually was a tee to be clipped. It was the thought that mattered, and an openness, based in conviction, to pretending.

He told struggling putters to give luck a chance by creeping the ball toward the hole with such modest speed — "like a mouse," Harvey said — that the ball would catch the side of the cup and tumble inside. He wanted everyone he taught to take dead aim — to have the penetrating focus to clear the mind of everything but the acute endeavor — and let go. He wished for his pupils the same thrill and joy he experienced in executing a shot perfectly imagined and smartly prepared for.

All of these ideas were grist for the notebook, but he wrote down only those that, to him, were as close to truth as they could be. Then, satisfied that he had done a service to his students, his profession, and himself, Harvey closed the Scribbletex and returned it to his desk, where only he knew it was hidden.

The UT golf team won the conference championship in 1932 with three lettermen — Gregg, Gross, and Tinnin — joined by newcomers Ferrell Daugherty and John Payne. It was a rising season in all sports. The football team, under sixth-year head coach Clyde Littlefield, finished as Southwest Conference runner-up. Head coach Edwin Olle and his varsity basketball team won their first conference trophy since 1924. Beloved baseball head coach William Disch, "Uncle Billy" on the UT campus, delivered his nineteenth championship. Swimming won. Cross-country won. In golf, "Texas exhibited its strength on the opening day of the Conference meet," the *Cactus* annual asserted. The Longhorns beat Southern Methodist, the defending champions, in Austin with a score of 309.

The team elected Tinnin as captain for the '33 team. Harvey had exceptional confidence in his senior. But he had an even better feeling about the next incarnation of Longhorn golf for a different reason.

He met a sharply dressed, coal-haired freshman from Bonham in the fall of 1932. Ed White, a student interested in the petroleum engineering program at Texas, was the son of a casket salesman and was also a two-time club champion in his hometown in East Texas. White had collected three aces by the time he enrolled in college. He could launch his long irons as high, as far, and as straight as Sam Snead. Freshmen were prohibited from playing on the varsity, but Harvey knew White had won the intramural singles championship in his first attempt. The third-year part-time coach waited for White to appear for team qualifying in 1933.

Meanwhile, Harvey kept playing. He shot a 63 at the club, a course record, with six birdies and an eagle. He was named captain of the 1933 Texas Cup professional team. One of 1,009 PGA professionals that year, Harvey was elected president of the Texas section, a position that allowed him to help select the U.S. Ryder Cup team. Hagen served as captain. The team, which included Sarazen and Harvey's friend Horton Smith, lost by a point in Southport, England, to J. H. Taylor's team from Great Britain. His election as section president earned Harvey a place already in PGA history: that year was the only one in which section presidents and the PGA Executive Committee selected the Ryder Cup team.

Back on the University of Texas campus, the Littlefield Memorial Fountain on the Main Mall sprayed water for the first time. Mae West selected the seven Bluebonnet Belles, the campus beauty queens. "It had to be seven — which is my lucky number — and seven it is," she wrote to the university. "I would like to see every girl personally . . . College people — particularly college men — interest me. After all . . . I'm just a bad woman with a good heart."

New fountains and flirtatious celebrities, however, were of little interest to Harvey. He had a star to chart. White swept the team qualifying matches as a sophomore with four rounds of 65 or better at the country club — a stunning feat that stirred disbelief among members, until the boys who played with White certified the fact.

White earned the number-one position that fall. He was everything Harvey had hoped he might be, returning from the conference tournament in Dallas with the singles medal and the team title with Payne, Tinnin, and Richard Snyder. The Longhorns went to the national tournament as a team for the first time since Harvey had become the coach two years before. They finished fourth behind Yale, Notre Dame, and Michigan at Buffalo Country Club in Williamsville, New York.

Harvey had his first truly dominant player in White. He also was on the cusp of his first dynasty. Texas swept its spring schedule, vanquishing Texas A&M, Rice, SMU, St. Edward's University in Austin, and TCU by large margins. The Longhorns won the conference in all three years White played for Harvey.

White won the individual medal each time. He was the 1934 NCAA runner-up to Charles Yates of Georgia Tech, who beat White 5-up with three holes to play at Cleveland Country Club in Cleveland, Ohio, as a junior. The team finished fifth in the nation that spring. The university properly rewarded Harvey and his team by establishing golf, for the first time, as a major sport.

Harvey was eager to see what White, playing as an experienced senior, might achieve in 1935. But first, Harvey played that year on the Texas Cup professional team, joining his mentor Jack Burke Sr., the former Austin Country Club professional Willie Maguire, the charming Houston professional Jimmy Demaret, and the Oklahoman Jack Grout, who later tutored a pharmacist's son in Ohio named Jack Nicklaus.

Harvey was approaching thirty years old that autumn. He was physically sharp, as capable as he had ever been of playing competitive golf. But his world beyond tournaments was far broader. His first child, a daughter named Kathryn, was now three years old. The club required more of his time — to organize events, monitor handicaps, and run the bustling golf shop. His lesson sheet was filled. And Ed White was about to establish a blinding standard for the Texas Longhorn golf team.

By the time the spring golf season arrived, the University of Texas was desperate for any measure of athletic triumph. The football team had lost all but one conference game, including a bleak shutout in Austin against SMU and its All-American quarterback, Sammy Baugh. The basketball team had upset "Tree Top Tall" Kelly and "Tightwad" Lodge of Rice, but San Marcos Teachers College beat the Longhorns by two, Arkansas nipped them by one, and other losses mounted. D. A. Penick had watched his men's tennis team go undefeated in the regular season but lose the conference title to Rice. There had been few celebrations around the athletic dormitories in Austin.

White qualified for the national amateur the summer after his junior year with Harvey. He lost in match play, but his momentum carried the Texas golf team to another conference championship, this one at Braeburn Country Club in Houston. He and Nelson Munger, along with Raymond Ramsey, Bill Welch, and Bob Battle, produced the finest season in the history of University of Texas golf.

A calamitous fire at Austin Country Club had distracted Harvey the previous summer. The two-story red clubhouse was destroyed in the early morning hours of March 19, 1934, after a fraternity dance the night before. Harvey lost $3,000 in inventory, including clubs, balls, and the tools he used to grind implements. All that remained was the charred steel of dozens of sets of irons.

The fire touched no part of the course. Members even played the next day. Harvey had to operate out of temporary quarters, however, until the board could determine when and how to build a new clubhouse. The inconvenience to its coach was of no consequence to the golf team, which sent two players, White and Welch, to the 1935 NCAA Championship. White roared through the first four rounds of match play at the national tournament in Washington, DC, beating every opponent before the sixteenth hole, including Yates, who had eliminated White in the finals the year before. Every match seemed to lift White to an even higher plane of conviction.

White met Fred Haas of Louisiana State, a tall and slender former champion of the Southern Amateur, in the thirty-six-hole final match. White was 1-down after the first eighteen-hole round. After lunch, he squared the score early in the second and felt lifted again. White went on to bludgeon his opponent, beating Hass five and four to bring Harvey his one — and, as it turned out, only — individual national champion. White played his 129 holes at mighty Congressional Country Club in 3 under par.

"When Ed lost to Charlie Yates in the finals of the intercollegiate the year before last, it was like someone hit me on the head with an ax," Harvey told *The Daily Texan*, the campus newspaper. "And then when he beat Fred Haas, I was on top of the world."

Members at the Bonham Golf Club, White's home club, threw a rollicking surprise party for the champion in late July. More than one hundred people attended. The president of the Fannin County Fair Association feted White with a new wristwatch.

White never strongly considered professional golf as a career. He understood that his engineering degree from Texas was worth far more than his golf skill. The stock market crash of 1929 depleted the supply of tournament sponsors, which financed competitions on the PGA Tournament Bureau (the forerunner of the PGA Tour). The dream of Henry Ford to put a car in every driveway in America had made traveling between sites a great deal easier. But tournaments could, by rule, offer as little as $5,000 in prize money. No one got wealthy playing golf in the 1930s. Paul Runyan, for instance, led all professional golfers in 1935 with $6,767 in earnings. Johnny Revolta won $9,543 a year later. Horton Smith, Harvey's friend and playing companion, earned just $7,682 in 1936. Tournament purses combined amounted to no more than $185,000 until after World War II, when Ben Hogan won more than $42,000.

White knew the financial consequences, and he also knew the social implications. Amateurs then had far more prestige than professionals. They were regarded as true sporting gentlemen of a higher station than the lowly professionals laboring in the golf shops. The names of amateurs carried courtesy titles in the newspaper golf agate. The names of professionals like Harvey did not.

After graduating from Texas, White moved to Houston, where he kept playing golf at a high level. He won the Mexican Amateur in 1935, captured the individual medal at the Little Rock Invitational the same year, and in 1936 accepted a coveted invitation to play in the Walker Cup matches against the best British amateurs of the day.

"I knew they'd have to," Harvey told a student reporter for *The Daily Texan*. "How could they leave him off?"

The U.S. team and its captain, the 1913 U.S. Open champion and former caddie Francis Ouimet, cleanly won the matches at Pine Valley, 9–0. White and his foursomes partner, Reynolds Smith, eliminated Jack McLean and John Langley, eight and seven. In singles, White beat Langley again, six and five. White then returned to Texas to start his career as an engineer. It was his only appearance on the Walker Cup team.

"I guess I owe most of the credit for wherever I am in golf to Harvey Penick," White said.

"Naw," Harvey objected humbly. "I didn't make him. He was a golfer the first time I saw him. All I did was to just polish him a little here and there."

More than sixty thousand people now lived in Austin. The city no longer exuded the brittle, always-under-construction feeling of the Western frontier. Swarms of Model Ts and some newer Model As sputtered up and down the newly paved streets of the widening downtown. The university had built its iconic twenty-seven-story tower near the Littlefield Fountain. The phallic landmark, a symbol of opportunity in a state and city that embraced adventure and risk, loomed over the southern skyline from the first tee at the Austin Country Club. Pedestrians saw a billboard atop the Bybee Drug Store touting American New Deal optimism: PROSPERITY'S ROSE BLOOMS AGAIN WITH ROOSEVELT. Meanwhile, golf had become increasingly popular with the arrival of each new spring and each new golf season in America. Both Austin newspapers frequently carried wire service reports about the new Augusta National Invitation Tournament in 1934 at a golf retreat for the wealthy built on an old orchard in eastern Georgia at the direction of Bobby Jones.

Harvey learned that his dear friend Horton Smith, whom he had seen three years earlier at the tournament in Harlingen, had beaten Craig Wood by a stroke in the first invitational in Augusta. Smith made a twenty-foot birdie putt on the seventeenth hole and a tense, downhill four-footer on the eighteenth to win. The manner in which Smith won came as no surprise to Harvey, for two reasons. Smith was the best putter Harvey knew. And putting was the best way Harvey knew to win a golf tournament. "A good putter is a match for anyone," Harvey liked to say to anyone who might listen. "A bad putter is a match for no one." Good putting — twenty-eight putts, for instance, in a round of 67 — constituted about 40 percent of the strokes played. Even on sloppy ball-striking days, a sound, graceful, and confident putting stroke could turn a 72 into a score at the top of the leaderboard. Years later, when Tom Kite was evolving from a good player into a great one, Harvey gave him a piece of advice that seemed strange at first. "Go to dinner with good putters," Harvey told Kite. That was it. That was all. But the more Kite considered it, the more that advice made sense. Like so much of what Harvey said, the truth of the words lay in the implication or the inference. In the stripped-down, logical way Harvey looked at the game, good putters are happy golfers. Happy golfers, the logic goes, are positive forces. They have a third of the game figured out. Kite began seeking out good putters as dinner companions.

Texas won the Southwest Conference again in 1936, even without the great White. Austin Country Club hosted twenty-four players, who arrived for the tournament that May from Baylor, Rice, Texas, Texas A&M, Texas Christian University, and Southern Methodist. Bill Welch, White's old teammate, won the individual medal. The Longhorns swept the team championship by eighty-three shots.

But the tournament carried far greater meaning for Harvey, one that he would not understand for a quarter-century: he met a Baylor student named Charles Crenshaw, who would settle years later in Austin to practice law, join the club, and have a son in January 1952.

He would name his son Ben.

That summer Harvey entered the sectional qualifying for the U.S. Open at Baltusrol. He finished fifth in the field of thirty-four, missing a spot by a single stroke. He also coached the golf team to a sixth consecutive conference championship, joining UT track, cross-country, swimming, and tennis — the program D. A. Penick had turned into one of the finest in the country — in the winners' circle.

Harvey taught many women at the country club, but women's golf in Texas and across the country was limping far behind what the game offered for men. The Texas Golf Association, established in 1906, had sanctioned the West Texas Amateur since 1925, a senior championship since 1937, and its marquee event, the Texas State Amateur Championship, since the year of its founding. The first state amateur competition for women was established in 1931. It was the only tournament of its kind in Texas.

The few women in the state who wanted to play competitive golf knew where to get their instruction. Harvey knew young Betty Jameson well before she enrolled at UT in the fall of 1937. The head professional at San Antonio Country Club, Tod Menefee, who often joined Harvey and the others at the Houston home of Jack Burke Sr., was Jameson's teacher at the time and told Harvey about her. For her part, Jameson had overheard other women at the San Antonio club praising the man who taught at Austin Country Club.

Jameson sought out Harvey as soon as she arrived on campus. He learned that she had won the Lakewood Country Club women's championship, the Dallas women's city title, and the Texas women's state amateur in 1932. That also was when she made sports history in Texas: Jameson shot a round of 82 at Stevens Park Golf Course in Dallas to qualify for the Sunset High School golf team, one of five players in a field of twenty-seven. No girl had ever made a varsity golf team in Texas. Jameson had done it at the age of thirteen.

She won her second state amateur in 1937, the summer before she moved to Austin. A women's golf team at UT was decades away still. But Harvey pictured his commitment to the university golf culture as an abiding stewardship that included both the men's varsity team and all women who showed potential and a willingness to work hard. He gladly accepted Jameson as a pupil in the fall of her freshman year.

Harvey's wife Helen picked up Jameson at her dormitory and drove her to her lessons at the club. There, Harvey traced her tendency to pull her iron shots to an exuberant left arm. He prescribed drills. She practiced after class. In 1938, as a freshman, she won the intramural golf championship at Lions.

Jameson won two more state amateurs, in 1938 and '39. She qualified for the 1939 U.S. Women's Amateur at Wee Burn Country Club in Darien, Connecticut, where she beat Dorothy Kirby in the finals. She repeated in 1940 at Del Monte Golf & Country Club in Monterey, California. She was the medalist a year later at The Country Club in Brookline, Massachusetts.

The champion that year was a beaming Southern Californian with a bow in her hair. Elizabeth "Betty" Hicks, who also swept the California and the Doherty women's amateur titles, was honored as the Associated Press Female Athlete of the Year. Harvey and Betty Jameson already had a deep respect for Hicks, a future golf writer and women's golf pioneer who would factor deeply in Harvey's life. She was eighteen years old, already a Long Beach city champion, when Jameson dispatched her in the national semifinals in Pebble Beach.

Jameson advanced to the finals of the first U.S. Women's Open in 1946. She lost, five and four, to Patty Berg. Three years later, she and a dozen other women founded the Ladies Professional Golf Association, of which she served as president, and she was in the first class of women inducted into the LPGA Hall of Fame. With Jameson, Harvey drew his first measure of fame as a teacher of women. She and many others ensured his place in the legacy of American women's golf. It was a legacy that would live longer than Harvey himself.

The game continued to grow in the United States. Some sixty million rounds were played in 1938, and a year later more than half a million spectators flocked to watch players such as Byron Nelson, Henry Picard, and Sam Snead compete for $172,000 in prize money at PGA Tour tournaments. By then, the PGA of America had swelled to more than 1,800 members, including Harvey.

Although the distant rumblings of World War II began to quell some of the enthusiasm for the professional game — fewer tournaments were scheduled, and fewer tournaments offered more than the mandated $5,000 minimum purse — the game had traction across the country as well as in Texas. The condition of the sport pleased Harvey considerably, especially as it related to men. Of all people in golf, however, it was Harvey who might have suspected that women's golf was about to blossom into something equally extraordinary and permanent.

Since 1923, the women at Austin Country Club had been drawn to their head professional for the same reasons elite players such as Jameson sought him out. Harvey exuded a spirit of equality, dignity, and fairness in his treatment of players that appealed to women who had long tolerated disdain from other teachers. Harvey had been nurtured at a country club that embraced women from its founding. His attraction to golf never hinged on whether a man or a woman was holding the club. He valued commitment and enthusiasm above all in a pupil.

The success of Jameson in the late 1930s tapped a deep and career-defining quality in Harvey: he was, by nature and circumstance, a man in the right place, at the right time, and in the right frame of mind for the inevitable rise of women in the game throughout Texas and the nation.

At the time, Alexa Stirling and Glenna Collett defined women's golf in the United States. Stirling was a childhood friend of Bobby Jones at East Lake in Atlanta, where she was the second of the three daughters of a Scottish-born ear, nose, and throat specialist who served as British consul to the city. She played with the great British champion Joyce Wethered. Stirling and Jones toured the South as the "Dixie Kids" during World War I to raise money for the Red Cross. She eventually won three national championships and finished second in three others in the 1920s, a few years after a strong and graceful girl from Providence, Rhode Island, joined her father at Metacomet Golf Club at the age of fourteen.

Glenna Collett watched the older men play a few holes, then asked if she could try. A tennis and baseball player on her brother's team, Collett lined a piercing shot down the center of the fairway. Her impressed father arranged for lessons that summer with Alex Smith of Shennecossett.

Their work together led to six national women's titles for Collett between 1922 and 1935. She won her last one at Interlachen over the young and petite Patty Berg, who later accepted an invitation from Bing Crosby and Bob Hope to play them along with a near-legendary woman from the Texas coast with a reputation in baseball, basketball, bowling, tennis, track and field, softball, and, finally, golf. The two entertainers were no match for Berg and Mildred "Babe" Didrikson.

They beat the celebrities in front of 2,500 spectators that summer day in California. Babe Didrikson Zaharias, as she would be known to the sporting world after her marriage in 1938, had roared into the golf consciousness on August 8, 1932, when she joined three sportswriters, including Grantland Rice, for a round at Brentwood Country Club after the 1932 Summer Olympics in Los Angeles. She had just won two gold medals and a silver with the U.S. track and field team and set two world records and one Olympic record. "She is an incredible human being," wrote Rice, who was on hand. "She is beyond all belief until you see her perform. Then you fully understand that you are looking at the most flawless section of muscle harmony, of complete mental and physical coordination the world of sport has ever known."

Now Rice wanted to witness her prowess with a golf club. She had boasted to him at the Olympics that she could drive a golf ball as long as the men on the tour. She told him she had shot 82. She also told him she had played only ten rounds of golf in her life. Rice wanted proof.

Using borrowed clubs, Babe pounded 240-yard drives through the dense California air. She scored poorly on the front nine, but rallied for a 43 on the back, winning her informal match. Rice could barely catch his literary breath. "She is the longest hitter women's golf has ever seen," he wrote, "for she has a free, lashing style backed up with championship form and terrific power in strong hands, strong wrists and forearms of steel." He added: "If Miss Didrikson would take up golf seriously, there is no doubt in my mind . . . she would be a world beater in no time."

Babe returned to Texas with a hot passion to conquer another sport. Harvey played with her a short time later in her first exhibition as a professional. The match pit Babe and Al Espinosa against Harvey and Vola Mae Odom, a member at Austin Country Club. Babe kidded Harvey about the firmness of the greens. She flirted with a judge in the gallery. Harvey gave her no formal lessons, but did offer a tip or two. He later regarded her as the second-best female golfer he had ever seen, behind Mickey Wright. The Babe later credited Harvey with part of her success, but the modest pro demurred. He said she was a player who made herself.

The arrival of Patty Berg, Betty Jameson, Babe Zaharias, and other skilled women in the 1930s signaled an energized level of interest from the public and led to early agitation for formalizing women's tournament golf. Their rise also brought Harvey a greater role in the game. Every woman he met, from nervous club members learning the grip for the first time to veterans seeking his renowned counsel, left their encounter with a connection of some kind to the gentle, well-mannered man who treated women with dignity. Soon all roads to the future LPGA traveled through Austin.

The Texas men's team, meanwhile, continued its steady escalation in the ranks of college golf under Harvey. The Longhorns repeated as Southwest Conference champions in 1937, the year Jameson arrived at Harvey's shop with so much potential. The trophy made six consecutive titles for Harvey and his boys, an accomplishment the Texas athletic department made the smart decision to promote.

Weldon Hart, a publicist for the university, asked Harvey to complete a brief questionnaire the following spring. In blue ballpoint pen, Harvey listed his height at six feet and his weight at 132 pounds. Under education, he wrote: "Finished Austin High." Under coaching experience: "I have been helping the University golf team for the last seven years."

He listed nothing under athletic experience. He cited no hobby. After reading the last question — "Can you recall the most thrilling incident of your athletic or coaching experience?" — Harvey left it blank. Perhaps he found it difficult to isolate just one. More likely, he blanched at the prospect of boasting. That rubbed against his nature. He was a proud man. But he was not a boastful one.

He welcomed Walter Benson Jr. to his team in 1938, a year Texas returned only two lettermen but nonetheless won the conference for the seventh consecutive time. The Longhorns beat Texas A&M that season at Austin Country Club, four matches to two. They swept Texas Tech.

A dark-haired sophomore who favored understated sweater vests and crisp creases in his trousers, Benson factored immediately into the Texas starting four. Harvey knew him before he even entered the seventy-two-hole qualifier to make the team. Benson's father, who owned a prominent publishing company in Austin, was a charter member of the club. A picture of him and other club founders hung on a wall in Harvey's golf shop.

The younger Benson caddied often for his father. After their rounds, he liked to poke his head around the door of the golf shop and see Harvey, toasted by the sun and sweating through his wavy hair, hunched over his bench, buffing irons and smoothing shafts with a plane. Benson had no inkling that he was looking at the man who would make him great.

Harvey one day introduced young Benson to Ed White. Benson watched White hit crisp, hissing shots—no fade, no draw, just climbing and unwavering arcs—that left geometrically perfect divots. Benson once asked Harvey what made White such a good player. "Because Ed takes a square divot," Harvey told him succinctly. Benson heard the message. He soon was taking square divots too. "Like a dollar bill," he said.

Benson later spent part of World War II in England as a communications officer in the Army Air Forces. Upon his discharge, he succeeded his father to lead the family owned publishing company in Austin. Benson won the Labor Day tournament at Austin Country Club and the Firecracker Open three times at Lions Municipal, carving dollar bills on the fairways he once played for the Texas Longhorns.

"Harvey would come out, drop a hint here and there, and probably give five million dollars' worth of lessons for free," Benson said. "Harvey didn't like quick cures and was turned off by people who came to Austin thinking they were going to take one lesson and knock ten strokes off their games. He liked people who worked over a period of time to develop their games."

Rice University snapped the Longhorns' conference streak in 1939, when Texas finished second in the field of five teams. It was an anomaly. Harvey and his team won all three of their team matches, and the Southwest Conference again, in 1940 and 1941.

The successful golf program wasn't the only reason the mood inside the athletics offices at the university was soaring. The 1940 football team — the "heroes of a new era" in "the dawn of a new day," trumpeted the *Cactus* yearbook — lost two conference games but shared third place with SMU and Texas A&M at the finish, which was reason enough for celebration. It was the Longhorns' best season since 1932. Making matters merrier, they beat both Oklahoma and Texas A&M.

Harvey played as often as his increasingly busy schedule allowed. He and Helen had seen their family grow by one in 1938, when Tinsley Penick, named after his uncle, joined his sister Kathryn at the new family home near the club.

The Great Depression during the 1930s had muted participation in golf. Americans returned steadily to the game as the economy brightened later in the decade, when more than a half-million people came out to watch professional tournaments. In addition, more than 2.35 million players patronized the nation's 3,705 private clubs, 1,050 daily-fee courses, and 606 municipal facilities like Lions in Austin. But World War II would threaten the sport's recovery and change American golf in deep and lasting ways.

The attack at Pearl Harbor not only threatened to dampen golf's economic recovery but also affected public opinion on the pastime. "The only justification for golf or any other sport in these times is that of providing earned relaxation for war workers and protecting and renewing the keenness of those who are doing their full duty on the civilian front," argued golf journalist and historian Herb Graffis, who edited *Golfing* and *Golfdom* magazines.

Everything in golf scaled accordingly. All PGA-sanctioned tournaments, even at the sectional and local levels, set aside 20 percent of their purses for defense bonds. Exhibition tours to benefit the Red Cross, like the one Alexa Stirling and Bobby Jones played across the South, replaced regular competitions. Manufacturers quit making golf

balls. The war effort needed the rubber. Some companies even recon-
ditioned old, damaged balls like the ones Harvey had around the clubhouse for practice. MacDonald & Son Golf Company in West Chicago
refurbished them at 84¢ a dozen. Gas rationing forced the cancellation
of competitions governed by the PGA Tournament Bureau. Harvey's
friends Jimmy Demaret, Ben Hogan, Horton Smith, and Sam Snead
joined different branches of the military. Nothing about golf resembled what it had been the year before.

Harvey saw the difference each time he drove the short distance to
the university for business involving the athletic department and noticed students walking to class in their dress uniforms. He also saw
changes at the club. Club members who enlisted and were dispatched
to Sicily or Guadalcanal were gone for months, some of them forever.
The PGA, meanwhile, waived dues for the 201 members who also
joined the war effort. Harvey tried to convince Helen that he should
report to the recruiting station. She reminded him that he was thirty-
eight years old, with crippling allergies.

The United States Golf Association canceled the 1942 U.S. Open as
a gesture of respect for the national war effort. In its place, the USGA,
the PGA of America, and the Chicago District Golf Association created the Hale America National Open, a benefit for the Navy Relief Society and the United Service Organizations, and scheduled it for that
summer at Ridgemoor Country Club. Harvey won the local qualifier
on May 25 at his country club, earning a handsome certificate signed
by Francis Ouimet, who represented the joint tournament committee.
But the path to the National Open ended there for Harvey; had he advanced, he would have competed against his friend Ben Hogan, who
won the Hale at Ridgemoor.

As he approached his fortieth year, Harvey had everything he
wanted. He loved Helen. More important to him, she returned that
love, reflecting commitment that Harvey sometimes found heroic
given the amount of time — six days a week, sometimes seven in the
summer — he spent away from their home and children. Harvey went
to work at first light. He returned after the sun set over the hills of Tar-

rytown. Helen made sure Kathryn and Tinsley had breakfast before school, a snack afterward, and dinner before homework and bed.

Her husband was a golf professional, a good and committed one. As his lesson sheet filled, his Scribbletex did too. Helen understood her husband and the sacrifices that he believed came with a life in golf. More and more, Harvey was asked to lead PGA teaching seminars throughout the state, and he considered these requests a noble privilege not to be denied. He was shaping the next generation of golf professionals and keeping his promise to his own calling, the one he heard as an eight-year-old boy the day he stood at Austin Country Club and felt the hot, open wind on his cheeks.

Harvey had two homes. Each required, in his mind, equal attention, though to Helen and the children it seemed the country club beckoned more. But Kathryn and Tinsley would long remember the one thing their father was sure to do each night after he got home. Harvey always made it home in time to kneel at their bed and say the Lord's Prayer before they went to sleep.

It was one small thing they could count on. It was something Harvey could count on too.

Chapter Four

THE SPRING OF 1943 nearly altered the course of Harvey's life and that of his family. The city, which now approached 100,000 residents, had given Harvey both a career and a legacy at the club, but he also felt a tinge of restlessness. He wondered, as he had done as a child, what more might await in golf. Harvey was never an overtly ambitious man. He achieved in small, quiet steps that over seventy years brought him a certain level of fame. But he occasionally thought about a life in golf beyond the city of his youth.

That winter, Jack Burke Sr., whose elegant home in Houston had served for many weekends as an informal teaching salon for Harvey and his peers, died at the age of fifty-two. That left River Oaks without a head professional for the first time since it opened in 1924. The club appointed an eleven-member search committee, which identified two preferred candidates. One was Jimmy Demaret, the gregarious and immensely popular touring professional who won the 1934 Texas PGA Championship and six tournaments in 1940, including the Masters. The other was Harvey.

The choice to be made by the River Oaks committee members reflected some stark contrasts. Demaret, then thirty-two years old, was from Houston. Like Harvey, he had started in golf in the caddie yard; unlike Harvey, Demaret was more interested in playing tournaments for purses than he was in teaching a membership and managing a shop. Demaret thrived on attention. He performed on the golf course as much as he played it. He bought his clothes in New York City and once described himself as sartorially partial to brick red, mulberry, royal crimson, pale pink, purple, hunter green, Nile green, heather green, and flaming scarlet. Demaret played the piano and sang. He spun mesmerizing stories for audiences that swelled as the punch line drew near. He was loud, magnetic, occasionally brash, eternally effervescent, a pleaser of crowds, an entertainer in metal spikes and snazzy plus-fours, always quick with a joke or a verse to croon. He was everything Harvey was not.

Harvey was six years older than Demaret. The River Oaks committee respected his reputation as both a builder of champions and an uncompromising steward of his club membership. Demaret had the name, but Harvey was the pure teacher, a consummate club professional who knew how to perform the job, from keeping a tee sheet to stocking a shop to fixing a bent wedge or a loose spike. Burke had been both, a touring and teaching professional. With Harvey and Demaret as the finalists, the next head professional would be one or the other.

The River Oaks committee convened on April 22 to consider two proposals drafted by chairman T. J. Ahern. The first: "That Harvey Penick be engaged as golf professional as of June 1, 1943, on the same terms as those which were in effect with Mr. Jack Burke at the time of his death." The second: "That the hiring of a professional be deferred until October 15, 1943, in the hope of hiring Jimmy Demaret if he should be available at that time, and that the present arrangement with respect to the golf shop be continued until that time."

The minutes of that meeting suggest that Demaret, who worked at Plum Hollow Country Club in Southfield, Michigan, would be unavailable by contract until the fall. River Oaks already had installed Burke's widow, brother, and son to continue the golf operations, so the club faced no urgent need to act quickly. But the committee could have voted to offer the position to Harvey, who presumably was available sooner, providing a more seamless transition and the likelihood of longevity in the position.

The committee voted. Because one member was absent, it resulted in a tie. Months of debate ensued. Finally, in November, the club elected to offer the job to Demaret, who accepted. "Some directors wanted a teacher; some wanted a name golf professional," said Ed Turley, who played at Texas from 1952 to 1956 and later became a prominent tax lawyer in Houston. "Demaret's *unbelievable personality* carried the day for him, plus he was a known personality, having worked in the golf shop as a teenager for Jack Burke Sr."

Contrary to an assertion repeated in many published accounts that Harvey was offered, and turned down, the position at River Oaks, a formal offer was never made to him. He later told Preston Moore Jr., an accomplished junior player at River Oaks who tried unsuccessfully to qualify for Harvey's teams at Texas in the late 1940s and early '50s, that River Oaks was the only job for which he would have considered leaving Austin.

The division among the members of the search committee in 1943 illustrates how narrowly Harvey missed an opportunity to advance to a bigger city, work at a more prestigious club, and teach a different population of pupils. He would have been forced to resign as head coach at Texas before he won the second half of the twenty team Southwest Conference championships his teams eventually earned. Harvey might never have met Tom Kite and Ben Crenshaw. And he might never have acquainted himself with the screenwriter, novelist, and journalist Bud Shrake. The *Little Red Book* might never have been published.

But this much is known: Harvey never had that choice to make. River Oaks retained Demaret. Harvey remained in the city where he was born, thus assuring his fame — and the salvation of swinging the bucket, clipping the tee, giving luck a chance, and taking dead aim.

The Longhorns, meanwhile, kept winning golf trophies. Rice took the conference championship in 1939, ending the seven-year run Harvey and his players had enjoyed at the top of the Southwest Conference, but Texas snapped back to form in 1940. Texas won that trophy and the next seven.

The state of Texas observed its centennial in 1945 without the revelry such an occasion would have commanded in peacetime. The university annual published the names of former students killed in action—in France, in India, in Italy, in Luxembourg, in planes, in automobiles, in skirmishes, in seas. The 1945 *Cactus*'s list of the dead ran for eight pages. There were first lieutenants with BBA degrees, captains with MDs, ensigns who left for duty before they could graduate. "The world which emerges from the present conflict will be ours to shape," the editors of the annual noted. "For this reason the 1945 *Cactus* is dedicated to no one man, but to the builders of Texas—past, present and future."

An Army Air Corps veteran from Wichita Falls named Bob Watson came to Texas in 1946, hoping to make a life in golf. Big and sturdy, Bob Watson had trained as a flight engineer for B-29s until the program ended, then ran the golf clubhouse for enlisted men at Maxwell Field in Alabama until his discharge. He enrolled at Texas, inquired about the golf team, and found himself one day at the country club, meeting the head coach.

Watson won the qualifier his first year on campus. Harvey liked everything about his new player but his grip. Harvey wanted Watson to play a right-to-left draw. "If you learn how to do that," he told Watson, "you can learn to do anything with the ball. You have to learn to draw the ball first."

Watson obeyed. He helped the Longhorns win the team conference championship in 1946 and '47, the latter at Lions Municipal. Watson claimed the individual medal by twenty-five shots as a junior, when Texas narrowly vacated the 1948 conference title, won by Texas A&M. A season later, Texas won thirty of thirty-six matches. No one could touch the Longhorns. Watson proved a formidable leader for Harvey with teammates Reece Alexander, Marion Pfluger, William Smith, and a winsome junior from Austin named Morris Williams Jr., a supremely gifted player Harvey regarded as fondly as a second son. Williams finished second to Watson that season in the Southwest Conference tournament. "The powerful one-two punch of Bob Watson and Morris Williams Jr. led the way to the SWC golf crown and bathed the tower in orange light once more," the *Cactus* yearbook noted.

Watson wanted nothing more from life than golf. He left the University of Texas before he graduated, certain his education was complete, and started a career, both playing and teaching golf, that brought him many low-level professional victories and elite club positions throughout Westchester County in New York. Years on, when he was a professional at the tony Westchester Country Club, Watson invited Harvey to New York for the 1959 U.S. Open at nearby Winged Foot Golf Club. They walked among the swells of the gallery, two friends deeply responsible for one another's success in golf, watching Ben Hogan and Arnold Palmer and Billy Casper, the eventual winner. Harvey "asked about Claude Harmon and Tommy Armour and Gene Sarazen," Watson said a half-century later. "He wanted to know what they were thinking about while they were playing, what they were teaching. He was always willing to learn and listen to other people."

The fall semester of 1946 brought another University of Texas freshman to Austin: a serious and science-minded woman with wavy hair parted on the side and a budding fascination with golf.

Betsy Rawls was born in South Carolina, lived the first three years of her life in North Carolina, and moved to Texas when the National Park Service sent her father to Burnet, a Hill Country town where the children, both girls and boys, played football, baseball, and cowboys and Indians in fields teeming with bluebonnets that rippled in the spring winds from the southeast.

She and her older brother, Bob, explored the craggy granite hills around Inks Lake, part of the Highland Lakes chain of the lower Colorado River, where their father was developing a state park. She barreled through her childhood with spontaneous vigor. Before she finished elementary school, Rawls had fractured one arm while swinging from a rope tied to a tree, pretending to be Tarzan, and the other arm after a tumble from a bicycle, which she attempted to ride while standing on the seat. Rawls relished even the most inconsequential challenge. But more than that, she burned to conquer it.

When her family moved to Arlington, between Dallas and Fort

Worth, in the early 1940s, Rawls took up tennis. She also cultivated a deep interest in books, and her father recommended she read Charles Dickens and Victor Hugo. Rawls finished the entire works of both before she turned sixteen. She never played football again.

Reading allowed Rawls a rich view of the world beyond Texas. But she found true joy in science, especially physics. She possessed a sharply rational mind and an aptitude for calculation, qualities she hoped to sharpen in a college science lab after high school. Then she discovered golf.

R. M. Rawls took his precocious daughter to the golf course with him when she was seventeen. Her first attempt to propel a ball with a club secured her unshakable calling. From that moment, Rawls sought absolute dominion over a game that repelled sovereignty. The prospect of winning at golf, of beating other people, held no particular appeal to Rawls. She wanted to push to be perfect. She wanted to own the singular, physical relationship between her and her golf ball.

A week after graduating in 1945 as valedictorian of her high school class, Rawls enrolled at North Texas Junior College. She remained there for a year, until her brother returned from service in World War II and her family moved to Austin. Rawls had just played her first tournament that summer, the West Texas Invitational, and she had qualified for the championship flight. But she lost her first match. She lost her first consolation match too. She was not perfect. Nothing was. "I went home with fire in my eyes," she said.

Rawls studied physics at Texas. Her coursework demanded a great deal of time in the lab, but she also committed more time than she ever had before to golf, patronizing Lions Municipal and its head professional, Tom Penick, who cooed to his younger brother about her organically pure form. Rawls never sacrificed her schoolwork for the practice. She was far too astute for that. But she learned that a disciplined routine on campus allowed enough time to fit in a round or two on the weekends and a couple of evenings on the practice green, where she sometimes was the only woman — and usually the one holing the most putts.

The regulars at Lions recognized promise when they saw it. She needed to meet Harvey, they recommended. Rawls soon made arrangements to secure her first lesson at Austin Country Club, where she saw the players on the men's team. She wished the university had a team for women, but it did not. Rawls was smitten the very moment she met the thin, polite, and shy man who insisted she call him Harvey.

He invited her into the clubhouse for a cup of coffee and a visit. He asked about her start in golf. He asked her what she wanted to accomplish in their venture together. He wanted to know why she wanted to play, and how much she was willing to devote to the craft, and whether she would work hard in between their visits. He asked to see her grip.

Harvey was honest with Rawls. He told her he would be delighted to help, but he wanted her to know that he intended to learn from her too. "I'm just practicing on you," he said often, notably when she inquired about the cost of a lesson, an overture he resolutely deflected. His sincerity touched Rawls. She was drawn to his modesty, "his interest in students for their own sakes rather than for the sake of his own reflected glory," she would write a decade later in *Professional Golfer* magazine. She detected his interest in a "mutual confidence," the feeling that their alliance functioned on a level of absolute belief in one another.

But her instant fidelity toward Harvey was about much more than that. It was the 1940s in Texas, after all. Rarely had Rawls encountered a man, especially one twice her age, who treated her with such dignity and in such a spirit of equality. With men, Rawls said, "he was one of the boys." But Harvey resonated with women on a different level. "He had that old-fashioned idea that put women on a pedestal. He gave them total respect. He was so kind."

They did not see one another often. Rawls came four or five times a year, between experiments in the physics lab or whenever she felt a tick in her swing. "It was a different world back then," she said. "The relationship between coaches and students was completely different." Harvey sought to fix her feet in a position that looked natural. He reminded her constantly to check her grip. He supervised a succession of shots without uttering a word. If they sailed well, he simply nodded and ambled away, leaving Rawls with the notion that nothing required his attention, which filled her with confidence. Harvey never bothered with small matters, like whether her wrists pronated or supinated, or how she held her finish for imagined photographers at some future U.S. Women's Open. "He wasn't the kind that overcoached," Rawls said.

Rawls won the second annual Austin Women's City Championship, played at Austin Country Club, in 1948. She won the Texas Women's Amateur title later that summer. She played in the Texas Open and, before classes began in August, traveled to California for her first competition outside of the state. There, she said, "I realized how far I had to go to become a good golfer."

In the spring, Rawls packed for Fort Worth to play in her second state amateur championship. She and Harvey had buffed her game to a fine polish, and Rawls won the trophy, beating established amateurs such as Betty MacKinnon and Polly Riley. Rawls played a full schedule in the summer of '49. She lost in the first round of the Western Open, but won the Trans-Mississippi Championship. She qualified for her first U.S. Women's Amateur that fall, but lost in the second round. Nevertheless, she smartly understood the deeper rewards that came with every competitive round, win or lose. Rawls was evolving into a force in women's golf.

Harvey recognized that. Their lessons became less pedagogical and more about fundamentals maintenance. It would remain that way throughout Rawls's blossoming career. "He was a teacher of how to play the game of golf," she said, six decades after she met him for that first lesson in Austin. "He wasn't a teacher of golf swings to [the] exclusion of everything else." Rawls and Harvey maintained their friendship — their mutually respectful alliance — for the rest of his life. Rawls somehow always knew they would. She was especially aware in the summer of '49 that she would need him occasionally, and that Harvey would be there when she did.

"He wanted no credit," Rawls said. "He didn't seek the limelight. He didn't teach for recognition. You never saw him on a practice tee at a golf tournament. He would never stand on a stage and give a lesson like some of those hotshots do today."

In the fall of '49, Rawls prepared for her final year at Texas. She would graduate in the spring with a degree in physics and math and a gold Phi Beta Kappa key.

Harvey often told Rawls how proud he was of her. For years, when someone asked him about her, Harvey might mention her elegant tempo, or her burn for perfection, or her discipline to practice the drills he gently suggested. He might say something about her role as a pioneer in women's golf. The golf anecdotes varied. But one fact did not.

He always mentioned the key.

As Harvey celebrated his team's second consecutive conference trophy in 1950, other matters occupied his mind. Austin Country Club, whose property north of the university had been such an important part of Harvey's life since he was a scrawny eight-year-old caddie, was making a move to the other side of the city.

It was an evolution years in the making. It also was inevitable. Readers of the *Austin Evening Statesman* had noticed a brief, vague article on March 3, 1945, under the headline "Country Club Property Too Valuable for Golf." The sentiment likely appealed to those well-traveled Austin Country Club members who had seen other prominent private courses in Texas, such as River Oaks, Houston Country Club, Oak Hills Country Club in San Antonio, or the gleaming parkland jewel of Texas: Colonial Country Club in Fort Worth.

Colonial opened in 1936 on the western edge of the city, along the Trinity River, just north of TCU. Designed by two distinguished course architects, Perry Maxwell and Harvey's friend John Bredemus, Colonial showed guests from Austin what a modern golf course should be. Its understated, red-brick clubhouse gave members sweeping views of a broad, muscular golf course with long par-4 holes and bentgrass greens, a rare privilege in warm-weather states such as Texas. Tall pecan trees lined the ribboning fairways. Precisely engineered water hazards, walled at the edges in stone, conveyed sublime harmony with the elements — and frightful challenges to players. Thoughtful bunkering multiplied the thrill. Every one of the eighteen holes exuded a mark of originality that the old Austin Country Club, charming though it was, thoroughly lacked. Colonial established a new standard for golf in Texas.

Members noticed. Their travels to Colonial, Oak Hills, Brook Hollow in Dallas, or River Oaks in Houston suggested that Austin Country Club was a marginal test of golf at best and, at worst, obsolete. When the USGA awarded Colonial the 1941 U.S. Open, momentum prevailed two hundred miles south in Austin: the time had arrived to modernize.

Austin Country Club announced in late 1946 its intention to sell "the old homestead" and find "commodious quarters" elsewhere in the city. A year later, it identified a treed, modestly flat, and available-for-sale two-hundred-acre former dairy farm near the Colorado River, five miles east of downtown. The tract was rich in soil good for growing Bermuda grass and close to the river, a reliable water supply in a region that invariably encountered harsh summer droughts.

Harvey favored Bredemus, his friend and occasional fellow competitor, as the architect of record for the new course. But club officials retained Maxwell, who also had designed Southern Hills in Oklahoma and Prairie Dunes in Kansas in addition to Colonial. The city bought the old club. Maxwell sharpened his pencils.

Harvey moved his family to a limestone ranch house on a short loop behind the tee of Perry Maxwell's new twelfth hole, a block north of Riverside Drive. The city later named the street Penick Drive.

To the family, the new club seemed to truly be in the country. Tinsley, now twelve, had become interested in raising stock, and he and his father built a pen behind the house for his Hereford steer. Harvey had long ago purchased a horse from a member for Kathryn, who was preparing for her freshman year at TCU. When Tinsley went outside to tend to the animals, he often found arrowheads in the dirt.

The move to the Riverside location added to Harvey's obligations, and so he curtailed his own competition schedule even more. It was Harvey's first experience with preparing and opening a club. With the new, bigger golf course and additional room for infrastructure, the club could build a larger membership. It could also serve as a site for the Texas Golf Association state competitions — a welcome development for the prestige of golf in Texas but yet another claim on Harvey's time. Byron Nelson, who later became one of Harvey's closest friends in the PGA community, came to Austin to survey the new course. He declared that it "will be one of the best in this section of the country . . . good enough for any championship tournament." Harvey appreciated the endorsement, but he also understood the implication. If the new Austin Country Club was good enough to please Nelson, so it would be for everyone else. The new club would be a busy place, and Harvey would be an even busier man.

Helen kept a scrapbook of her husband's accomplishments as a player. The neatly trimmed headlines taped to the pages reminded Harvey of how good he used to be. "Course Record Established by Penick." "Penick Pushes by in Tourney." "Penick and Burke Leading State Tourney." "Penick Enters Los Angeles." "Penick Honored by PGA." "Penick Elected to Lead Pros."

Yet Harvey knew his time as a player was reaching its inevitable end. He was forty-five years old when the club moved to East Austin. Now he was traveling farther, beyond the boundaries of Texas, to lead teaching seminars for the PGA. He bought a small farm in Lockhart, thirty miles south of Austin, where he and Tinsley drove the only car the family owned to clear brush and care for a modest herd of cattle. His lesson sheet, meanwhile, remained full. And the Scribbletex notebook in his rolltop desk contained fewer blank pages.

He continued to enter state PGA-sanctioned events, but he no longer regularly attempted to qualify for the Texas Open and other tournaments. His identity began to shift. The caddie who became a player who became a club professional who became an instructor now was becoming ensconced, firmly and forever, as the guardian of golf's simplest truths. They were there, in the notebook seen by no one but Harvey.

Occasionally he appeared in exhibitions, as many local professionals did in Texas. None was more celebrated than the one on May 13, 1950, at Lions Municipal in the prosperous West Austin neighborhood of Tarrytown, where his brother Tom was the pro.

More than a thousand spectators gathered for that bright morning in Austin. It was the largest crowd ever assembled in the city to watch a golf event. Each patron paid $2 that day for the privilege, but not to watch Harvey, or even Morris Williams Jr., the NCAA runner-up in 1949, or Ed Hopkins Jr., the runner-up the year before.

They came to see Hogan.

Harvey had arranged for Ben Hogan — now thirty-seven years old and the cagey winner of a U.S. Open and two PGA championships — to participate in a golf clinic and exhibition four-ball match sponsored by the Austin Junior Chamber of Commerce. The appearance drew enormous interest. Hogan had nearly died fifteen months earlier, when his car collided with a bus in West Texas. But he had recovered and was now thriving. He had just tied a tour record of 21 under par the week before, winning the Greenbrier Open in 259 strokes.

Hogan was on his way to Hollywood to film a movie when he stopped that Saturday morning in Austin, where he and Harvey were set to play Williams and Hopkins. A parade of Fords, Dodges, and a few new Cadillac convertibles lined Enfield Road that morning where it intersected with Exposition Boulevard. Traffic was thick, and so was the excitement. "The Hawk" was in town to play a round of golf.

The exhibition began at 1:30 P.M. Hogan wore a gray alpaca sweater with muted tan trousers and the extra Hogan spike in the center of the sole of his right shoe. The small man with the cutting dark eyes seemed to be in a pleasant state of mind as he performed his repertoire of shots on the practice range, starting with his wedges, finishing with his driver. He noticed a dark-haired young woman he appeared to recognize and invited her to participate. Betsy Rawls, the reigning state amateur champion, smiled coyly. Absent golf shoes and golf glove, and using Harvey's driver, she laced a shot downrange that drew robust applause from the hometown crowd. Then another. Then another. "Good ones, too," noted the golf writer for the *Sunday American-Statesman*.

The theatrics were only beginning. On that spring afternoon in Austin, spectators saw a jovial, even mischievous, side of Hogan.

The match began at two o'clock on the first hole at Lions. Without letting anyone in on the joke, Hogan staggered through the wall of spectators, then feigned a wobble, as if he had ordered one too many mimosas with breakfast. He doffed his cap when introduced on the crowded tee and replaced it crookedly on his head. He teed his ball unsteadily. He stumbled to his knees. "What's wrong with Hogan?" gasped someone in the gallery. "Why, it looks like he's drunk," offered someone else. Hogan rubbed his eyes, squinted down the fairway, and tripped backwards. He persuaded himself into position to swing.

He took an exaggerated lash at his ball—*and missed*. The Hawk grunted loudly. No one spoke. No one knew what to think. Hogan clumsily knocked his ball from the tee with a backhanded swipe. His caddie scurried to replace it. Hogan took his address again, teetering on his heels. He topped his shot.

Harvey, Hopkins, and Williams hit theirs down the fairway. The group trudged to Hogan's ball, which he sliced like a once-a-month player trying to reach the moon. His hat fell off this time. He replaced it, sideways. On the green, he slapped his first two putts twenty feet past the cup. He holed his third for a score no one dared calculate.

Silence.

Hogan fetched his ball, scanned the stunned spectators surrounding the green, and smiled.

"Okay, partner," he said to Harvey. "It's up to you on this hole. I'll do better from now on."

This was a new Ben Hogan. Harvey had always admired Hogan's intensity and focus, but he appreciated his wry sense of humor just as much, so he laughed too. Harvey clucked when his partner ripped a sublime drive to the center of the fairway on the next hole. He sensed a shift in the mood. This was no U.S. Open, Colonial Invitational, or even Sunday afternoon Nassau. But it was golf against someone else. The game was afoot.

"Harvey," Hogan said as they walked down the second hole, "I flew over a lake coming in here. Which way is that lake?" He also wanted to know which direction was west. Someone pointed south, to the Colorado River, which they could not see through the trees. But Hogan now knew one truth about Lions: how the greens broke. Slopes, Hogan understood, always lean toward the low point of the land, or west, all other conditions being equal.

Hogan and Harvey were tied with the amateurs through two holes. Then Hogan birdied the third, giving the professionals a 1-up lead. The spontaneous vaudeville production continued later when a movie camera whirred at the top of Hogan's swing. In competition such a distraction would elicit a hard, accusing stare. This time Hogan merely grinned.

Hogan was Hogan now. He shot 3-under 32 on the front half. He birdied the tenth and eleventh to dip to 5 under par. A bogey on the back nine gave him a 4-under 67, and with Harvey's 2-over 73, the professionals beat the amateurs, two and one.

"The Fort Worth ace was impressed with the Austin Municipal, classing it one of the best public courses he's played," Morris Williams Sr. wrote for his *American-Statesman* readers the next morning. "It's so good, it makes you think you're not in Texas," Hogan said as he worked his way down a line of autograph seekers extending admission tickets for him to authenticate. Decades later, when Harvey included a chapter about the exhibition in his second book, he recalled with clear fondness the humanity Hogan shared with Austin that afternoon. "Few people remembered the result of the match," Harvey wrote. "But everyone that day remembered Hogan on the first hole. They talked about it for years."

Harvey continued: "The rest of the way, Ben played that charity match as if it were the U.S. Open," he wrote, which was true. "The college boys beat us 1-up," which was not.

Maybe he forgot. Maybe that's how he remembered it. Or maybe he recast the truth because he wanted the world to know how good his boys, Hopkins and Williams, really were. Especially Williams. Because the world never would.

Chapter Five

HARVEY NEVER COACHED a black player on his teams at Texas. It would be decades before the country club accepted its first black member; moreover, Harvey, as the head professional, had nothing to do with the composition of its membership. His attitudes about race therefore remain a mystery.

A city of more than 132,000 at midcentury, Austin was patently segregated. Having long since designated the east side of Austin a "Negro district," the city provided municipal services to its black citizens, such as schools, sewerage, and parks, in these limited areas. The African American community included 150 businesses at the time, along with thirty churches and two colleges. If a black family wanted to go out for dinner in 1950, stay in a hotel, use a city bus, or attend school, the established Jim Crow laws, enforcing separate-but-equal status, required them to do so apart from their white peers.

Golf punctured that inequity a year after the Hogan exhibition at Lions. What happened in 1951 suggests that the members of the golf community in Austin—a group that definitely included Tom and Harvey Penick—showed surprising tolerance, even acceptance, for the times.

Taylor Glass, the Austin mayor at the time, was informed one morning that two black youths were playing golf at Lions. There is no indication whether the two had paid the fee to play or had snuck onto the grounds, as many youths did then. But the fact remains that they were on a city-operated golf course in the Jim Crow era, when the doctrine established by the 1896 U.S. Supreme Court decision *Plessy vs. Ferguson* continued to be used in the South to justify segregating municipal facilities.

"This was before there was any mixing of the races in restaurants, schools, or anywhere," Glass said two decades later. The 1954 *Brown vs. Board of Education* case, which ended official segregation in the United States, was still three years away.

Glass deliberated that day in 1951. He had the authority to direct Tom Penick or any other city employee, including the Austin police, to order the two African Americans to vacate the course. But he did not. "I don't see why it ought to bother anybody," Glass said in response to the news about the two youths playing at Lions. "I'm for leaving them alone." No one objected. No police officers were dispatched. No one at Lions was ordered to chase the players from the course. "We went on and let them play," Glass said, "and never heard a word."

If two black golfers wanted to challenge Jim Crow attitudes in Texas, Austin may have seemed like the place most sympathetic to their cause. The segregationist climate had begun to shift by 1951, given the U.S. Supreme Court's landmark decision in June 1950 to allow Heman Sweatt of Waco, Texas, admission to the University of Texas Law School. Sweatt, an African American, had met every qualification but was denied admission to the school in 1946 based only on his race. The Court determined that the equal protection clause of the Fourteenth Amendment required that Sweatt be allowed to attend UT because the state law school for African Americans in Houston failed to offer a substantially equal education. Sweatt and another black student, the future architect John Saunders Chase, were waiting in line at the registrar's office the next day, permanently integrating graduate education at the University of Texas.

The two newspapers in Austin had trumpeted the news in bold headlines in 1951, but neither mentioned, a year later, the city's quiet refusal to disrupt the golf game of two black youths playing at Lions.

The significance of that statement of tolerance went unrecognized for fifty-seven years. In 2008 a group of Lions players, wondering how many other municipal golf courses in Texas had become desegregated by 1951, learned that it was the first municipal course south of the Mason-Dixon Line to verifiably integrate the races. The discovery made national news.

It also led to a push to commemorate Tom and Harvey Penick's stewardship of the course for three decades, including the period when the two black youths were allowed to play there. The Texas Historical Commission placed a marker at the entrance to the club in 2009, noting the distinction. Mary Arnold, a longtime advocate for Lions Municipal Golf Course—which was also known as "Muny"—spoke at a small ceremony in October of that year. "In the wide, open spaces of Muny, everybody gets to play," Arnold said that day.

Not everyone got to play at Austin Country Club, however, in 1951. There is no record of whether African Americans were denied membership, just as there is no record of whether any applied. But a number of black youths caddied at the club, where they were embraced by Harvey and his golf staff, said former caddie Lawrence Byrd.

Byrd and his older brother Jesse lived in Montopolis, the black and Mexican-American neighborhood that had been known as the Negro district. Austin's only private golf course had effectively relocated to the center of the city's minority population. The Byrd boys, known as "Big Weasel" and "Little Weasel," were among twenty to thirty regular caddies at the club—which they reached through a cut in the trees—who earned $1.50 a round, and $2.50 for carrying two bags.

"That's how we survived," Lawrence Byrd remembered more than fifty years later. "That money went a long way."

Harvey allowed no acts of bigotry or racism in the caddie yard, Byrd recalled. He let his caddies roam anywhere on the property—excluding the locker room, which even the golf staff avoided. The caddies had a small, white building behind the shop, under a sweeping oak. Between jobs, they pitched washers, hunted the woods for balls, gambled with dice, and created a crude pitching course along a shallow gulch. The Byrd brothers felt welcome to participate. Harvey gave them old clubs to use, and he allowed them to watch him teach. Harvey even gave the Byrd brothers rides to and from the club. "He took an interest in all of us," Lawrence Byrd said.

The caddies tried especially hard to loiter behind the practice tee when the Texas men's golf team came to the club to practice. Harvey and his surging Longhorns had won their second consecutive Southwest Conference championship in the spring of 1950, and they appeared ready to stage another long run of titles.

That was the year Morris Williams Jr., the Texas senior who lived across the street from the original Austin Country Club, faced a cocksure sophomore from Texas Christian University named Dan Jenkins — later an accomplished novelist and journalist for *Sports Illustrated* magazine — in an epic match at Colonial Country Club in Fort Worth. "Morris was a really nice guy," Jenkins said years later, "but when he got in competition, there was an ax murderer trying to climb out of his heart."

Williams and Jenkins stood all square after fifteen holes at mighty Colonial, the host course for the 1941 U.S. Open. "I was playing the round of my life," Jenkins recalled in 2010. The match between the top players for Texas and TCU that spring had started on the back nine in deference to the Colonial members; as a result, Jenkins and Williams faced a long, straight, and pecan-lined corridor as they prepared for the final three holes. Hogan happened to be on the grounds. He and Colonial founder Marvin Leonard met Williams and Jenkins on the tee of the par-4 hole to watch.

The story of what they saw in the next quarter-hour is still told today from Fort Worth to Austin.

Playing cautiously, Jenkins blocked a 1-iron into the right rough, behind the soaring pecans. Williams rifled a wood to the middle of the fairway. Jenkins studied his circumstances and considered all the possible outcomes, giving equal weight to the need for courage or discretion. A shot to the green required the distance of either a 7-iron or a 6-, depending on who was telling the story. (Harvey remembered the 6-iron; Jenkins, in 2010, said it was the 7-.) What remains beyond dispute is this: Jenkins needed to curve the ball sharply from right to left—a lilting boomerang from a campy lie—to make a shot to the green even possible from the tangle of grass and dense trees at Colonial.

Jenkins knew Williams faced no such obstacles and enjoyed a clear view of the wide green. He knew Hogan stood nearby. He knew the fate of his team's finish rested on his deliberation and choice. He also understood the vagaries of match play. In stroke play, in which each shot matters as much as any other, Jenkins might never have attempted such a bold and risky execution. He might not have tried to reach the green against an inferior player in the center of the fairway. But this was match play. That player was Williams. And there stood Hogan. So Jenkins addressed his shot, waggled, and swung.

Jenkins watched his ball climb cleanly over the limbs of the pecans. The shot landed without incident and swerved toward the hole. It came to rest six inches away. "Nice shot," Jenkins heard Williams say.

The next sound he heard was the *whoosh* of Williams's swing. Moments later, the ball tumbled into the hole for an eagle two.

Shaken, Jenkins three-putted the seventeenth hole, the secluded par-3 along the Trinity River. He lost the match, two and one. Williams shot 68 on a U.S. Open course that day, perhaps the most difficult course in the state, maybe the entire Southwest. "He was one of the greatest young amateurs in the history of Texas," Jenkins remembered a half-century after the match.

Buddy Weaver of Rice, a whip at 140 pounds, earned the individual medal that spring at the 1950 Southwest Conference tournament at Lions. He shot 4-under 280 to beat a field of thirty-one players, including Williams, whose rounds of 73-70-70-68 left him one behind Weaver.

Weaver holed three shots from the fairway in the final round, including his second for an eagle on the first hole. But Texas finished with five players inside the top ten. In addition, Williams, Reece Alexander, Wesley Ellis, Billy Penn, and Marion Pfluger gave Harvey the seventeenth team conference title of his career as the part-time coach of the UT men's golf team.

The Longhorns played unevenly at the NCAA Championship in Albuquerque, where North Texas won again, having beaten Texas and Purdue in 1949. Harvey's squad left New Mexico a year later no longer in the top ten — a crushing disappointment, given their runner-up finish the season before and, most significantly, the end of Williams's historic four-year career at Texas.

Williams seemed unstoppable in his chosen pursuit. Long-limbed and lanky at six feet and 135 pounds, darkly handsome and unnervingly quiet, he cuffed his khaki trousers twice at the hem to keep them unsoiled on the course. Williams had taken the Longhorns to three conference titles under Harvey, who considered Williams one of the purest, most naturally endowed players he'd ever seen. Harvey wondered if Ed White's records would survive the reign of Morris Williams Jr.

Williams was the only son of the golf columnist at the evening newspaper, the *Austin Statesman*. The Williams family — Morris Jr., his father, and his mother, Thelma — lived in a small, handsome single-story house at 517 East Fortieth Street, across the road from the seventeenth hole at Austin Country Club. An earnest student interested in fast cars, fast boats, all sports (including table tennis, at which he excelled), and almost as many girls, Williams won four city junior championships and often beat the best amateurs at the country club. No one, not even Harvey, could predict how far he might go in golf. His potential seemed limitless.

Williams absorbed every word Harvey spoke. He devoted himself to golf and the ways Harvey prescribed it in his secret Scribbletex notebook. As happened with many of his junior players, Harvey saw a reflection of himself in Williams. When Williams had been old enough to cross the street by himself, he had waited until early evening, then shimmied through a barbed-wire fence, carrying a canvas bag of shag balls. He scattered practice shots with a 7-iron to the green of the seventeenth hole. By the time he entered high school, Williams rarely curved a shot unless he meant to. He displayed professional-level expertise with a pitching wedge and "was a wizard with the putter," said longtime Austin Country Club member Bill Gainer, a teammate of Williams's at Austin High.

Harvey imagined so many destinies for Williams. He liked playing with his pupil, and did it often, because he learned from Williams's grip and divots. His swing — elegant, upright, eerily repeating, as if assembled at a drafting table with calipers and strain gauges — was the marvel of the Austin Country Club range and "all built by Harvey," Gainer said. Williams possessed uncanny hand-eye coordination. He carried himself quietly and smoked Chesterfields, like Hogan.

He rarely lost a match. Williams's 1-down loss to future two-time U.S. Amateur champion Harvie Ward on the final hole of the 1949 national championship in Ames, Iowa, devastated his coach and long-time friend. Harvey wanted Williams to win everything. He thought he could. He thought he should.

He nearly did too, in a magical span of golf between 1949 and 1950.

Williams entered the 1949 Texas Junior before his senior year at Texas. He churned through match play to face Bert Weaver of Beaumont in the thirty-six-hole final that July at Brackenridge Park. Williams birdied six of the first nine holes. Weaver made two birdies of his own, but "couldn't match the brilliant putting of his opponent," the Associated Press reported from San Antonio. Williams led 1-up after the first eighteen holes.

The afternoon round remained knotted through the front nine. Williams won the thirty-first hole. Weaver, two years younger than Williams and far less experienced at executing in the final stages of an important competition, faltered. Williams won, three and one.

He and Harvey then traveled to Midland late in May 1950 to compete in the Texas PGA Championship, a competition carrying a $5,000 purse and open to professionals and amateurs alike. The field of 123 players included Harvey, Williams, and his Longhorn teammate and close friend Marion Pfluger of Austin, as well as some prominent and colorful players of the young game in Texas: Shorty Hornbuckle of nearby Odessa, Bunny Plummer of Galveston, Smiley Rowland of Fort Worth, Shirley Robbins of Big Spring, and a kindly full-time rancher and part-time golfer from Roanoke named Byron Nelson.

Nelson had retired from full-time professional golf by this time. He'd crafted his historic eighteen-win season in 1945, when he made thirty starts and won eleven consecutive tournaments. Nelson finished that year by winning the Seattle Open and the Glen Garden Open in Fort Worth, where he had begun, as Harvey did in 1912 in Austin, as a caddie. Nelson started the 1946 season with victories in Los Angeles and San Francisco. He won four other times that year, his last on the tour. Nelson cruised into the 1946 U.S. Open at Canterbury Golf Club outside Cleveland and ended up in an epic, thirty-six-hole playoff with Lloyd Mangrum and Vic Ghezzi. Nelson missed a short putt for par on the seventeenth hole in the second playoff round and accepted privately that he would win no more major championships. He wanted to go home to his wife and ranch and church. He was thirty-four years old and finished.

Nelson rarely played competitive golf after 1946. But he entered the 1950 Texas PGA Championship, most likely out of kinship with the state section, but also because he liked playing with club professionals and college stars. The tournament started with a pro-am on Wednesday, May 31, at the nine-hole Midland Country Club, which stretched to 6,641 yards and was played twice around from different sets of tees.

A squall burst over the grounds late in the afternoon, and some players failed to finish. Nelson was one of them. Harvey shot 73. Williams played the meaningless round in three fewer strokes, a 2-under 70, six behind professional Tucker Bowles of Bay City, who won with Williams as his partner in the best-ball format. Bowles kept the prize to himself. Williams, still an amateur, was entitled to no money.

The next day, Texas governor Allan Shivers, who knew and admired Harvey, donned a dark suit and white hat for the Sixteenth Annual World Championship Midland Rodeo. Shivers ate a plate of West Texas barbecue at an event attended by four hundred people in his honor, and he posed for pictures with Harold Smith, who represented the Mid-Continent Petroleum Corporation. The governor later participated in a parade, but there is no record that he made it to the country club to watch his friends from Austin.

Harvey matched the 73 he shot in the pro-am, five strokes out of the lead of the tournament. With a 68, Williams shared the lead with Roane Puett, a senior-to-be at Midland High School and future Texas Longhorn under Harvey, as his caddie. Billy Maxwell, his rival from North Texas, also posted 68. "Both played a sharp game all the way," wrote Shorty Shelburne, the sports editor at the *Midland Reporter-Telegram*.

Nelson recorded a 3-under 69. "Nelson's game was alternately hot and cold," Shelburne observed. "He had three birdies on the first nine holes and was going strong with a 33 at the turn. But on the tenth he caught a bogey five." (Nelson tamped any alarm among the considerable gallery with a thrilling eagle at the eleventh, a par-5. If he had cared like he used to care about winning golf tournaments, Nelson would have gone to sleep that Thursday night in Midland with the assurance that another trophy was very much within reach.)

Williams executed beautifully in the second round, which he completed in sixty-six swings, which "set off a lot of tongue wagging among the galleryites," Shelburne wrote. The reigning Texas Junior champion and recent Texas graduate tied with Dallas pro Ray Gafford and amateur Joe Conrad of North Texas for the lead after thirty-six holes. "Williams has played the most brilliant golf of the tourney the last two days," noted Shelburne, who mentioned Harvey in the "Sport Slants" column inside the section: "Penick tutors golfers at the University of Texas and has done one of the best jobs at it that we can remember."

That was the last time the sports editor of the newspaper mentioned Harvey that week. But he would write the name of Morris Williams Jr. many more times.

Williams lost a stroke to the lead Saturday in the third round when Maxwell, with a 66, claimed the lead. Williams shot a credible 70, earning brief mention in the news the next day: "Maxwell and Williams are the class of the amateurs and there is little chance they will be overtaken by anyone but Nelson, Gafford or Joe Conrad," all of whom finished at even-par 206. Maxwell, at 203, started the final round Sunday with a one-shot lead over Williams. Nelson, Gafford, and Conrad trailed the young Austinite by two. The *Reporter-Telegram* predicted a "torrid race" on the last day of the Texas PGA. "The largest gallery in the history of golf here is expected to turn out," readers of the newspaper learned that Sunday morning, June 4.

The final round of the Texas PGA coincided with the fourth annual Celebrities Golf Tournament across the country in Washington, DC, where two Texans seized the lead in a competition among golfers, politicians, and entertainers at the Army-Navy Country Club. More than 7,500 spectators in the nation's capital watched Hogan sign his scorecard for a 65 and Didrickson Zaharias sign hers for a 69. Bob Hope, Milton Berle, Danny Kaye, and Frank Sinatra participated. So did elected officials — Representative Sydney Yates, an Illinois Democrat with a swing that crossed party lines, posted 76 to lead the "Official Washington" division of the tournament, which also included cabinet members, Supreme Court justices, other congressional leaders, and high-ranking military officers. A soft mid-Atlantic shower soaked the affair.

Coincidentally, more than an inch of rain — as rare as a cool breeze in the Permian Basin of West Texas that summer — soaked the Texas PGA golfers that Sunday in June. The storm stretched across much of the state, all the way to Victoria and the Gulf Coast, plunking hail that cracked windshields in nearby Odessa. Nelson, Williams, and Maxwell, the leaders in the Texas PGA, evaded the weather, owing to the late starting times reserved for contenders. Williams's trousers, cuffed twice at his ankles, looked flawless as he held his club with his Harvey-built grip at the first tee that historic afternoon.

Nelson and Gafford shot the rounds of the day, 3-under-par 69s on the soggy grounds of Midland Country Club. Gafford, the defending champion, made a bogey five on the eighteenth hole; Nelson holed a ten-foot putt for a birdie three. Williams stared at a nine-foot putt to win. "Make it, boy," Nelson encouraged.

Williams planted his feet, squared his hips, folded his fingers over the handle, and guided the shaft back through his line. Wrote Shelburne for the *Reporter-Telegram:* "It was perfect." Sam Schneider, one of the professionals at River Oaks in Houston, watched the proceedings from the rim of the green. "That was courage," he said.

Shelburne's story the next day included this line: "The win by Williams and a tie with Gafford and Nelson by Billy Maxwell reversed the popular selections. Saturday, everybody thought Maxwell was a cinch to win and add more glory to the North Texas State golf team's great record. But Williams took down the top honors for the University of Texas, from which he graduated this year, and for himself. Both the amateurs are identified with their schools in every breath." With his triumph that afternoon, Williams assumed custody of two of the three most significant trophies in Texas golf. The twenty-year-old champion of the Texas Junior and Texas PGA would soon return home to practice for the Texas Amateur Championship, scheduled for later that month in San Antonio.

Harvey was deeply moved. He cared little about the 77 he shot that Sunday in the Texas PGA, a score that gave him a 15-over-par, middle-of-the-leaderboard 303 for the tournament. His week in Midland mattered only because his pupil and prodigy had beaten a field that included college rivals, the finest playing professionals in the state, and, above all, Nelson. "Byron Nelson still is the old master and the Mr. Golf in Texas to me," Williams said after the tournament. "I couldn't have beat him with a stick if he had been putting good all the way around."

The young winner posed wearily for a picture with Dr. Allen Coffey, a prominent Fort Worth physician who had furnished the enormous trophy since 1935. Williams held the gleaming cup, waist-high, with slender, tanned arms. His rolled-up khakis, secured by a narrow black belt, barely reached the tops of his white socks. He personified American 1950s-era innocence straddling the moment between boyhood and whatever awaited him as a man. He looked content. He looked like he was ready for Hogan. Williams smiled broadly for the photographer that afternoon in Midland. "I was lucky," he said.

Williams won the Texas Amateur too, beating a field of more than 180 players and a captain at Lackland Air Force Base, five and four, in the final two-round match. Williams played the thirty-two holes at Oak Hills Country Club in 2 under par. "I was hitting the ball real good, probably my best of the tournament," he said. Williams took home the silver, ninety-nine-pound T. L. Edwards Trophy, gathered the other two that he had won, and brought all three to the country club, where Harvey could see them. They posed for pictures and celebrated a feat that had never been accomplished in the history of Texas golf, and never would be seen again. Williams's father joined them for the occasion. "You did it, son," he said. "You did it."

The next time he returned to Midland, Williams had joined the country club as an assistant professional and was living in the garage apartment of the family of his Texas PGA caddie, Roane Puett. Williams was determined to polish his game for the tour.

He entered as many tournaments as he could afford to play that summer. He played alongside Nelson again, and Don January of North Texas State, in the pro-am at Odessa Country Club, a better-ball competition in Permian Basin that attracted the best players in West Texas and gamblers with oil money to wager. The Calcuttas reached frightening levels at Odessa Country Club. The riches at stake in the ample side bets attracted huge galleries, most of them there to monitor the progress of the golfers they had bet on, not the quality of golf being played. Puett caddied for Williams when the young Texas graduate was paired with Nelson and January. Puett proposed a match-play wager with Nelson's caddie: If Williams hit his approach shot closer than Nelson, Puett would win the hole. If Nelson's ball finished closer, the other caddie would win.

Puett won the bet.

Williams played professional tournaments up and down California. He drove to Arizona, where Gary Nixon, a professional at Sam Snead's course in White Sulphur Springs, West Virginia, reported to his starting time and met Williams on the tee. "This boy had the sweetest swing I ever saw," said Nixon, whose point of reference included Snead himself as well as the tour players who came to West Virginia each year for the Greenbriar Open. "The old pros were really sold on [Williams]," Nixon said, adding that they believed he was "one of the most promising youngsters in the game." Williams played in Tucson. He finished in a tie for eighth at the Mexico Open.

Harvey saw him infrequently by now. Williams returned to Austin in December for an exhibition match at the country club and played with Alice Bauer against Harvey and reigning Texas women's amateur champion Betsy Rawls. Williams and Bauer won, four and three. Williams shot 66 on his own ball. Harvey shot 75. He marveled at the maturity of Williams and the potential he seemed to be realizing. Harvey missed him so much. But the duties of teaching others and running the new golf shop at the Riverside location kept him busy enough to forget how much he wished he could see Williams at the club each day, as he had for so many years.

Nelson, meanwhile, remained in retirement at Fairway Ranch, caring for chickens and three hundred head of Hereford cattle. He spent little time anymore on the paved roads that connected tour stops and more time outside in the North Texas wind, watching after his stock. He and his wife, Louise, used the car only to go to services at the Church of Christ and not much more. "I don't miss much about being on tour," Nelson told a reporter in those early days.

Hogan flourished. Two years after his near-crippling car crash, twelve months after the majestic 1-iron shot to the eighteenth green at Merion that helped him win the 1950 U.S. Open, Hogan repeated the championship at oppressive Oakland Hills outside Detroit. Williams's old rival Dan Jenkins, early in his career as a sports journalist, documented the historic conquest for the *Fort Worth Press*. "Those who watched the golf at Oakland Hills saw the greatest player in the game win on what may have been the toughest Open course ever devised," Jenkins wrote.

It was Hogan's third U.S. Open Championship. Harvey and Williams appreciated Hogan's accomplishment as much as anyone in golf. They knew about the accident on February 2, 1949, that had injured Hogan and his wife Valerie. It had happened in Texas, after all, near tiny Van Horn, a couple of hours east of El Paso. The Hogans' Cadillac collided with a Greyhound bus on Highway 80. No one knew if Hogan would survive his first night in the hospital. But nine months later, two weeks before Thanksgiving, Hogan began easing full shots down the practice range at Colonial, where he once had watched a Texas Longhorn named Williams rip the spirit of a normally irrepressible TCU Horned Frog named Jenkins.

When the news from Oakland Hills in the summer of '51 reached Texas, Williams was convinced of his destiny. He knew more than ever that he wanted to be a part of the tour life, to compete against Hogan and Sam Snead and the rest at places such as Oakland Hills and Canterbury and Merion and even Augusta National. Harvey certainly supported Williams, whose swing mechanics and psychological composition seemed ready for the rigors of tournament golf. But like any young player with boundless dreams, Williams needed help. His father chiseled a modest living for himself and Thelma, but the salary of a newsman could not accommodate a son who wanted to travel in cuffed trousers to professional golf tournaments from California to Florida, no matter how good his prospects for success happened to be. Williams needed a plan to finance his dreams of playing golf.

So he enlisted in the air force. The United States was at war in Korea, but the conflict had reached a position of stalemate by July 1951, at which time the Thirty-Eighth Parallel of the Korean Peninsula had returned to a demarcation line separating the two Koreas and their allies, the United States and China. The conflict continued only in small skirmishes. Military leaders on both sides broached the topic of peace.

The newly commissioned Lieutenant Morris Williams Jr. was trained as a pilot at Lackland in San Antonio, where he had won his last Texas Amateur two weeks after defeating Nelson at the Texas PGA. The military knew an asset when it saw one. The commanders nominated Williams to represent the branch at the annual Interservice Golf Championships, a competition among soldiers, sailors, airmen, and, from 1950 to 1953, a Coast Guard yeoman from Pennsylvania named Arnold Palmer.

As in his civilian life, golf consumed Williams's earliest months in the air force. That changed when he was selected for the Aviation Cadet Program. Williams spent eleven days in Austin over Christmas 1951, returned to flight school, and barely had time to contemplate Harvey's lessons anymore. "We are right in the middle of the busiest phase of the whole Cadet program — instrument flying, which is a good deal nerve-wracking; inane classes all morning and every morning; inspections every day; drill and physical training; and night flying starts next Monday," he wrote in January 1952 to an aunt and uncle in Fort Worth. "But, then I think of Korea; and even the merest mumble seems facetious and a little bit childish. This is only a picnic if you consider emergency to be a natural state of existence."

In 1953 Williams learned that he would be training to fly F-86 Sabre fighters out of Eglin Air Force Base, near the sugary Gulf Coast sands of Fort Walton Beach, Florida, and Choctawhatchee Bay. The twenty-three-year-old officer left the 436th Fighter-Bomber Squadron in California for his special detachment to Eglin. He arrived in Florida to the seismic whine of Sabre jets, menacing silver warplanes that recorded 757 air victories above Korea. Williams would be among the next batch of Sabre pilots.

His mother and father traveled that summer to Washington, DC, to watch him compete in the Interservice Golf Championships. They saw him capture the title, beating Tom Nieporte, representing the army, and Jon Gustin of the navy. The two-day, $15,000 Celebrities Golf Tournament commenced directly after, with President Dwight D. Eisenhower, Vice President Richard Nixon, General Omar Bradley, and the entertainer Bob Hope in the field. Morris Williams Sr. returned home with more clippings for the pair of scrapbooks about his son's rise in the game Harvey taught him.

Morris Williams Sr. had just observed his twentieth anniversary as the golf writer at the newspaper in Austin. Young Morris — "Papoose," his father called him — was three years old when his father, a linotype operator, heard the editor of the *Statesman*, Charles E. Green, shout across the newsroom: "We've got to have a golf writer. I don't care whether any of you know anything about it or not, but we've got to start covering the sport. It looks like it's a sure comer." Williams Sr. spoke first. He'd read the stories in his newspaper about Harvey and the country club and the famous characters who played there. Watching golf seemed like a pleasant way to spend afternoons in the sun, away from the dank offices of the newspaper. "I'll try it for a week," Williams Sr. told Green.

The new golf writer appeared soon after at Willow Springs, the nine-hole sand-green course managed by Harvey and his brother Tom behind St. Edward's University in South Austin. Williams Sr. remembered at his anniversary celebration the thrill of playing his first hole there in par, an accomplishment he repeated three other times before purchasing the single-story house on East Fortieth Street, across from the country club. Fred Williams (unrelated to Morris) wrote the "Top O' Morn" column for the *Statesman*. He penned a warm, affectionate toast to Williams's journalism career on the day of the celebration, organized by the Austin Golf Association at the old club, known since the relocation as Hancock Park.

"Things have changed in those 20 years," Fred Williams wrote. "The black-haired golf writer being honored today now has a handsome shock of gray hair streaked with black. But that twinkle in his blue eyes and that heart bigger than a Halloween pumpkin are still there."

Williams considered his life and liked what he recalled: Twenty years in the company of golf. A tidy house on a corner in Central Austin, across the street from a country club. A son, his only child, a lieutenant in the U.S. Air Force and a pilot, as well as a University of Texas graduate. The only player in the history of the state to hold the Texas Junior, Open, and PGA trophies in the same span of time. One of Harvey's boys. These were the countable blessings that Morris Williams Sr. remembered, in his quiet but assured way, as he read those words the morning after his day at Hancock Park, written by his friend and colleague.

The father was grateful.

On September 16, 1953, Harvey and the members were still telling stories about the annual Labor Day tournament at Austin Country Club. The club had honored Harvey at a testimonial dinner, attended by Governor Shivers and other dignitaries. Harvey and his assistant, Charles Ranly, were in the golf shop when the telephone rang.

The caller asked for Harvey. "His face went white," Ranly remembered years later.

Morris Williams Jr. had been killed on a training flight over the Florida Gulf Coast. His Lockheed F-80 Shooting Star, a jet he had spent twenty-three hours flying in preparation for his training in the Sabre jet, had made a "low-angle strafing pass at Range #2," according to air force records made public in 1996.

The conditions were mild that day: a 25,000-foot ceiling, visibility of ten miles, an outside temperature of eighty-two degrees, calm winds, no birds. The circumstances were normal: altitude at 3,200 feet, the strafing angle at twenty degrees, the airspeed at 350 to 370 knots, the power at 85 percent. Williams had been airborne for about fifteen minutes when the aircraft made its third pass over the range as the last plane in a four-man formation.

The report suggested that Williams began a steep ascent and "aggravated a high-speed stall," dipping the jet's left wing, then the right. The Shooting Star "reverted to a left snap, striking the ground in an inverted position." The air force investigated a variety of suspected causes. Officials ruled out structural failure, engine failure, hypoxia, ricochet damage from ammunition, and ricochet injury to the pilot. They concluded that Williams perished after an "accident due to high-speed stall and subsequent violent snap roll." The report also noted that Williams had played in a golf exhibition the afternoon before his death. The day was otherwise unremarkable.

Word spread quickly and somberly at Austin Country Club. "Everybody knew," recalled Ted White, one of Harvey's players on the

1953 Texas golf team. One of only a few out-of-state golfers for the Longhorns—he came from Roswell, New Mexico, where he later returned to farm cotton and alfalfa—White was on the practice range when Harvey answered the telephone in the golf shop.

"It was all over the club right quick," White said, remembering that Harvey appeared for a brief time, meeting quietly with the members limbering for their games, then staring at the ground, looking alone and confused and suddenly empty. Harvey turned back to face the clubhouse. Then, White said, "Mr. Penick just walked on into the pro shop with his head down."

Harvey accepted the agonizing task of informing Morris Williams Sr. When Harvey told him at the newspaper offices downtown, the stricken father collapsed in his arms. "Harvey always said the toughest day of his life was when he had to tell his dad," Ben Crenshaw recalled one October evening in 2010 at San Antonio Country Club, where Williams Jr. was enshrined, fifty-seven years after his death, in the Texas Golf Hall of Fame.

A military escort brought the body home. Harvey served as a pallbearer. It seemed like the entire city attended the 4:00 P.M. funeral at Weed-Corley Funeral Home. Williams received full military honors. A bugler blew "Taps." The occasion seemed to break the lieutenant's parents. Harvey watched in silence with reddened eyes.

Williams Sr. wrote a letter a month later to a family member in Fort Worth. "We will be eternally grateful for your thoughtfulness, kindness and generosity at a time when it seemed the world had ended for us," he wrote. "It is still that way, but we gotta go on somehow. Right now my eyes are full of tears and it's so hard to be bright, brave and gay." Williams informed the recipient that he intended to return to work soon. "All I have to do is write my column and cover what game I want during the football weekends. Not hard at all—just takes a little time. I think maybe it would help me, too."

Williams Sr. never recovered from the loss of his son. In March he and his wife attended the basketball game between Texas and Texas Christian University at Gregory Gymnasium. At halftime, the Williamses accepted a small replica of the Morris Williams Jr. Memorial Golf Trophy from Major General E. J. Timberlake, who noted, "The expression 'officer and gentleman' means much to the military service. Taken in its fullest meaning, Lieutenant Williams was every inch an officer and a gentleman."

The dead airman's parents regarded the trophy with pursed lips. Williams Sr. managed a forced smile. Harvey's friend and putting mentor Horton Smith, the two-time Augusta National Invitational (later the Masters) champion and now the president of the PGA of America, sent a telegram to be read to Morris and Thelma Williams: "It is with deep personal regret that I will be unable to attend ceremonies honoring Lieutenant Morris Williams. As an American I am humbly touched by his offering of himself that we might continue to live in freedom." Smith added: "I say that golf has lost a dear friend and a genuine symbol of true greatness." The trophy was later sent to the George Air Force Base in California, where it remained until the next branch championship.

Harvey and other officials at Austin Country Club dedicated the twentieth annual Labor Day tournament that September to Morris Williams Jr. They changed the format to stroke play, aligning with the game's move in the United States away from the ancient form of match play. The new seventy-two-hole configuration attracted a field of 143 players. The club also invited airmen from four bases in Texas: Bergstrom, Lackland, Gary, and Connally. Don January, the former North Texas State star who played in that summer of 1950 with Williams Jr., was elected captain of the Lackland team.

Homer Thornberry, a University of Texas law school graduate and U.S. congressman from Austin, suggested to Mayor C. A. McAden that a new municipal golf course be named for both of the Williamses, Jr. and Sr. "Morris was a fine example of young American manhood, aside from his abilities as a golfer," Thornberry wrote. "I think this would be a fitting tribute to him."

Morris Williams Sr. died four years after his only child was buried at Memorial Park Cemetery. His wife, Thelma, survived until 1985.

She lived long enough to see the dedication in 1964 of Morris Williams Golf Course, built for $85,000 on 100 acres near the municipal airport in East Austin. To memorialize both father and son, city officials decided not to include the words *Jr.* or *Sr.* in the name of the course. U.S. Representative Homer Thornberry wrote a letter to Austin mayor C. A. McAden in support of the name: "Morris was a fine example of young American manhood, aside from his abilities as a golfer, and I think this would be a fitting tribute to him."

The Texas men's golf team staged its Morris Williams Spring Invitational there for decades. Some of the best players of the old Southwest Conference — Kite, Crenshaw, and Justin Leonard of Texas; John Daly of Arkansas; Payne Stewart of SMU; Bob Tway of Oklahoma State; Jeff Maggert of Texas A&M — competed there. The course remains one of the most popular venues in the city, accommodating tens of thousands of rounds a year. The community affectionately knows it as "MoWillie." Low handicappers consider it the most demanding municipal course of the five in Austin — making it worthy of its name.

Chapter Six

THE DEATH OF WILLIAMS haunted Harvey for the rest of '53. He never stopped missing his young friend.

But he managed the loss with the accepting perspective of a man who knew he had to adapt. He was nearing fifty. He had lessons to administer. He had a membership to satisfy. He had a notebook to maintain. He returned to his career because that was what he knew. Golf gave him comfort and routine. He needed both to feel complete again.

Harvey and his UT golf team won nearly every match they played that season, as well as another conference championship. Texas senior Wesley Ellis beat Don Addington of SMU that May in Dallas by eleven shots for the medal. The early 1950s represented a period of crushing dominance for Texas golf. Williams had won his Texas triple crown. The Longhorns had defended their conference title a year later, in 1951. Then along came the '52 squad, one of the best ever built in Harvey's career at Texas—and a team connected at the soul. The talent assembled for that team, which included two of Houston's finest young players and a sophomore from Vernon who was shaped entirely by Harvey, assured the Longhorns of a conference trophy, either for the team or for a medalist, through 1954.

Texas and SMU, with its dominating Addington brothers from Lamar High School in Houston, defined college golf in Texas for the next three years, along with North Texas State in Denton, which won four consecutive national championships, from 1949 to 1952. The "Mean Green" played outside the Southwest Conference, but Harvey was well aware of Don January, Billy Maxwell, and the rest of the players groomed by North Texas head coach Fred Cobb. There simply was nothing like college golf in Texas in the early 1950s. And it was a time like no other for Harvey. His teams, forged of deep friendships and unwavering esprit de corps, brought a whiff of understated royalty wherever their black Ford team sedan carried them to compete.

There was Julian Oates of Waco, who came to Texas to play tennis for Harvey's cousin. He won the individual conference championship twice for D. A. Penick and used his last year of eligibility to compete on the golf team. Oates suspected that his tennis coach, a golfer of some repute, encouraged Harvey to invite Oates to the qualifier on a wintry pair of days more ideal for a fireside game of checkers than two rounds of golf. Harvey never once considered postponing the qualifier, in which Oates finished second.

He won the conference medal.

Then there was Ed Turley of Beaumont. He made the team as a freshman, ceded to better players through his brief and unremarkable career as a collegiate golfer, and left the university with an abiding affection for the coach who treated him as an equal to the starting four. Turley kept the letter Harvey mailed him one September day, a single page of cursive with sweeping capitals: "Dear Edward," it read. "I can take your application for a place in the athletic dorm at the University." It was Harvey's way of telling Turley he belonged.

There were Moncrief and Riviere. They were the comets of their classes, the best of the best. Bobby Moncrief came to Austin with a polished swing crafted on the privileged practice line at River Oaks. Bernard Riviere learned the game under Robbie Williams at Memorial Park, the municipal course designed by Harvey's friend John Bredemus and the home of the Houston Open. The older brother of the future professional and golf-course architect Jay Riviere, Bernard was Don Addington's teammate at Lamar, and he thought about joining his friend at SMU. But Harvey's countenance and paternal manner convinced him that Austin was where he needed to be. He never once regretted his choice.

They arrived on campus with reputations as two of the most complete junior players in the state. Riviere came right from high school, but Moncrief played a year on the freshman team at SMU. Moncrief weighed less than 120 pounds. What he lacked in power he balanced with a tremendous short game, honed on the practice green and sand bunker between the caddie shack and tennis courts at River Oaks. He appeared one summer day at Austin Country Club while Harvey was watching one of his son's cows graze near the barn.

"Mr. Penick, my name is Bobby Moncrief," the small boy said. "I want to play golf for you."

Harvey looked him over, up and down. He told Moncrief to wait. Harvey fetched a 7-iron and a 3-wood from his shop, returned, and told the youth to swing them for him. Moncrief did as he was told.

The coach needed nothing more. "I hadn't seen Bobby hit a ball," Harvey wrote years later. "But I had seen his swing and looked into his eyes. I could see he was a player."

So were the rest of those charmed Longhorns of '52.

The team won twenty-nine matches that spring and plowed through the conference tournament. Circumstances were different now for the varsity. The game was bigger, their sport more esteemed. They carried canvas bags with TEXAS stitched on the side. They played nicer courses. Even the competition to make the team had toughened, to the point that five-time Houston City Junior champion Preston Moore, possessed of as assured a pedigree as Moncrief and Riviere, failed to qualify in every attempt he made.

Moore learned the game under Willie Maguire, the early Austin Country Club professional who had left years before for Houston Country Club, and later Dick Forester, the assistant to Jimmy Demaret at River Oaks. Moore had met Harvey at a qualifier for the national Jaycee tournament, and he instantly was smitten with the loving handshake, the care in his voice. "He had a way about him," Moore said. He could go anywhere to play golf in college. He chose Texas.

No better junior had ever stepped to the first tee at River Oaks. The club, which thought it knew a future ambassador on the professional tour when it saw one, even granted Moore a complementary membership. But he wilted at the qualifier to play for Harvey at Texas. "I choked," he said. "It meant so much to me." Nevertheless, Harvey embraced Moore as if he had won every time he teed a ball. He wanted to surround himself with young men like Moore, who devoted so much to making the Longhorn team. "He never told me this, but I got the feeling that it hurt him more than it hurt me," Moore said in 2013.

"He never said that," Moore added. "He wouldn't. He wouldn't acknowledge failure." But Harvey did acknowledge his affection for Moore. He referred to him as one of his college players, despite never having made the team, for the rest of his life. Moore, who rose to become the chief financial officer of the U.S. Department of Commerce under President George H. W. Bush, referred to Harvey as the teacher who made the biggest difference in his life.

Moore knew Moncrief and Riviere from the junior circuit in Houston. The three of them became Harvey's acolytes and devotees of his methods — they cheerfully shared their enthusiasm with whoever would listen. They would describe his unusual algorithms: teaching the swing with the image of a bucket of water, teaching the grip with a common yardstick, teaching a mental trompe l'oeil with three words: *take dead aim.* The boys would explain how that message meant everything — when they invested completely in it, they often played the golf of their dreams.

"He had this way about him," Riviere said. "If you listened carefully, you got some gems."

Moncrief noticed that Harvey accepted blame for his team's failures so his boys wouldn't have to. He thought about how, before every out-of-town match, a telegram arrived. It would read, "Take dead aim," and be signed, "Harvey."

Moncrief noticed also how much the thirty-four USGA rules of golf mattered to his coach. One afternoon, after a home match at Lions against Oklahoma, Moncrief confessed to Harvey that he had lost,

1-up, because he had called a penalty on himself on the seventh hole. Harvey put his hand on Moncrief's shoulder and said, "That was exactly the right thing to do." Moncrief left the course with the pride of a winner.

But his affection and admiration for Harvey prevented Moncrief from telling him, after his sophomore year, that he was leaving school and the golf team. Moncrief had been caught having another student take a test for him in a history class. He fled to Houston. "I was so embarrassed, I didn't go see him," Moncrief said. "I felt like I had let him down, that everything he had taught me I had violated."

Moncrief never wrote Harvey, never called or visited him in Austin, until years later.

When he showed up, Harvey greeted him with the same gentle handshake Moncrief remembered from that day at the club, when Harvey was minding Tinsley's cow. "It was like I'd never been gone," he said.

Unlike Moncrief, Moore, and Riviere, Joe Bob Golden had no prior reputation when he entered the freshman-team qualifying tournament in the spring of 1951. He had no competitive experience outside of Vernon in North Texas, where he played on his ragtag high school team. Harvey granted six players a place on the freshman team. Golden finished seventh. But one of the six qualifiers was deemed ineligible, opening a place for Golden, who suddenly found himself surrounded by players expected to win in the Southwest Conference. He was filled with pride. He was haunted by doubt.

Golden asked his new coach for help. He wanted a golf swing he could believe in. Harvey invited Golden to the club, where he could watch him more closely on the range, and scattered a few practice balls at his feet. Harvey said nothing as Golden, a freshman trying to show the poise he did not yet have, took his stance.

Harvey never mentioned to Golden that he rarely gave this kind of intimate, wholesale lesson to a player on his teams, because so few needed or wanted one. He chose not to reveal that most of his players appeared in Austin with tournament-ready mechanics. Nor did he tell

Golden how much he typically learned from his players, how he often wrote in his notebook a move or adjustment advocated by a teacher from another club that he learned from one of his players. Instead, Harvey just watched Golden hit practice shots until he thought he had an answer that might help.

Harvey thought a lot that day about the length and tempo of Golden's swing. He wanted it shorter and slower, more repeatable, especially under pressure. He also wanted Golden to put away his driver. But if Golden shelved his driver, what else would he use?

"Come on to my house and let me see if I can't find you something," Harvey told Golden.

The two of them went to Harvey's home on Penick Drive. Harvey clawed through a barrel of clubs in a closet and returned with a Jimmy Thompson brassie, the equivalent of a 2-wood in the modern era. It was typical of Harvey to steer his players away from their drivers for a short period of time. He considered the driver one of the three most important clubs of the fourteen available, but he also thought players should earn the option of using it only after many hours of persistent practice. Most players, Harvey said, would play better golf if they used a fairway wood instead.

Golden used the Jimmy Thompson brassie for his entire freshman season and also shortened his swing. He earned a place as a sophomore on the varsity team, which won the conference with Riviere, Moncrief, Wesley Ellis, and Lee Pinkston. Two years later, Texas took the conference championship, and Golden won as an individual, beating teammate Roane Puett by a shot. He shot 68-69-71-70. Harvey allowed him to use his driver.

"Harvey made me the player I was," Golden said more than fifty years later. "He had me slow down my swing. He had me hitting a three-quarter shot with every club in the bag." Harvey trusted Golden so much that years later, after a stint as an intelligence officer in the air force and a return to Texas for law school, his old coach hired him to travel with the golf team from tournament to tournament, part chaperone, part chauffeur, part mentor, part extension of Harvey himself.

"He was the greatest teacher in the world," Golden said. He meant the compliment well beyond golf.

Golden went on to a long and distinguished career as a jurist in a town of eight thousand in East Texas. He was known as a compassionate, committed, and sensible judge — a reflection of Harvey, but with a gavel. Golden kept a placard on his desk in the Jasper County Courthouse, where he supervised cases in the First Judicial District until his semiretirement in 2008. The placard read: KINDNESS . . . PASS IT ON. He chaired the judicial probation board. He served cake and ice cream to delinquents who completed their sentences. He rarely wore judicial robes, not even when, in 1999, he presided over the trial of one of three white men convicted of dragging to death a black man named James Byrd on a rusty chain before dumping his remains in front of an African American church and driving to a barbecue.

Golden played golf long and well enough to teach his children what he had learned from Harvey. He took both of them to Austin when he had taught them all he could. His daughter Kate was about thirteen, Golden recalled, when they arrived at the country club and found Harvey in a golf cart, collecting range balls and wearing a wire range bucket on his head to protect him from the incoming. He stopped and watched Kate Golden hit about a dozen balls.

"Kate, that's all I need to see," Harvey said. "You're going to have people telling you what to do, showing you how to swing. People will want to give you tips. What I want you to do is say, 'Thank you.' And then go right back to what you're doing."

Kate played golf at Texas. Her brother Joe played at Stephen F. Austin State in Nacogdoches. "I knew that he would teach them the right way, and I wanted them to learn all about Mr. Penick," Golden recalled. But the lessons he arranged for his children had to do with so much more than golf. "I just wanted my kids to know him," Golden said.

The country club planned a special dinner for Harvey and Helen in the fall of 1953, to observe his thirtieth year as its head professional. Governor Shivers attended and posed for a picture with Harvey, who wore a size-too-big suit with enormous lapels. The city established

September 5 as Harvey Penick Day in Austin, certified by the hand of the mayor, C. A. McAden.

"Whereas, it is deemed altogether fitting that the signal example of Harvey Penick as a citizen, a friend, and a sportsman, who has won and held the hearts and admiration of all Austin citizens who know him, should be recognized in an appropriate manner," the proclamation read in part. Club officials enthusiastically endorsed a $3,000 bonus check.

The torrential teams of the early 1950s and the '54 twin conference championships for Texas represented the last true dynasty for Harvey as a college golf coach. The churn of managing the team, compounded by his work for the Texas section of the PGA, which had him traveling all around the state for teaching seminars, began to wear on Harvey.

His energy waning, Harvey was beginning to feel his age. He wanted to keep coaching out of loyalty to the university, but he also wanted to loosen the ever-present tugs on his time. He began to contemplate an exit. But he wasn't ready yet.

His team finished sixth in conference in 1955, beating only Baylor in the league of seven teams. Davis Love Jr., his driven player from Arkansas who wore alligator shoes and lived for the sport ("He didn't study," said Turley, "he didn't date, he was consumed with golf"), finished third individually. But Texas rarely celebrated a third-place finish in any sport, especially not for a team accustomed to championships.

It was an aggravating year altogether for sports in Austin. The football Longhorns won four games. The basketball team won four games too. The baseball team finished fourth in conference. Only Harvey's cousin saved the university from wholesale chagrin. D. A. Penick and his reliable tennis team won their eighth straight conference trophy.

Away from campus, at the humming grounds of Austin Country Club, Harvey continued to thrive. He now had an assistant, a young man from Robstown named Charles Ranly, who supervised the shop while Harvey was teaching for $2 a lesson. "He showed me what to do, and I was always there," said Ranly, who later bought his own golf course in North Texas. "I loved it. I never missed a day of work."

When Jack Burke Jr., the son of Harvey's mentor, won the Masters in 1956, Harvey noticed his putter, which was manufactured in Alabama. He instructed Ranly to order a dozen to sell at $9.50 apiece. They sold out in two weeks. Harvey placed another order. Then another. He stocked his shop with Spalding irons and Wilson Staff persimmon woods. He sold Titleist and Maxfli golf balls with balata covers, the kinds the tour players spun on soft bentgrass greens.

Harvey was evolving into the modern PGA professional: teacher, manager, customer service specialist, part-time agronomist, full-time merchandise consultant. Harvey preferred teaching above all. But this was 1956. Golf was booming, with more than 6,000 courses in the United States. The jobs of its 3,798 professionals were broadening to meet demand, and Harvey had to adapt. So he adapted with the kind of loyalty and good cheer that had made him, by his fourth decade as a presence at Austin Country Club, an icon.

Powerful golf people trusted Harvey. The unassuming professional from Austin never inserted himself into the emerging national golf scene, but he held great influence, especially among people who had a stake in the careers of the students who learned under Harvey. He was the remote intersection through which important roads coursed.

For instance, in the summer of 1955, L. G. "Plug" Osborne, director of the professional golf division of the Wilson Sporting Goods Company, the Chicago-based manufacturer that supplied high-grade clubs to tour staff, including Betsy Rawls, was growing concerned about Rawls. Osborne corresponded regularly with Harvey, and he wrote to him on June 24, wondering if Rawls had been "listening to some bad advice along the tour.

"To be perfectly frank with you, and I hope you will talk to her about it if you ever get a chance, I am a little afraid she lets Betty Hicks influence her to [sic] much," Osborne continued. Rawls had objected to that suggestion, Osborne acknowledged, but he wondered if she was being truthful. The company had a great deal riding on her success.

Osborne wanted to ensure that Rawls remained on the path to great-ness that so many predicted she would achieve.

"You have been wonderful to her and I guarantee you she appreci-ates it very much," Osborne wrote. "She thinks you are about the best guy in the world and I am not so sure she isn't right."

Though Rawls won only one tournament that year, she would win three more in 1956. The next season looked promising for the Phi Beta Kappa who never quit. Meanwhile, back in Austin, the golf team fin-ished third in 1956. Harvey's service to his club and the Texas sec-tion of the PGA, however, was neither third nor second to anyone else teaching golf in Texas. The section named Harvey the "pro who did the most for the section" at its annual meeting in Houston. As Mor-ris Williams Sr. noted in his *Sunday Austin American-Statesman* golf column, "The honor could have been bestowed in 1946, or in 1936, or even in 1926. For Harvey has been around the Texas golfing scene for a long, long time."

Buck Luce, a former player at Texas and one of the men who saw Jimmy Demaret establish the course record of 60 at the Hancock site in a friendly game with Harvey, hired Wesley Ellis in 1956 as his assis-tant at Greenwood Country Club in River Vale, New Jersey. Ellis had played for Harvey's conference championship teams in 1950, '51, and '52. Luce credited his old coach with shaping Ellis and many other for-mer Longhorns now spreading his teaching ideas on ranges through-out the country.

"Wesley is another product of the greatest professional in the game," Luce wrote in a letter to a friend. "Harvey is such a great credit to the game. Much has been said of the fine [amateur] players he has turned out, yet very little has been said about some of the fine professionals that he has turned out and is turning out."

Others in the game, including those who wrote about it, also ac-knowledged Harvey's considerable influence — even his legacy, which by his fifty-first birthday had begun to carry the weight and heft of an entire career. "Penick is one of an old and vanishing school of golf pros who moved up from caddy, to shop to teaching," Tom Davison of the *Houston Post* wrote in 1956. "He has probably developed more championship golfers in this state than all the other Texas pros combined."

One of those championship golfers, Betsy Rawls, the object of concern for Harvey and others just two years before, roared into the summer of '57 like the wavy-haired freshman consumed with perfection Harvey had met in the fall of 1946.

Rawls won the Tampa, Lake Worth, and Peach Blossom Opens. She finished a shot behind Jackie Pung in the U.S. Women's Open that summer at historic Winged Foot Golf Club, but Pung was disqualified for signing an incorrect scorecard. Pung had been playing that Saturday with Harvey's friend Betty Jameson, who was out of contention early. Both players made bogey six on the par-5 fourth hole. Both of them also, mistakenly, recorded a par 5 on the scorecards they were keeping for each other. Neither discovered the error when they were checking their cards later.

The ruling left an indelible cloud over the grounds: "You will probably never see an unhappier group of people at a golf championship," the august golf writer Herbert Warren Wind noted from Mamaroneck, New York. Even officials from the USGA, which had enacted the regulation the year before, regretted the decision. The USGA and Winged Foot members took up a collection promptly after Pung was disqualified. They raised more than $2,000 on the spot.

Pung was circumspect after the announcement. "Winning the Open is the greatest thing in golf," she told the gathered golf press. "I have come close before. This time I thought I'd won. But I didn't. Golf is played by the rules, and I broke a rule. I've learned a lesson. And I have two broad shoulders." Pung did not disclose the fact that Rawls had edged her in her last close brush with the U.S. Women's Open championship, in a playoff in the summer of 1953 at the Country Club of Rochester.

Rawls modestly and somewhat reluctantly accepted the trophy at Winged Foot. The circumstances were imperfect. But she had her fourth major championship. More than that, she was winning with regularity again.

Her fifth and final victory that year came in Reno, Nevada. She occasionally wrote to Harvey from hotels in tournament cities, and when the LPGA dropped into Texas for the Betty Jameson Invitational at Brackenridge Park or the Dallas Open at Glen Lakes, she would try to fit in a quick drive to Austin to see him. All of his women players did.

"Everyone in Texas knew Harvey" by that time, Rawls explained. "It was the first thing you asked another Texas golfer. *Do you know Harvey?* People from West Texas, South Texas and Houston, they all knew him. He was the reason there was a great bond between Texas golfers on the tours. You'd mention Harvey, you'd always smile and tell stories."

In addition to his stewardship of the golf team, the 1950s represented the apex of Harvey's wide, paternal influence on the LGPA circuit. Betty Jameson continued to contend, but she was nearing retirement. Rawls won thirty titles that decade. Her most dominant season came in 1959, when she won ten times, including two major championships. Harvey found reasons to be proud nearly every week he opened the *Sunday American-Statesman* to check the golf agate.

He had no way of knowing, of course, that his reach was about to deepen even more.

Early in the summer that saw Rawls return to form and win at Winged Foot, a mother loaded her seventeen-year-old daughter into the family car for a 450-mile trip from Jal, New Mexico, to Austin. It was the first of many hot drives across the flat plains of Texas that Dama Whitworth and her young daughter Kathy would make to see Harvey.

The small town they left that morning had given all it could to Kathy. The youngest of three sisters, she came to golf late, having been occupied for much of her childhood with roaming the property her grandparents homesteaded, chasing calves around the barn, and swimming with her friends in shallow ranch tanks. Life for the Whitworth girls orbited the four sacred entities of small towns: church, family, school, and neighbors, whose kids went to the same school and probably the same church. Their father operated a hardware store. Their mother volunteered with the local Democratic Women's Club and kept active at the First Baptist Church. They lived in a small frame house on South Fourth Street.

The community of 2,675, a speck on the bleak and brittle flatlands near the Texas border, thrived on cattle ranches on the outskirts until the late 1920s, when the El Paso Natural Gas Company appeared, bringing in a new batch of jobs. Jal had none of the big-city attractions that kept kids occupied in faraway places such as Austin. But it did have a nine-hole golf course.

Whitworth first played there at the invitation of a friend whose family had a membership. She borrowed her grandfather's clubs. She flailed down the scorched fairways and cottonseed greens, chopping at a little ball that never behaved the way she willed it to. She lost count of her strokes. She felt foolish and inept. She wanted to go sit down inside one of those green fiberglass shelters, handy for the rain that rarely fell, with her head in her hands. She also learned that day what she wanted to do with her life.

"Oh my God," Whitworth said later. "I was just so bad. I couldn't believe it was so hard." From that day, she shaped her entire life around golf.

Morris and Dama Whitworth joined the Jal Country Club for their daughter, who rarely chased calves anymore or swam in the tanks at the ranch. They paid Dode Forrester, who gave lessons at the country club in Hobbs, New Mexico, to teach her the foundations, including the powerful firing of the hips she often credited for the snap in her swing. The Whitworths eventually retained Hardy Loudermilk, the professional in Jal, who detected a potential in his new student that was both thrilling and rare on the plains of eastern New Mexico. Loudermilk decided to call Harvey. "I've taken her as far as I can," he told his friend in Texas.

Harvey agreed to meet Whitworth, as he would have done for any committed player recommended by a fellow professional, especially one he respected as much as he did Loudermilk. Whitworth and her mother arrived at the country club and entered Harvey's shop, which seemed to the girl like a cave, with a picture of Bobby Jones on the wall and a small photograph, angled on Harvey's rolltop desk, of Tommy Armour sitting on a bench. Harvey suggested they go outside.

He liked Whitworth the moment he watched her handle a golf club. They started, as Harvey always did, on the practice green. He admired her intuition there, how every putting stroke seemed calibrated, in both speed and direction, to the correct path to the hole. Harvey examined her grip. He was unimpressed. But he wanted to see her take full swings before deciding what he wanted to say and exactly how he wanted to say it.

Harvey surveyed his five-foot-nine pupil as she emptied a bucket of balls on the range. He knew this much from his purview: Whitworth was strong and built for golf, all levers and torque and quick-twitch fiber. She was big for her age, overweight even. But she used her mass like a catapult. Harvey sensed he could turn a good player into a great one in Whitworth. But she had to invest in him.

"Most people don't want to hear that," she said. "Because it's so hard to change."

Whitworth and her mother stayed in Austin for three days. Harvey met her each morning at the club, prescribed a drill or single thought, and left her alone while he attended to his other duties. Then he came back. Another drill. Another thought. They rebuilt her golf swing stage by stage, like the concrete steps that led to the new clubhouse on Riverside Drive.

Harvey gave Whitworth a molded grip so she could memorize the position Harvey wanted her hands to assume on the club. At night, she sat on the bed in front of a mirror in her hotel room, cradling the molded grip, absorbing the sensation. She closed her eyes and concentrated. She believed in Harvey. She thought a lot about the humility of Loudermilk, the professional back in Jal, who accepted his own limitations and deferred to Whitworth's best interests, an act that led her to

Harvey. She felt pulled toward him. She felt centered. "I wasn't going to question anything," Whitworth said.

She returned home with restless conviction. She won the New Mexico State Women's Open that year in Farmington. She won it again in 1958. She was barely getting started.

She enrolled at Odessa Junior College, but full of restless plans, she quit early. She wanted to play with the LPGA Tour, whose stars, including Mickey Wright and Betsy Rawls, scheduled frequent exhibitions in Amarillo, Lubbock, or Pecos, Texas. Whitworth often joined them. She could play with those women. Whitworth confided to Wright that she thought she was ready, but Wright tried to persuade her to wait. To spend another year with Harvey.

Whitworth was unconvinced.

She formed a syndicate with her father and two Jal businessmen, who agreed to finance her career for three years. They offered to give her $15,000. She averaged eighty strokes a round as a rookie, earning a little more than $1,200 in twenty-six tournaments.

Whitworth limped home to Jal and cried. Her father told her to spare him her tears.

His daughter heard the message. She returned to the tour, camped on the range, and watched Wright, Patty Berg, and Louise Suggs, trying to parse their swings, from waggle to impact to finish. Whitworth started playing well. She was having fun. She lost in a couple of playoffs, but she was playing well enough to get there. "There were times when I came close to winning," she said. She sent a bottle of champagne to South Fourth Street in Jal. She instructed her parents to pull the cork when she won her first tournament.

"I still marvel at how all this started, how lucky that was," Whitworth said, describing that first encounter with Harvey in 1957 at the country club. "When you look back on it, it's like fate. It seemed preplanned."

Harvey, meanwhile, attended to his notebook in the rolltop desk. He planned lessons, gave them, sat through church with Helen, fed the stock, cleared mesquite on his farm, watched the agate in the Austin newspapers for golf scores, played a little, hoped for rain, and spent time with his children, Kathryn and Tinsley, when they came home for a visit. He started reading a new magazine series that ran in that year of '57 in *Sports Illustrated*.

The series was written by Ben Hogan, Harvey's old Texas friend and former Texas Cup teammate, with the most famous golf writer in the country, Herbert Warren Wind. It was called "Ben Hogan's Modern Fundamentals of Golf." It struck Harvey as too complex for the average player but essential for the championship contestant to absorb. The series featured illustrations of panes of glass, swing planes, theories about intricate ballistic kinesiology, and the like. It changed the way a lot of people thought about the golf swing. It changed nothing about Harvey.

Harvey still believed, as much as he ever had, in the simplicity of imagery, gentle direction, incremental advice, and small words. He wanted to strip the swing to its most primitive essentials. The grip. The stance. The position of the body. When those three elements were aligned, the ball almost always went where it should.

Harvey had been watching golf shots for more than four decades. He only prescribed what he believed to be true, and truth rose from exposure. Harvey sought small measures. He found fact in buckets of water and weed cutters and three words that applied to anything in the human experience — *take dead aim*. He admired and respected Hogan in profound ways. But there was only one Hogan.

PART II

THE BOOK

Chapter Seven

BY NOW, HARVEY had been giving thought to some kind of book. His friend Betty Hicks tried to convince him to write one with her. Hicks won the 1941 U.S. Amateur and later gave lessons for $83 a month at a municipal course in Long Beach, California. She helped to found the Women's Professional Golf Association, the precursor to the LPGA, in 1944. She also could write.

Hicks contributed sports stories to the Long Beach newspaper in the late 1930s, and she later wrote freelance stories for *Sports Illustrated* and the *Saturday Evening Post*. She could string words together as well as she could string birdies.

Hicks and Harvey mulled a book project in the mid-1950s. She wrote him one July day in 1958 from Los Coyotes Country Club in Buena Park. "Golf Digest just wrote me with a plea for a good instructional series," she informed Harvey, who had written to her earlier about a writing partnership. "Could you put a few of those down, so we could collaborate on some articles?" Hicks asked.

She continued: "I think it's a shame that you haven't been able to put some of your ideas in print before—and extensively. So let's go to work on it. We never did get around to writing that book, did we?"

Harvey did end up submitting a collection of short instructional articles to *Sports Illustrated*. He wrote four paragraphs in the spring of 1958 about the "Proper Use of All Clubs" in which he suggested that golfers not fret over subtleties. "The average player wonders whether to play the ball off the right foot, from the center or off the left foot," he wrote. "The manufacturer has tried to solve this for the players who will let him . . . If a golfer can master the one sound swing that is best suited for him, it should suffice for all clubs." Simplicity reigned for Harvey. He spread a gospel of sensible logic.

That fall, a lanky and long-driving player named Terry Dill, who later claimed to be the first golfer put on full scholarship at Texas, joined the Longhorns from Odessa Junior College. Harvey immediately wanted to change Dill's grip. He refused to allow his tall new competitor from Fort Worth to play an actual round for a month.

Dill thought Harvey had the answers to every question. He became one of his most curious, if not excessively persistent, students. When Dill developed an acute hook, he summoned Harvey. When he read a new tip in a golf magazine, he wanted to know what Harvey thought. When he needed to know the answer to the complex question of whether a player developed confidence *from* hitting good shots or whether confidence *resulted* in good shots, he asked Harvey. "He was perplexed," Dill said.

Dill later enjoyed modest success on the PGA Tour and the Champions Tour, including three Masters appearances — 1965, '66, and '67 — for which he traveled with Harvey to Augusta. A half-century after playing for Harvey, as he prepared for a Champions Tour tournament in Austin, Dill scribbled notes on six loose-leaf pages — in twenty-seven distinct entries — on what he learned from his teacher:

He believed a player should hit five chips and putts for every long shot in practice.

Sometimes he thought a player should aim out of bounds to not hit it out of bounds.

He had some secret drills for controlling the clubface I have never seen in print. They were pretty complicated, and he didn't want to confuse anyone.

When I started [the] senior tour and had been playing two years, he asked me when I was going to quit playing a slice. I believed I was playing a fade. He believed fades turned into slices. He was correct.

I asked Mr. Penick why he didn't play more professional tournaments. He said, "Two words: Sam Snead." I asked Mr. Penick why Sam Snead went over the top. He said, "Because Snead lined up ten yards right of his target. Snead was such a good athlete he could have lined up twenty yards left and still been one of the best.

In college I was hooking the ball terribly on the course. I came in and told him I needed a lesson, [and] he said go up to the range and hit a few balls to get loose. I did, and I must have made some adjustment. Started hitting the ball straight. I was waiting for him to give me the lesson. Out of the corner of my eye, I noticed him and he watched me hit three shots. He turned around and went back into the golf shop.

Harvey had his own way of teaching. If players accepted the idiosyncrasies, as Dill did, it simply worked.

Dill never won a Masters, but Arnold Palmer, who played service golf with Morris Williams Jr., won his first in 1958, his first major championship title. Augusta National absorbed heavy rains after the third round that year, and the tournament committee designated a special rule for Sunday that allowed embedded balls to be lifted and dropped with penalty. Palmer exercised the rule at No. 12, where his tee shot on the par-3 hole lodged in the steep bank behind the green.

Palmer and the rules official agreed that Palmer should play two balls: his original and a second one, which he dropped according to his understanding of the new rule. He made a double-bogey five with the first ball and a par with the second. He holed an eighteen-foot eagle putt on the par-5 thirteenth. The tournament rules committee deemed his drop a proper execution of the special rule. Palmer won by a stroke.

Hogan's collaborator on *Modern Fundamentals,* Herbert Warren Wind, who wrote in that era for *Sports Illustrated,* wanted to capture the arresting complexity of that elbow in the Augusta National property where the expansive eleventh green, the entire span of the twelfth hole, the debut of Rae's Creek, and the secluded, alone-with-your-thoughts back tee of the thirteenth converge in a magnificent arrangement of nature and nerves. It was the place where Palmer seized his first Masters and so much more.

Standing alone in his signature tweed jacket in that corner of Augusta National that spring, Wind remembered a jazz record he listened to once in college. One of the songs, a spiritual, was called "Shoutin' in the Amen Corner."

Perfect, Wind thought. He named the place Amen Corner.

The Texas golf team limped through the sour remainder of the 1950s and the early seasons of the '60s. The football team, meanwhile, had a new head coach, a former quarterback from Oklahoma named Darrell Royal. He and the Longhorns beat the Sooners in 1959, opened the season 5-0, and stunned Texas A&M, 27–0 to conclude the season with seven wins and three losses. It was the team's best record in five years. Harvey watched his players finish fifth in the Southwest Conference.

But Harvey had reasons to be proud. His friends and pupils shined on the LPGA Tour, which had formed after the 1950 U.S. Women's Open at Rolling Hills Country Club in Wichita, Kansas. His earliest star, Betty Jameson, was one of the thirteen founders of the organization. Betsy Rawls had won at least one major since 1951. Harvey's friend Babe Didrikson Zaharias captured twenty-nine titles in the decade. His web of influence on the women's tour had broadened to include players such as Judy Kimball of Sioux City, Iowa, and Mary Lena Faulk of Thomasville, Georgia, one of Jameson's closest friends. The former Curtis Cup team member had won shelves of trophies, among them the 1953 U.S. Women's Amateur, by the time she arranged her first lesson with Harvey at the country club. She did not let too much time pass before she saw him again.

Faulk wrote Harvey on March 28, 1960, to schedule another visit. "Since we have a week before Beaumont without a tournament, I thought it would be especially fine for me if I went out to Austin for a few days," she told him. "I can't think of an atmosphere that would be more helpful and thoughtful for me and my game than to be in Austin."

The sweet summer of 1962 reunited many of those pioneering women. The Austin Civitan Open, a onetime LPGA tournament played that July at the country club, returned Rawls, Jameson, Whitworth, Judy Kimball, and Mickey Wright to Austin—and to Harvey.

His students, current and former, filled out a stout field. Sandra Haynie, Mary Lena Faulk, Carol Mann, Ruth Jesson, and Peggy Wilson—all of whom had won on the LPGA Tour—joined LPGA cofounder Bettye Danoff in the first week of July to compete for the $7,500 purse at Austin Country Club. Harvey watched Wright finish three rounds in a tie for second place, two shots behind Haynie, who shot 69-73-72 on his course. Haynie would play in the last group in the final round, with one of the best women in the game in close pursuit. Harvey wanted both of them to prevail. He and Wright were just beginning their work together, a relationship that would last for many years. And Haynie was a friend.

Haynie spent the first twelve years of her life in Fort Worth, where she took lessons from A. G. Mitchell at River Crest Country Club. When her family moved to Austin, Haynie naturally sought Harvey as a replacement. She and her father had heard of him in Fort Worth. Everyone had. "He had a very good name," she said.

She arranged a meeting with him and mentioned Mitchell from River Crest when she introduced herself. "You're working with one of the best," Harvey told her. "Why would you switch?"

His answer made sense. Everything she knew she had learned from Mitchell, and there was no reason to change, not while they worked so well together and she continued to improve. Haynie and Harvey became friendly through golf. They saw one another often at tournaments and on the Austin Country Club range. Many years later, after Harvey became famous, their names were linked as if she were one of the women, like Whitworth and Rawls, who rose in the game under his guidance. But she never took a lesson from Harvey. "I think it's interesting that my name comes up with Mr. Penick," she said years later. "I always felt good that I knew him. I feel blessed to have had him in my life. I think just knowing he was there, that was special."

Haynie turned professional at seventeen. She was nineteen years and six days old on Sunday, June 10, 1962, the day of the final round of the Austin Civitan Open. That hot and humid afternoon Haynie shot a 75. She won by a shot over Wright.

She earned $1,200, which seemed like a life savings to someone barely old enough to be out of high school. Haynie eventually won forty-two LPGA titles, including four major championships, earned more than $1 million in her career, and was elected to the World Golf Hall of Fame in 1977. She bought and read the *Little Red Book,* retired to North Texas, became a golf instructor, and infused her own methods with the ideas and simplicity of the man she knew as a friend. "Believing in good, basic fundamentals can never go wrong," she said.

Haynie had achieved the improbable in the summer of '62, at the only Austin Civitan ever played. Mickey Wright was almost untouchable at the time. She was nearly as good as Byron Nelson had been in 1945. Wright's reign began in 1958, when she won the LPGA Championship and the U.S. Women's Open at the age of twenty-three. She captured her second Open a year later. She lost her bid to win a third when Rawls won her fourth U.S. Women's Open in 1960, but Wright responded a season later with a record-breaking run, winning the Open, the LPGA Championship, and another LPGA major, the Titleholders Championship. "If she didn't hit the ball in the center of the clubface every time, she thought something was wrong," said Louise Suggs, who played the LPGA circuit with Wright.

Tall and willowy, Wright grew up in San Diego, the poised daughter of a lawyer who recognized her aptitude before she turned ten. He took her to see Harry Pressler, one of the best teachers in California. Pressler had seen Wright win the Southern California Junior. He offered his help. Their first lesson amounted to four hours in front of a mirror in the living room of her home. Wright and her mother made the 250-mile round trip for lessons with Pressler "every Saturday for the next two years," Wright said. "All I did was practice."

Wright turned professional in 1955 after an All-American collegiate career at Stanford. She won her first tournament a season later. Her rise led to an inevitable friendship with Rawls, who suggested one day in the early 1960s that the two of them stop in Austin between tournaments. Rawls wanted to introduce Wright to Harvey.

Wright knew and understood her own swing, which was fundamentally flawless. It was the one Pressler built, the one Ben Hogan called one of the finest he had ever seen, the one that had won nineteen tournaments and three major championships by the time she shook Harvey's hand. Wright had no reason to seek another teacher. But she wanted to meet the quiet golf oracle of Austin. Rawls, Whitworth, and so many other women on the LPGA Tour spoke of him as a shaman. Wright felt as honored to have Harvey watch her swing as he did to be invited to do so.

The first time Harvey saw Wright hit balls, he wondered how she ever finished second. Every swing was a reflection of the one before and a preview of the one after. With high hands and a tight turn, she played a soaring, delicate fade that landed like a cottonwood seed. She was one of the few players Harvey never tried to persuade to play a right-to-left draw. Harvey knew when to leave alone something so close to divinity. He stood silently as she carved the Austin sky with balls.

To Harvey, Wright's swing represented everything he tried to teach his pupils and everything he tried to capture in his notebook. It was elemental. It was explosive. It seemed as organic as the stride of a sprinter and as potent as black powder. The way Wright swung a golf club was the motion Harvey imagined when he lay in bed at night, staring at the ceiling, trying to picture a connect-the-dots image of purity in motion.

"I treated hitting a golf ball as an art form," Wright once said.

She rode that thought and her celebrated swing through historic ten-win seasons in 1961 and '62. But nothing compared to her charmed summer of 1963. Playing a set of Wilson Staff Dynapower irons and an eight-year-old Acushnet Bulls Eye putter that would carry her through her career, Wright won thirteen tournaments that year, earned an unprecedented $34,000 in prize money, and was named the Associated Press Female Athlete of the Year. Wright played a game no one had yet seen in women's golf. "When Wright was over a shot, it was a dictatorship," journalist Bill Fields wrote three decades later. He called her swing "equal parts satin and steel." Her shots resembled those of no other woman on the LPGA Tour.

"When someone told Wright she hit it like a man," Fields added, "she smiled."

Harvey saw Wright when she crisscrossed Texas for tournaments. Her sound swing never required much work, but she liked hearing Harvey's thoughts, and Harvey was happy to share them, ever so carefully. He might observe that her divots were slightly deeper than last time, an indication of a creeping steepness in her swing. He might spend an hour staring at her grip. He sometimes seemed to be in a trance. Then, when he was ready to speak, he might simply tell Wright that he liked the alignment of her hands on the club handle. "I was always struck by the simplicity of his teaching," she later wrote. "He insisted on a good grip as the prime determinant of the swing and tried to impart to his students the feel of a good swing."

Harvey kept writing. His red Scribbletex was filling up. He contributed more short instructional articles to *Sports Illustrated,* including one in September 1960 that suggested how much he had evolved as an instructor. In his fourth decade as a teacher, Harvey was beginning to accept that there were mysteries in golf he would never solve. He was both confident and humble enough to be at peace with that.

In an article called "Crispness in the Short Game," Harvey noted the differences in the way higher-handicap players and those closer to scratch played finesse shots around the green. Average players used longer backswings on pitches and chips, Harvey had observed. Better players used shorter ones. Pressed for an explanation, Harvey demurred. He had seen other golf instructors try to explain what they did not fully understand, a flaw of conceit that often got them in trouble. They would confuse their students, complicating what should have been simple — a violation of a golf version of the Hippocratic Oath. Harvey would never commit such a violation, which went against everything he loved and respected about golf. His aim was to clarify, using buckets and benches and small words to carry big ideas. So when he wrote for publications such as *Sports Illustrated,* he took great care to retreat when he had reached the limit of his understanding. Why do average players take long backswings around the green? Why do better players take short ones? "Why this should be I don't know," he wrote, "except, maybe, that the better player thinks that shortness produces decisiveness." Harvey had the answer but not the reason, which was acceptable to him because he knew the truth. The cause and its explanation were largely unimportant. Only the effect — the result — mattered.

The acute slumping of the Texas men's golf team resulted in no lack of interest from fine players from around the state. They wanted to play golf for the Longhorns because Harvey was the coach. One such player was Billy Munn, a confident, square-jawed youth from Midland who joined the Texas team expecting to incite the renaissance of Texas golf in the Southwest Conference. But Munn barely swung a club until his senior year.

Bad knees, pulverized by years of basketball, limited Munn in ways for which he later became forever grateful. He underwent four surgeries at Texas. Instead of hitting balls at the country club or qualifying for dual meets at Lions Municipal Golf Course, Munn spent the early part of his college career recuperating in the golf shop, scented with shellac and balata, listening to Harvey tell stories about Demaret and Hogan, Rawls and the Babe, past Texas and Houston Opens with Hagen, or the time he qualified for the 1928 national championship at Olympia Fields and played a practice round behind Bobby Jones. Munn sat enraptured as Harvey told and retold his distinct memory of watching Sam Snead rifle long irons on the range at Memorial Park. Harvey thought himself a pretty good player at the time, with the will to make it on the tour, until he saw Snead pound balls into the horizon. It was on the train home to Austin that Harvey decided to commit his life to teaching, not the tour.

Munn preferred going to the country club rather than to class. He felt like Harvey's presence was an education in and of itself. "I had this unusual relationship," Munn said. "Not because he picked me. But because we kind of picked each other."

Munn was there in 1961 when a television executive from ABC named Bud Palmer approached Harvey about sharing his golf knowledge for considerably more than the $3 per lesson he was charging at that point. The network wanted to hire Harvey to provide televised instruction during golf broadcasts. Harvey considered the offer but declined. Palmer retained Byron Nelson instead. "The reason he [Harvey] said no, politely, was that he didn't give group lessons," Munn recalled. "Had he taken that, imagine the students he would have had."

Munn entered his junior year ready, at last, to compete. The Longhorns finished third in the Southwest Conference. Texas A&M, which never used to win, was the Southwest Conference champion for the fourth consecutive year. No Longhorn had been the conference medalist since Terry Dill in 1960, and the Longhorns had last won the tournament as a team nine seasons before.

Harvey, meanwhile, had just completed his thirty-second year as the golf coach at Texas. In October he would turn fifty-nine. Obligations pulled at him—from his club, from his pupils at the club, from the top amateurs in Texas who came to Austin for his help, and from his players on the LPGA Tour.

He felt burdened, pressured, and unable to meet the requirements of his position with the club, which always took precedence with Harvey. The longtime Texas coaches in the other spring sports at Texas had resigned: Billy Disch had retired as baseball head coach long before, in 1939; his cousin D. A. Penick retired as tennis coach in 1956;

and Clyde Littlefield announced in September that he was retiring as track coordinator. They were his peers, and now they were gone. The atmosphere seemed different at the university. Harvey sensed that it was his time to go too.

He made an appointment to see Darrell K Royal, now the athletic director at Texas as well as the football coach. He met with both Royal and his assistant, Edwin Werner Olle. He told them he was ready to resign.

Harvey left a program that had won twenty conference championships, produced nineteen individual conference medalists and an individual national champion in Ed White, and finished eight times in the top ten in the NCAA tournaments. Harvey had regrets. His team had come so close to a national title in 1949, for one. Morris Williams Jr., gone now for a decade, had nearly won the individual medal, as did Ed Hopkins Jr. in '48. But Harvey had given all he could. He needed to simplify. His career at Austin Country Club and his desire to teach mattered most.

"The association at the University of Texas has meant a great deal to me," Harvey said. "But handling all the lessons that I do, and running this club and coaching the golf team is just more than one man can handle."

Billy Munn and his teammates were welcome at the club. They always would be. Harvey was happy to greet them, invite them inside, even give them a look on the range.

But he never again watched a round of college golf from behind the branches of a bush.

Harvey did keep writing. He had even more time to write now. He also began to think about what he would do with his notebook of golf truths when he was finished with it, if he ever did finish it. He had started it for himself, never once thinking that it might become important to anyone else, but he now wondered whether his son Tinsley might find it useful in his own young career in golf.

Tinsley had become a golf professional like his father. He took his first job at Huntington Country Club on the north shore of Long Island, where he lived in a New York City banker's weekend house near the beach. He gave lessons and ran the shop as an assistant in the summers on Long Island, returned home to work for and alongside his father in the winters, then went back to New York at the first sign of bluebonnets on the road to Lockhart, where he and his father kept a herd of shorthorn cattle on 380 acres of mesquite trees and limestone outcroppings they didn't get to see as often as Tinsley wanted. Harvey had never forced golf on Tinsley. His son preferred caring for his animals over spending an entire day on the range, staring at divots and trying to sort out the best ways to execute certain shots. But when it was time to decide on a career, he chose golf over the farm. It was the only job he ever had.

One day when Tinsley was home from New York, Harvey showed his son the notebook he had been keeping for thirty years. Tinsley read it with interest. The contents appealed to him more as a golf instructor than as a son getting his first glimpse at what would become his father's legacy. The notebook gave Tinsley ideas for his teaching. It helped him in practical ways, but nothing about it suggested its future as a sensation among sports books. "You could make it up," Tinsley said fifty years later, "but that's not the way it was."

Meanwhile, in early 1963, Austin Country Club management began planning a black-tie ceremony to acknowledge Harvey's fiftieth year as a servant to the club. The invitations for the May 25 dinner and dance were embossed in gold. Organizers invited hundreds of guests, including club professionals throughout Texas, as well as Jimmy Demaret and Byron Nelson. They arranged for the Dutch Sheel Orchestra to perform until one o'clock in the morning. Former governor Allan Shivers, who had presided over a similar dinner a decade before in honor of Harvey's fortieth year at the club, was chosen to present Harvey and Helen with a silver service. Organizers also solicited letters of congratulations from golf royalty.

Ben Hogan sent a telegram. Francis Ouimet sent a letter of admiration. Jackson Bradley, the professional at River Oaks in Houston who

later would teach with Harvey at Austin Country Club, sent his regrets, adding: "You are indeed fortunate, and so are we, to have Harvey
as a friend."

Executives with the Ben Hogan Golf Equipment Company in Fort
Worth and the Massachusetts-based Acushnet, which made Titleist
clubs and balls, praised Harvey in their letters. Penrose B. Metcalfe,
the president of the Texas Golf Association, complimented Harvey on
his service to the game. "When I look back over the many, many years
since I first knew you as a caddie, and then as a most capable golf
professional, it seems you have established many records for golf that
place you in a very special niche in the hearts of golfers, not only in
Texas, but throughout this country," Metcalfe wrote. The minister at
Central Christian Church, where Harvey was a deacon, said: "There
are some rare occasions in our world where genius and modesty seem
almost to be married. They seem to live together in one person's life
all his days. Harvey, such a person I think you are." By the end of the
decade, Harvey would be elected to the Longhorn Hall of Honor at
the university that employed him for thirty-two years. The club would
give him an honorary lifetime membership. The annual Labor Day
tournament, one of the biggest in the city, would be christened with a
different name. From then on it would be known as the Penick Classic.

Thanks to his retirement as the Texas golf coach, Harvey had more
time now to reflect on his career as a teacher. But his lasting attachment to the university program was about to get deeper in ways he
never predicted.

It all started shortly after the anniversary dinner at the club. An Internal Revenue Service bureaucrat named Thomas Oliver Kite moved
his family from Dallas to Austin. An avid golfer in Dallas, Kite was a
member of Riverlake Country Club who had wasted no time getting
his young son onto a golf course, hoping that he might enjoy the game
as he did. His son was on a golf course before he went to kindergarten.
"I carried him out with me to practice when he was three, and when
he was five I got some little chopped-off clubs," Kite said.

The father saw his dream realized. Tom Kite Jr., a slight and fair-skinned youth with wiry reddish hair and a punishing work ethic, became enchanted with golf, especially the discipline required to play it better than anyone else. The younger Kite found as much joy on the practice tee with a big bag of range balls as he did on the golf course with one bag of clubs. That commitment had produced a fine little junior player at Riverlake.

Kite won his age division in the Riverlake two-day handicap in October 1961, the first recorded trophy in his future World Golf Hall of Fame career. Kite shot 153 over thirty-six holes. He was eleven years old and beat every twelve-year-old in the field. He discovered that day how much he liked winning.

The Kite family — senior and junior, his mother Mauryene, and sister Karen — arrived in Austin two years later when the IRS transferred Kite Sr. to its service center in the growing capital city of 205,000 people. They moved to North Hills Drive in a shady and affluent north-central Austin neighborhood zoned into McCallum High School. The family joined Austin Country Club. Harvey soon introduced himself to the intense, analytical, bespectacled boy with the exhaustingly energetic routine and so many questions. The two formed an exquisite pair.

Harvey marveled at Kite's devotion. He stood back at the range and watched the boy pound ball after ball, always with purpose, rarely with a smile, with a burn that seemed to weekend players at the country club to border on manic. But Harvey understood. He knew what his young study wanted and needed. When harsh weather chased the recreational golfers indoors, Harvey expected Kite to come to the course anyway, because he knew his career in golf would require him to learn to play in rain, wind, and glove-and-knit-cap weather with three layers of clothes and discipline that seemed rare and enviable. Kite never failed to be there.

On those wet and sloppy afternoons, Harvey would supply Kite with enough balls to last until suppertime. He occasionally would check on him, peeking around a corner so as not to be seen by Kite. There Kite was. Every swing splattered perfect, shallow divots. He was in no hurry. He worked as if the sun was shining and he had no other obligation to distract him. Harvey hoped that someday Kite would have the opportunity to use the good form and attitude he was learning in the rain and the mud and the chill of those infrequent poor weather days in Austin.

Harvey appreciated the way Kite embraced everything else about golf. Harvey had done so himself, all those years ago, and he saw a little bit of himself in Kite. He noticed how Kite molded his identity around his rigid ideal of what an aspiring tour professional should look like. He wore the right shirts. He played the right irons. He carried the right bag. He wore the right steel-spiked shoes. Kite was acutely conscious of his image as the newest member of the Lamar Middle School Scottie golf team on Burnet Road. He wanted to project absolute resolve. Kite tried hard. He always would, even into his early sixties, when he played a full schedule on the Champions Tour.

Kite's arrival in Austin coincided with the majestic parallel rise of a young Ben Crenshaw. Crenshaw had met Harvey when he was six years old. His father brought him to the country club and asked Harvey to acquaint his son with a proper grip. Harvey placed Crenshaw's fingers on the grip of a cut-down iron and marveled at what he saw. It was like the boy's hands were created for golf. When he watched him swing, Harvey admired Crenshaw's fluid attack on the ball, the way his arms and shoulders seemed to flow from his hips and feet. He was like a blooming flower facing the sun, possessed of an uncanny sense of rhythm and an innate grasp of the metaphysical connection between time, space, and the sweet spot of a clubface. Harvey was mesmerized.

Crenshaw won his first tournament when he was in fourth grade at Casis Elementary School. He shot 46 over nine holes at Lions Municipal Golf Course. He made two holes in one, three days apart, when he was eleven. He also shot a 74, an achievement that merited having his picture published in the *Austin American-Statesman*. His father remanded him to the back tees after he turned thirteen. "Stay there," Charlie Crenshaw told his son. Crenshaw stayed there.

Kite and Crenshaw, their futures so inevitably braided, played their first round together one Saturday in 1963, shortly after the Kites moved to Austin from Dallas. Crenshaw had been playing—no, dominating—the course for years. He had a reputation. He was as good a young player as anyone at the club had ever seen. He could shape shots like he was drawing them with pencil. He could drive beyond the eyesight of the older men, who cooed at his swing. He could do everything, but what the better players admired the most was Crenshaw's putting stroke. Fluid and graceful, it appeared as simple as a footstep but was impossible to imitate. Crenshaw was a born athlete. He could instruct his body what to do and his body would do it, beautifully.

On that Saturday in 1963, the differences between Crenshaw and Kite were as obvious as the colors of spring and fall. The apple-cheeked boy from Dallas with the rust-colored hair had to work hard for what seemed naturally given to Crenshaw. What no one understood, however, when Harvey paired the boys that morning was that what Kite had could not be seen. Harvey sent them to the tenth tee, where they were joined by Crenshaw's brother, his father, and another excellent amateur named Wally Scott. A small crowd assembled to watch.

It was a consequential collision of future rivals and friends. The two would soon compete against one another for city championships. They would play on the same University of Texas team that would sweep NCAA titles. They would account for thirty-eight victories on the PGA Tour, including a U.S. Open for Kite and two Masters titles for Crenshaw. They would captain U.S. Ryder Cup teams. They would be elected to the World Golf Hall of Fame. They would represent the best of what Harvey could do with a boy willing to give everything to golf. Crenshaw and Kite were like siblings that way: the Penick boys of Austin.

But they were not brothers, even though, like brothers, they had a relationship neither easily defined nor easily understood. That was the way it would always be. That they were eternally finding themselves compared, especially by fans and the media, was frustrating to both of them at times, but beyond their control. There was Crenshaw, the spirited one who drove throaty muscle cars and wore fashionable shirts and kept his hair long and summoned command of a golf ball without so much as a practice swing. People adored him for what he was. And there was Kite, the dogged one who lacked the Paramount Pictures looks and the Fifth Avenue clothes and the Detroit coupe, but had a fire smoldering inside that Crenshaw would never feel. Kite's dominion in golf seemed more like stewardship. He wouldn't think of swatting a shot in competition until he'd spent an hour on the range. People admired him for what he was not. And there they were on a Saturday in 1963, joined for the first time by Harvey.

Kite pegged his tee.

He unleashed his coil with the ferocity of a May tornado. He knew better than to attack a golf ball with such abandon, but he wanted desperately to impress. "I was the new kid on the block and trying to scratch my way in," he said decades later, telling the story as if it had happened the weekend before. On that day in 1963, Kite was going to make Austin Country Club aware that the junior championship had a new contender and that Crenshaw had met his match. Instead, he made them aware that even the winner of the Riverlake two-day handicap was capable of completely whiffing a drive. "I had the prettiest, most beautiful divot," Kite remembered, "laying right over the ball."

Crenshaw looked at his father and brother. No one spoke. Kite managed a wan smile and recovered gamely. The two boys, eleven and thirteen, finished their round, the first of thousands they would play together, from after-school Nassaus to junior championships to college tournaments to tournaments on the PGA Tour. It was the start of something magical. The names Kite and Crenshaw would become two halves of a whole — the pair of Hall of Famers from the same city, the pair shaped by Harvey Penick into two of the greatest players ever.

Kite redeemed his inauspicious debut at the country club many times over. He qualified for the 1966 U.S. Junior at California Country Club, where he lost in the semifinals. He won an individual medal at the 1967 Texas 4A State Championship with a final-round 70 at Morris Williams Golf Course, then again in 1968, with the same score.

Kite strapped himself to the range. He lost himself in hours and hours of practice. "I spend most of my time on the practice tee, trying to keep my swing grooved," he said in 1967. "By grooved I mean one that can be repeated time after time, with a minimum of difference. I also believe there is a difference between practicing and just hitting balls. Practice requires concentration, while hitting balls does not."

He was listening to his new teacher. He had found his muse in Harvey.

Kite also had found a new friend at the country club, another promising high school player who, like Crenshaw, would make him better by playing with him. Terry Jastrow, the son of a prosperous oilman in Midland, flew to Austin in 1965 to spend the summer before his senior year at Midland Lee High School working for Harvey.

George McCall, a club member, had told Harvey about Jastrow. The winner of the Midland Country Club Championship had used Jastrow as his caddie, McCall knew. He recommended the boy to Harvey as a potential pupil with tremendous promise. Could you put him to work this summer? McCall asked Harvey. Could you give him lessons instead of paying him a wage? Harvey agreed to the arrangement.

Jastrow had never even seen Harvey when the taxi delivered him to the clubhouse off of Riverside Drive. But the good players in Midland who knew golf in Texas told Jastrow that he had never met a man like him, and never would again.

Jastrow noticed Harvey's hands first. Wrinkled like wadded paper, etched by years of exposure to the sun and the wind, those hands told Jastrow that he was in the presence of someone who cared about his trade. Harvey looked very old to the boy. Ancient. He was almost sixty that summer, but he appeared to be eighty, until he spoke. Harvey noticed the boy in his shop. *Are you Terry Jastrow? I'm Harvey Penick. You can call me Harvey. Mr. Penick is my father. Nice to meet you, son.* Harvey held out his etched hand. Jastrow was startled by how gently Harvey took his.

Then "he put me to work," Jastrow said. He never called him anything but Mr. Penick.

Harvey instructed Jastrow to pick the range in the morning. He provided him with a cylindrical canvas bag attached to a tube, reminding him to work fast so they could get to their lessons. Jastrow carried a club with him as he picked, and when the range was lightly used, in the dead of a July afternoon, he ditched the bag to hit balls back toward the tee. When the range was clear, Harvey sent Jastrow to the bag room, where he cleaned clubs until the afternoon shift arrived. He then was free to play.

Jastrow spent much of that summer and the next one walking the course with Kite and Barbara Puett, who had coached Kite at Lamar Middle School. The new friends talked between shots about Harvey, who never allowed either of them to eavesdrop on the other's lessons. They spoke in awe of Harvey's ability to address a ball, pivot 180 degrees, then twirl around, and flush it with the authority of Ben Hogan. "Look," Jastrow remembered Harvey's saying, "if *I* can hit this ball dead solid doing that, I think *you* can hit it looking at it."

Hearing that, a beginner might quit the game in fear or frustration. But Jastrow was no beginner. He accepted the message Harvey wanted him to hear: *You can do this.* "You believed you could play because Harvey said you could play," Jastrow said.

The two of them worked together for the entire summer of '65. Harvey struggled to lighten the pressure that had invaded Jastrow's grip, the evidence of which Harvey could see in the boy's palms. Harvey scratched at Jastrow's callouses with long, sharp fingernails. "I held the grip captive," Jastrow said. They worked for weeks on that one simple lesson. Soon there were no callouses on Jastrow's palms for Harvey to scratch.

Harvey started Jastrow with a 9-iron. He soon allowed him to practice with the 7-. Harvey never let Jastrow use his driver on the range. The longest club he hit was a fairway wood. Harvey sometimes picked at the boy's hands again. Sometimes he just watched him deplete a bag of balls and said nothing. Jastrow thought it odd, this unnerving silence. But he trusted Harvey.

"I held him in such regard, I had such a fondness for him, that he could do no wrong," Jastrow said. "When he spoke, I literally hung on every word." The same was true when Harvey didn't speak.

Jastrow qualified for the Texas Junior that fall at Brackenridge Park in San Antonio. He advanced to the finals, where he lost. After his school year back in Midland, he returned to Austin for another summer with Harvey. Jastrow dug ditches at the club between lessons, held the club lightly, and won the state junior in 1966, dispatching John Mahaffey in the finals. He was the low scorer in the qualifying rounds at the U.S. Junior Championship in Whittier, California. Lanny Wadkins beat him in the quarterfinals.

He left that fall to play for Dave Williams at the University of Houston. Harvey later saw a copy of *Sports Illustrated,* and there was Jastrow, on the cover, photographed with Williams in a posed lesson. When Jastrow drove back to Austin from Houston, he approached Harvey for a lesson. Harvey declined.

One teacher at a time is plenty, he told Jastrow. And they said good-bye.

Chapter Eight

CRENSHAW, MEANWHILE, won the 1967 Texas State Junior Championship at fifteen, hitting tee shots off of rubber mats at Brackenridge Park in San Antonio, imagining the old Texas Opens of the past, when Snead and Hogan and Hagen and Harvey's mentor, Jack Burke Sr., had conquered Old Brack. He qualified for the 1968 U.S. Junior Championship, becoming one of 1,599 entrants invited to The Country Club in Brookline, Massachusetts. The trip, and the place, would alter his life.

Crenshaw could barely contain his excitement about the trip to New England. His father planned excursions to walk the Freedom Trail and the Liberty Trail. They bought tickets to a Red Sox game. The younger Crenshaw had never been farther east than St. Louis, Missouri. But he knew from reading his favorite book, *The World of Golf* by Charles Price, that he would be playing the course where Francis Ouimet, a twenty-year-old former caddie, won the 1913 U.S. Open in a rain-streaked playoff over the famous English professionals Harry Vardon and Ted Ray.

Crenshaw had never played bentgrass fairways. He had never putted on bentgrass greens. The variety of The Country Club's holes left a profound impression on his young imagination. "I had never seen comparable natural relief on a course," he remembered two decades later. "Such rolling fairways, such deep bunkers, such shallow greens, like the one on the seventeenth hole, which Francis Ouimet birdied on the last regular round and again in the playoff."

He lost in the quarterfinals. Larry Griffin, the junior champion of New Orleans, beat him on the eighteenth hole. But Crenshaw gained so much more. His reach now extended beyond Texas. His points of reference seemed to multiply in one week. "Even though I didn't win," he later wrote, "I grew up a lot." Brookline altered the world profoundly and permanently for Crenshaw. The experience emboldened his golf. Crenshaw returned to Brackenridge Park in 1969 for his second Texas junior title. He won the annual Firecracker Open at Lions in July, one of eighteen tournament trophies he collected in his dizzying senior season at Austin High School.

And he began to think about the crisp and certain promise of the beyond. He wanted everything in golf. He burned to compete. He yearned to see and play and be charmed again by places like The Country Club. Harvey had polished Crenshaw well. The boy who wanted to be the best was close enough to want the best the game could offer.

"If you were a young player and thought you were pretty good, all you had to do was watch Ben swing and see how much farther he hit it to wonder about your own ability," said Terry Jastrow, an excellent junior player at the time from Midland. "There was something else that convinced you. A bunch of us would be on the practice range beating balls. With everybody else, Harvey Penick would spend an hour. But when he got around to Ben, he would look at him for a minute or two, smile, and tell him to go play golf."

Kite and Crenshaw challenged Harvey to think carefully and creatively about his role in their golf lives. He understood that his two young charges had almost opposite needs. On one level, Crenshaw and Kite were mutations of the same strain. They were born to fathers who witnessed the rise of Hogan and Nelson. They were sons of a robust, independently minded state ideally suited — in climate, wealth, topography, and untethered ambition — to nurturing young players of a sport whose identity was emerging in Texas at a furious pace. Crenshaw and Kite simply came along at the right time and into the orbits of the right people. They were children of tremendous privilege, not only because they were wealthy, but because their support systems made so much possible. Their families gave them every opportunity to do what they wanted to do. If that meant chasing golf balls down the gilded fairways of Austin Country Club, let them, by all means, chase golf balls.

Kite and Crenshaw may have been fundamentally brothers in many important ways, but Harvey recognized that they were not the same boys at all. He saw Kite's basic need for order and answers. He knew Crenshaw responded better to abstraction and questions. Harvey decided to prohibit them from witnessing one another's lessons because the message he wanted to impart to Crenshaw might hurt Kite, and vice versa.

But his pupils learned together in one important sense. Kite and Crenshaw grew as players because they so often competed together. They learned from one another how to lose. And they learned how to win.

The two entered the 1967 Jaycees Junior Golf Tournament at Morris Williams Golf Course, where Kite had won his state championship. Crenshaw was in the ninth grade at O. Henry Middle School. He was the reigning Austin men's city champion. Kite shot 70 to lead him by two after the first round.

Kite shot 2-under 34 on the front nine on the second day. Crenshaw flailed, making the nine-hole turn at 3-over for the round, five behind Kite. He lost another stroke at the par-4 tenth.

They were young and cocky and imminently capable of anything, which explains how Kite played the next eight holes at 4 over par and Crenshaw, settling into a trancelike rhythm, played them at minus 3. Kite lost by a stroke.

Crenshaw won the Texas State Junior later that year, beating Wayne Fenick of Brownsville, nine and eight, over thirty-six holes of match play. Kite was a favorite to win that summer at Brackenridge Park, but Crenshaw intervened. Kite won the consolation match instead.

Kite did win the Texas-Oklahoma Junior in June 1968, by a staggering eleven shots. He took the Firecracker Open a month later in Austin. A month after that, Kite delivered a final-round 66 at Lions to capture the Austin junior title. "It was about time I played good," he said brusquely. "I haven't felt that I've played good in the tournament until today."

One more significant tournament remained on the Austin amateur circuit: the biggest trophy in Austin golf, the 1968 men's city championship, was won each year by the best amateur in five counties. The golf community buzzed. Kite entered the tournament with three recent trophies and momentum. Crenshaw, now at Harvey's old high school, Austin High, came to Morris Williams as the defending champion.

Kite shot a blazing 7-under 65 in the opening round. Crenshaw shot 70. He followed with another 70 to Kite's 71, then shot 69 in the third round. Kite wavered there, shooting 75.

Crenshaw nipped Kite by a shot in the fourth round, his 70 to Kite's 71. People actually came out to watch. They felt like they were seeing the future of the PGA Tour. And they were.

Harvey's boys finished in first and second place. There was Crenshaw from old West Austin, with his cascading hair and his charmingly crooked smile and his disdain for the monotonous humdrum of practice, again holding a trophy every dreamer in Central Texas sought to win. There was Kite, with his relentless quest for precision through practice and his enduring itch to prove so much, watching the newspaper photographers take pictures of Crenshaw with the trophy he wanted to be his.

"He's a tremendous putter," Kite said that day. "The best in the state."

"I made the putts I had to make," Crenshaw said.

They were the humble, accepting words of boys in golf about to become men in golf. To those who lingered for the trophy ceremony that afternoon at Morris Williams Golf Course, their achievements so far seemed wonderful and promising and intriguing. No one — not Kite, not Crenshaw, not Harvey himself — could have predicted how much more Harvey's boys would accomplish. But everyone at the golf course that afternoon felt the ground shifting.

Kite had committed during his senior year at McCallum to playing golf at Texas, a decision that pleased Harvey immeasurably. A former pharmacy student at Texas named George Hannon had succeeded Harvey as the golf coach. Harvey considered Hannon a dear friend, even a protégé. The retired coach wanted his successor to carry the Longhorns to heights he had never reached. Harvey knew a player like Kite could factor into getting there.

Harvey had worked closely with Hannon at Lions Municipal Golf Course, where Texas had played many conference matches, and he respected Hannon's ability to lead. Hannon regarded Harvey as a mentor. "Harvey taught me all the golf I know," Hannon said.

The two met in 1942. Hannon was a freshman at Texas, uninterested in trying to qualify for the varsity golf team but eager to play on weekends and after class. Harvey liked Hannon, who caddied for him when he played with Hogan at the Lions exhibition in 1950. Harvey also asked Hannon to accompany him at teaching seminars for the Texas section of the PGA. The two of them created scripts for the visits to other Texas golf clubs; Hannon, the confederate in the crowd, asked the predetermined questions. Harvey answered with rehearsed aplomb. They were a brilliant road team.

Harvey often asked Hannon if coaching at Texas might interest him someday. The obligation was light: recruit, arrange qualifiers, organize a tournament schedule, make sure the station wagon had a tank of gas, give each player three golf balls per tournament, $6 a day for meals, and $10 for a hotel room. "They would make a little money off of that," Hannon said.

When his opportunity came, Hannon accepted with deference and grace.

"There is a certain amount of prestige involved," he said when his appointment was announced. "It's always tough to take over another man's job, and it's doubly hard to step into a big pair of shoes," he said. "But I wouldn't have taken the job if I didn't think I could do it."

Like Harvey, Hannon had a long Texas pedigree. He was born in 1924 in Kemp, enrolled at the university briefly, interrupted his education for three years to join the Army Air Corps, and returned to UT in 1945. Hannon never played on the Texas golf team, but he became friendly with Harvey's players when he returned to college from the service and worked as the starter at Lions Municipal. He became a golf professional in 1950 and eventually joined Dallas Athletic Club as an assistant. It was a fortuitous opportunity for Hannon, who was asked to assist the Southern Methodist University golf team between lessons and given other duties at DAC. Hannon drove the team station wagon.

Hannon left Dallas in 1960 when Tom Penick, Harvey's older brother and the man who allowed the two black youths to play in 1951, announced his retirement as the head golf professional at Lions. Hannon got the job. The two years he spent there — between his appointment as Tom Penick's successor and his appointment as Harvey's with the Texas golf team — allowed him to watch Harvey on the lesson tee.

"He has an almost uncanny knack of being able to spot defects in a student's swing and give him a maximum amount of help," Hannon said. "I have tried to pattern my teaching after him."

Hannon understood that the Texas golf team needed to return to prominence, especially given Texas A&M's rise in the conference, and he accepted the challenge of his new undertaking, which paid $500 a year. His duties with the city included running golf operations at the new municipal facility under construction near the airport on the east side of Austin. Morris Williams Golf Course, named for the father and son whom Harvey considered family, was scheduled to open in 1964, Hannon's first year as the UT golf coach. Hannon was certain to be busy.

The transition went as smoothly as anyone could have imagined. The Longhorns won the 1964 Southwest Conference Championship in Lubbock, led by medalist Pat Thompson. The team repeated in 1965. Randy Geiselman of UT won the individual title. Hannon took particular pride in the championship that year (and so, privately, did

Harvey): the Longhorns had won the championship in College Station — the home of Texas A&M.

University of Texas golf was on the rise again. The Longhorns had a new coach and a new home course at Morris Williams. Hannon had changed the fortunes of the Texas golf program.

Harvey, meanwhile, had a good feeling of his own about what lay ahead for the Longhorns.

Kite and Crenshaw were getting better and better. They developed a natural and lasting kinship through golf that would endure through every stage of their careers. But they also were creating a formidable personal rivalry. Each wanted to be the best player in the city. And that meant beating the other. They lived to win.

That much was clear when both of them had only innocent, boundless dreams. One early evening in 1964, Kite and his father, Tom Sr., were driving home to North Hills Drive after a devastating finish at a junior golf tournament. Long before they had established their pattern of alternating glory, Kite had just lost to Crenshaw. He was nearly in tears. Crenshaw was thirteen years old at the time, and Kite was fifteen.

He had told his father many times how desperately he wanted to play the PGA Tour. Good, Tom Kite Sr. would tell him. Keep working. But that evening the father looked at his son with sympathy and blunt disbelief. "If you can't hold your own with him [Crenshaw], how are you going to make it on the tour?" he asked.

Kite had no answer. But the question filled him with even more resolve. He would learn to hold his own against Crenshaw. He would learn to hold his own against the world. The boy who believed in working hard knew that this belief could take him where he wanted to go.

He would make it.

At the university, meanwhile, Hannon was gradually changing the entire scope of the Texas golf program. He installed a fall season, making golf a year-round sport. His teams won four conference championships in his first six years as head coach. But a different coach at a different school was beginning to put pressure on the preeminent golf program in the state. Texas was losing its footing.

Dave Williams, the head coach at the University of Houston since 1952, had won seven national championships from 1956 to 1970. The Cougars had competed in three different small conferences until 1960, when Houston went independent. Houston wanted to join the Southwest Conference, with Texas and the other big schools, but there was a complication: the Southwest Conference played tournaments in the match-play format. Williams believed that his teams had a better chance to succeed in stroke play, which involved thirty-six holes on the first day of a tournament and eighteen on the second. The evidence for that belief was his record and his team's results: in the spring of 1970, at the Border Olympics tournament in Laredo, Houston beat Texas by eighteen shots.

Hannon often had coffee with the other Texas coaches each morning on campus. At one such gathering in 1970 (another year Houston won the national title), athletic director and head football coach Darrell Royal asked Hannon: "What do we have to do to compete with Houston?"

"They play a different game than we do," Hannon replied.

Hannon was certain that Texas could challenge Houston if the conference adapted its tournament system to the prevailing format of the times. Match play, the ancient British style of competition, was vanishing. The PGA Tour no longer did match play, and few recognized competitions beyond the USGA national amateur championships did either. "We need to play stroke play," Hannon told Royal.

Royal suggested that Texas boycott all Southwest Conference matches, playing only invitational tournaments, if the other schools refused to switch. "If they don't change it, we'll pull the whole thing out," Royal told Hannon. The other schools declined. Hannon kept his word. The Longhorns played a full schedule of tournaments that season, but no round-robin conference matches. And they advanced all the way to the final round of the national championship with a faint chance to win.

Ben Crenshaw never thought seriously of playing golf anywhere but Texas. He could have signed with any school in the nation, but he loved his hometown and wanted to live and play near friends and family. He also wanted to be able to see Harvey as often as he could.

With Crenshaw as a dazzling freshman and Kite as a junior runner-up to Lanny Wadkins at the 1970 U.S. Amateur, Texas had been ranked number one in the nation for most of the season. But the Longhorns finished three rounds at the NCAA Championship in the spring of '71 a distant fifteen shots out of the lead. The mood the night before the final round was grim. Hannon told his team he thought the Longhorns needed a team score of 12 under par to stand a chance.

"I thought at the time that if we shot twelve under, the other teams will start choking a little," said George Machock, a senior. His teammate William Cromwell hoped Texas could fight into a top-three finish. Florida had the lead, with Wake Forest and Houston in close chase. The miracle in the desert of Tucson, Arizona, was less than twelve hours from beginning.

Kite opened the last round in a fury. He birdied the first four holes at Tucson National. He eagled the fifth. After nine holes, Texas trailed Houston by five shots and Florida by four. Playing in the last spot for the Longhorns, Crenshaw played the eleventh through fifteenth holes in 4 under par. He holed out a wedge on the eighteenth for eagle. His 7-under 65 was a formality for the team. Texas won by seven shots.

Crenshaw shot a tournament-record 15-under-par 273 and won the individual medal, the first for Texas since Ed White did it for Harvey back in 1935. The team's 13-under score of 275 set another NCAA Championship record.

"The spark was Kite," said Machock. Kite shot a final-round 68 after his torrid start. "What he did was phenomenal." The team postponed its sixteen-hour drive back to Austin and spent the evening in Tucson to celebrate. Houston, which finished second, was long gone by the time the first UT national championship team retired for the night.

"It was one of the best — no, make that the greatest — team performances I've ever seen," Hannon said.

Texas repeated in 1972. The Longhorns again beat Houston, this time in Cape Coral, Florida. Kite shot a final-round 68 for the individual lead, then watched Crenshaw, the sophomore All-American, hole a twenty-five-foot putt to tie him. The two shared the individual NCAA championship, a first in the seventy-five-year history of the tournament, because the NCAA allowed no playoff. "Both are disappointed," Hannon said after the championship. "They're teammates and good friends, but no one won."

After the trophy presentation, Kite searched for Crenshaw. "You've got to be the world's greatest putter in the clutch," he told him when he found him. "Tying is like kissing your sister."

"No," Crenshaw corrected. "It's like kissing your brother."

The two shared a laugh. Then they began to think about their futures. Crenshaw would go home to Harvey, return for his junior year at Texas, and win a record third NCAA individual championship. Kite had played his last collegiate tournament. He would go home to Harvey and prepare for the PGA Tour — just as he had promised his father he would do, all those years ago in the car.

"I'm glad it's over," Kite said. "Coach Hannon is a super coach and I owe him more than I can ever repay, but now I can get on with the pro tour, and what I've been building toward."

He announced his plans that summer of '72.

He had just finished nineteenth in the U.S. Open at Pebble Beach Golf Links. He was the second-lowest amateur on a California course that would figure profoundly in his career in golf. He had played on the U.S. World Amateur Cup team in Spain. He had been amateur runner-up at the Masters the last two springs, and he had played in a Walker Cup at St. Andrews in Scotland.

"I've met my first goal by completing four years at the University of Texas," Kite told a student reporter with *The Daily Texan* upon his announcement.

He had so many more.

"He is a talented, committed golfer with every reason to succeed as a professional," Harvey told the *Texan*. He had no idea how right he would be.

Harvey maintained a full teaching schedule into the early 1970s. When Kite and Crenshaw were traveling, he saw Whitworth or Rawls, whose career was nearing its end. A steady parade of new and old members filled his practice range on Riverside Drive. Harvey returned to his notebook often.

He began to enjoy a broader national profile. In the summer of 1970, he was invited to the All-American Golf Dinner in New York, where the best college golfers in the nation were honored. Harvey had to rent a tuxedo. He appeared with his old friend Byron Nelson. Vice President Spiro Agnew attended. Harvey and Helen stayed in an apartment on Fifth Avenue. "I think this is a nice honor," he said modestly.

He conducted a growing series of seminars for the PGA. Most of them were in Texas, but Harvey sometimes ventured to Arkansas, Alabama, California, Florida, Georgia, New York, and Tennessee. He traveled one summer weekend to Cedar Ridge Country Club in Tulsa, Oklahoma, for a three-day workshop with other club professionals. "When I started playing golf, it was not the business that it is today," he told them. "We played in tournaments solely for fun."

Harvey joined his longtime friend Jimmy Demaret at a seminar in Houston. Speaking in front of 150 fellow professionals from the Southern Texas section of the PGA, they led a discussion about the golf swing. When they finished, Demaret smiled. "Harvey has been speaking two hours and used the word 'I' once," Demaret said. "Such humility. I wish Jack Burke was here."

But Harvey's humility was accompanied by a growing fatigue.

Harvey was sixty-six years old in the early winter of 1970. He had been associated with Austin Country Club for nearly six decades, and he'd been the head professional for nearly five of them. The thought of retiring left him uneasy. But Harvey sensed a need to slow down.

He told his son Tinsley, who had been his assistant since leaving a teaching professional position in Colorado in 1969, that he was ready to relinquish his title. He planned to maintain his teaching schedule, but he wanted to spend more time at home with Helen and less time monitoring inventory in the shop. Harvey thought it was an ideal time to bring another Penick to Austin Country Club. The club voted to approve Tinsley Penick as the successor to his father. Tinsley accepted gladly.

By this time, Harvey's reputation as a teacher of great players had exceeded his more modest one as a consummate club professional who had devoted his life to his membership. Jim Trinkle, reporting for *Golf* magazine, came to Austin to interview Harvey for a profile. "Harvey tightens nuts, bolts and screws in the golf games of people we see in golf's weekly television dramas," Trinkle wrote. He noted that Harvey seemed "made of leather, barbed wire and India rubber." Trinkle studied Harvey's wrinkled skin, crinkled by decades in the sun. "You can read the Dead Sea Scrolls in that chipped, weathered face," he advised. Harvey had no interest in discussing his features for the golf writer. "Here," he blurted, rising from his chair and handing Trinkle a putter. "Hit this ball toward that hole."

Trinkle's story about Harvey occupied five pages in the April issue of *Golf*. It was the first large-scale feature published about the Austin Country Club professional. Trinkle mentioned Kite and Crenshaw and the many women Harvey had taught, including Rawls and Whitworth, and shared anecdotes about Davis Love Jr. and Canadian PGA champion George Knudson, who said of Harvey: "Harvey is the only man I really believe knows all there is to know about this game." The story included a sidebar listing nineteen observations Harvey had made about practice, putting, chipping, club selection, and the idea that every player should have what his friend Jimmy Demaret called "a choke stroke." Like the low cutoff fade that Jack Nicklaus later made famous in major championships, a choke stroke "repeats under pressure," Harvey told Trinkle. "If you can make a good, basic shot you'll rarely have to attempt a fancy one."

The club announced the transition from Harvey to his son Tinsley on January 1, 1971. Harvey insisted that his son issue the remarks. "I couldn't be happier with my promotion," Tinsley told the Austin newspaper. "Austin is the greatest place to live in the United States and we have a fine membership at this club." The brief article included no statement from Harvey.

The dynamic in Austin golf was shifting in other ways. The city was nearing 300,000 residents. There were two other country clubs in the city, both of them on the more prosperous west side, and a second municipal course had been built. Austin Country Club remained one of the best golf courses in the area, but the dining and banquet facilities, largely unimproved since 1950, were barely used by members. Revenues were sinking.

Another country club was beginning to take shape on twisting, flood-prone Onion Creek in the southeast corner of the city. Demaret had started work on the early stages of what would be the Onion Creek Club, which retained the three-time Masters champion as the principal designer of its eighteen holes.

The owner of the bald cypress- and pecan-lined property had met Demaret years before at Champions Golf Club in Houston. Rex Kitchen, the president of a construction company in Austin, had gone to Houston in the early 1960s with Austin Country Club members Jimmie Connolly and Charlie Crenshaw, Ben Crenshaw's father, to watch the annual Champions Cup matches.

Founded in 1957 by Demaret and Jack Burke Jr., Champions was the site of the 1967 Ryder Cup matches and the 1969 U.S. Open won by Orville Moody. The club staged its invitational matches as a way to attract the finest amateurs in the country. The competition brought spectators from around the state, including Kitchen, who had a 750-acre cattle ranch in South Austin along Onion Creek.

Kitchen was not a golfer, but he did appreciate the beauty of Champions. "He said, 'You know, I have a pretty piece of property in Austin. I would like to have something like this in my memory,'" Demaret recalled before Onion Creek Club opened.

After Kitchen died in 1965, the idea continued to intrigue Demaret. He said he circled the land four times in an airplane and saw a golf course waiting to be discovered. "God designed it," he said, "and we loaned some equipment to finish it." Demaret also knew an opportunity when he saw one. Austin had only three private golf clubs — not very many for its size — and the city was growing south. Onion Creek seemed both a chance to capture a market and a certain way to make money.

Connolly and Demaret created a partnership to buy the land in 1969 for $812,500. Demaret routed the holes, construction began in 1971, and the course was complete in 1973.

A celebrity outing christened Onion Creek Club on June 2, 1974. The cast included Bob Hope, Mickey Mantle, singers Phil Harris and Tennessee Ernie Ford, professional golfers Jack Burke Jr. and Jay Hebert, country-music crooner Willie Nelson, and Darrell Royal, the folksy, immensely popular head coach of the University of Texas football team who had won three national championships.

None of them imagined that the new course they played that day would matter as much as it did to American golf in 1978, when a small group of retired players from the PGA Tour traveled to Austin for a reunion.

Back at his own country club, where he no longer worried about the daily operation of the golf shop, Harvey gave more thought to writing. The notebook in his rolltop desk resembled nothing coherent, but he began to see a void in his own library of instruction books, which he maintained and displayed with great pride at his home behind the twelfth hole.

When he looked at his collection, he saw *Rights and Wrongs of Golf* by Bob (Bobby) Jones, published in 1935. He saw *Down to Scratch* by Abe Mitchell, published two years later. There was *How to Play Golf* by Ben Thomson, *A New Way to Better Golf* by Alex Morrison, *Sam Snead's Natural Golf,* and a personal favorite, *How to Play Your Best*

Golf All the Time by Tommy Armour, presented to him in 1953 by one of his earliest elite women, Betty Jameson. "Fore!" Jameson had inscribed inside the cover. "Harvey, with fond affection and deep gratitude — both for you and your ability as a great teacher."

Harvey cherished the book because Jameson gave it to him near the end of her decorated career, a season of reflection if there ever was one. But he also treasured it because he revered the author. Armour, an original Scottish-born professional from the Braid Hills of Edinburgh, had won the 1927 U.S. Open, the 1930 PGA Championship, and the 1931 Open Championship at Carnoustie. He also had been an influential teacher. Like Harvey, he believed that good golf began in the hands. "Get it right, and all other progress follows," Armour wrote in the book on Harvey's shelf.

Harvey never forgot Armour. He kept a fuzzy black-and-white photograph of the "Silver Scot," sitting on a bench with a club between his dark stockings, on the surface of his rolltop desk, where he could see it every day. Under the photograph were Armour's words: "I can tell you all you'll need to know in ten minutes." Armour had spoken those words, but Harvey lived them.

Harvey noticed a clear theme among the books in his collection. They were written for players, not teachers, and mostly beginning players at that. He wondered why there were so few books for teachers. Harvey understood that reading about how to play golf could help an aspiring player. But he also knew that the golf swing needed to be rehearsed, to be *felt*, in order to become efficient.

He'd had opportunities earlier. Betty Hicks, the LPGA professional who corresponded often with Harvey, tried to persuade him to write a book of instruction, but Harvey rejected the idea. "I told her the publishers wouldn't give anything for a good one," he said in 1974. "They would want something controversial."

Harvey had no interest in controversy. Friction ran against his gentle, pacifist nature. But sharing his ideas in published form intrigued Harvey, especially the prospect of a book written explicitly for golf teachers. He appeared to be thinking seriously about that possibility in the summer of 1974 when he and Helen traveled to Levelland to visit their daughter and son-in-law.

Billy and Kathryn Powell moved to Levelland, on the Llano Estacado west of Lubbock, when Harvey's son-in-law joined South Plains College as its first athletic director and women's basketball coach. They joined Levelland Country Club, where Harvey met Charles Richards, the editor of *The Surveyor* newspaper, for an interview on the country club grounds. A picture accompanied the article: Harvey, in his seventy-first year of life, looked tan and sinewy in his white golf shirt. His face wore an expression of patient accommodation—he was getting accustomed to these reporters and their questions—as the *Surveyor* photographer snapped the shutter in his face.

In the interview, Harvey discussed his insights into his own limitations as a teacher—limitations he recognized, accepted, and even, with self-effacing modesty, valued. The interviews he'd granted over the years customarily teemed with deferential humility. Harvey took great care in his public statements to deflect credit for the success of his students or for his reputation. He referred to himself many times as a "guide"—a word suggesting that his involvement in, say, the rise of Rawls or Whitworth or Crenshaw or Kite had amounted to little more than providing supervision, like a parent standing nearby to catch a child learning to ride a bike. (His students, however, bestowed much of the credit for their successes on Harvey. It's likely that at one and the same time everyone was right and everyone was wrong.)

The editor of the Levelland newspaper asked Harvey pointed questions about the nature of golf. Why should older players avoid long irons? Why should beginners practice their short shorts to develop their full swings? "I don't know why," Harvey replied, declining to speculate. "Except having seen more shots in my life than anybody else, I just know that it's true."

The editor pressed Harvey for answers. Harvey provided none.

"Again, I don't know the reasons," he said. "I never say I know anything will work. Anyone who says he knows something, I'm leery of them."

The notebook Harvey maintained in Austin never masqueraded as a repository of reasons. The notes he made did indeed represent answers, but not to questions involving the nature of things. Harvey knew what he knew because he had seen it work.

He knew taking dead aim worked. But could he explain it? He knew swinging the bucket worked. But could he unpack its physics? He knew giving luck a chance gave players a high probability of scoring. But could he explain luck or chance? Could anyone? Harvey's methods functioned on the simple premises of reliability and repeatability — two critical dimensions, both physical and mental, of playing good golf. He was almost childlike in his approach to helping others grasp the game. He was far more interested in effect than cause. If you do *this*, he seemed to say, *this* will happen. Why question truth?

Decades later, long after Harvey had died, Tom Kite said that his longtime teacher knew far more than the Levelland interview implied. "He understood the way the body worked," Kite said one winter morning in 2014. "He understood the limitations that people had in their bodies. He totally understood what made the golf swing work."

Kite often solicited other instructors, but Harvey taught Kite the fundamentals. He knew Harvey as a golf teacher as well as anyone. "Just because he didn't share that with his students because he didn't want to clutter their minds doesn't mean he didn't understand it," Kite said. "If you came in and said you were hitting the ball too high, he knew multiple ways to get it down. He knew the *best ways* to get it down."

Kite told a story about one of his part-time instructors, Chuck Cook, who later worked with Payne Stewart and Jason Dufner. Cook apprenticed under Harvey. He once told Harvey that he was struggling with a nasty hook. Harvey never asked to see Cook's swing. Instead, he asked Cook to retrieve his persimmon from the trunk of his car. Harvey examined the wear spots on the grip of the club. He studied the streaks of color on the sole, determining how the club brushed the wooden tees. He angled the face of the club in the light, so he could see the wear marks from contact with the ball. He then prescribed adjustments. Harvey never saw Cook swing but identified problems in his grip and release, Kite said. "That's knowing what's going on," he said.

As the interview wound down that July afternoon in Levelland in 1974, the editor asked Harvey to remember the finest round he'd seen Kite or Crenshaw play, or their best tournament. Harvey said nothing.

"A shrug of the hands," Richards wrote.

"Dates and scores, things like that, don't stick in my mind," Harvey said. "If I ever saw you hold a club or hit it, I'd remember that. A year or two from now, if I saw you swing a club in another fairway, I might not remember your name. But I'd remember you as the fellow from Levelland."

The fellow from Levelland reminded Harvey that he recently had been on a show with his friend Cactus Pryor, a famous broadcaster in Austin. Pryor had asked Harvey to recall his best round of golf. Harvey told Pryor he couldn't remember it. But Pryor could. It was a 63, the course record at the Riverside location of Austin Country Club. "Things like that don't stick to my mind," Harvey told Richards in Levelland. "Golf swings do."

Richards had one more question: Would Harvey ever write a book?

"I wouldn't mind, later on," Harvey said. But he then clarified his answer: "It would be to help teachers teach," he said. "I don't think I'd do one for golfers, as far as how to play."

Chapter Nine

BACK HOME, fame accumulated slowly for Harvey, like a trickle into a cistern.

In 1975 an oilman named Howard Sutton of Shreveport, Louisiana, learned from a friend that Harvey could make any player better, regardless of sex, age, or ability. His son, an astounding ball striker and tenacious scorer, had won the Louisiana State Junior the year before. But Sutton and the teaching professional at Northwood Hills Country Club in nearby Blanchard, where the Suttons played golf, wondered if the boy might learn even more about his swing from Harvey. Sutton bought a pair of tickets to Austin and arranged a lesson with Harvey.

Sutton and his seventeen-year-old son Hal were greeted by Harvey at the Austin Country Club clubhouse. He invited the pair inside his shop. Hal had never met Harvey. "I didn't even know what he looked like," he said. The gentle old man he met that morning looked ancient, wrinkled in the face and stooped at the waist. Harvey leaned in and studied the positions of the callouses on Hal Sutton's hands. He approved. Harvey suggested they go outside, just him and the boy. "Well, Howard," he said, "we won't be needing you."

On the range, Harvey asked Sutton to hold the club, and Sutton obliged, revealing a three-knuckle grip. Harvey approved. He ordered Sutton to never change it, no matter who told him to. Harvey turned to amble to his golf cart.

"Hit three drivers," he instructed. Hal didn't know why Harvey wanted to see three drivers. Why not five? Why not ten? He didn't ask. He just hit three balls with his driver and waited for Harvey to speak.

Harvey sat in a cart and watched. He said nothing. Sutton wondered if the old man had forgotten why they were there. Then Harvey rose slowly.

"Here," he said. "Now watch." Harvey took a club and demonstrated a swing, from address to finish, posing at the top of the swing and at follow-through. He wanted Sutton to notice the handle of the club, how it remained in front of his chest throughout the arc of the turn, never ahead, never lagging. "That's what I wish I would've understood better at the time," Sutton said nearly four decades later. Harvey wanted him to synchronize.

Harvey ended the lesson after his demonstration on the range. Other teachers might have been tempted to do more, but Harvey appreciated the soundness of young Sutton's grip, stance, and swing. It wasn't that he didn't know how to help. It was that he knew how much help to give. Sutton's father asked Harvey many questions about his son's mechanics. Harvey demurred. On the flight home, Hal Sutton himself wondered what good the trip had done, given how little Harvey had said or demanded. "I don't know if we got anything out of this or not," he told his father.

Sutton played twenty-three years on the PGA Tour. He won fourteen titles, including the 1983 PGA Championship. Harvey recounted his visit in 1975 with Sutton — the only encounter the two of them had — in his book, but he neglected to mention the postscript.

"As time goes on," Sutton said, "it's maybe the most powerful lesson I ever had. I wasn't smart enough to take it at the time. I thought more was better. Isn't that what every young person wants?" Sutton slumped, left tournament golf for a few years, and then returned to compete on the Champions Tour. At that point, he said in 2013, his morning with Harvey made more sense than it did when he boarded the flight home to Louisiana as a teenager.

"I went there expecting a lot," Sutton said. "And I got a lot — in a small package, if that makes any sense. I think he was telling me that 'you want to make it too complicated, and your dad wants to make it too complicated.'"

He added: "Isn't that kind of life right now?"

Crenshaw had risen to every expectation at Texas. He won five tournaments as a freshman and won eleven times as a sophomore, including the Trans-Mississippi Championship and the Porter Cup. He finished a stroke behind Vinny Giles in the '72 U.S. Amateur, where he shot 288 at Charlotte Country Club. He had two NCAA individual championships when he returned the year after Kite left. He was the best player in college golf.

His junior season at Texas told him everything he needed to know about his future. He won the Western Amateur, the Northeast Amateur, the Sunnehanna, and a second Southern Amateur title. Crenshaw finished the collegiate season with a third consecutive NCAA medal.

It was a historic and pivotal year. Crenshaw made fifteen starts. He won eleven times. He weighed the consequences of remaining at Texas for his senior season or going to the PGA Tour qualifying tournament. If he waited, Crenshaw could attempt to win a fourth NCAA title with the Longhorns. He would have another chance to play the U.S. Amateur.

He also was likely to qualify for the Walker Cup team. That possibility held special appeal for Crenshaw. The matches that year would be played at The Country Club in Brookline, which had charmed him forever after he qualified for the U.S. Junior there at the age of sixteen.

But he also considered this: he had tasted the tour and come away thirsty. He'd finished tied with John Mahaffey as low amateur at the 1970 U.S. Open at Hazeltine, third as an amateur at the Heritage Classic at Harbour Town, and seventh at the Houston Open at Champions Golf Club. He remembered his tie for nineteenth at his first Masters, in 1972, and how he'd held the lead briefly in 1973 at Augusta. Crenshaw wanted to play the Masters forever. He decided the best way to do that was to try to qualify for the PGA Tour. He left for Myrtle Beach to play those 144 holes and never cast a glance back toward Austin. He won by twelve.

Crenshaw entered his first tournament, the San Antonio Texas Open at Woodlake Golf Club. He won, beating George Archer and Orville Moody. He tied for second two weeks later at the World Open, an eight-round tournament at Pinehurst No. 2 in North Carolina. "He's the best that's come along since Nicklaus," said the winner, Miller Barber. "I knew when I beat him that I'd done beat somebody."

Dan Jenkins wrote the first lengthy profile of Crenshaw for the February 11, 1974, issue of *Sports Illustrated*. Editor André Laguerre liked it so much that he made it the cover story. "Make Way for the Kid" read the title, superimposed over a color picture of Crenshaw with his tongue out, watching the flight of a drive.

When he found the magazine in Austin, Harvey clutched it in his hands and felt that familiar swell of pride, just as he had felt watching Ed White, Ed Hopkins, Morris Williams Jr., and so many others. There was one of his boys—a man now of twenty-two years, the sunlight bleaching streaks in his over-the-ear hair, a steel-shafted persimmon driver sliding through the glove on his left hand, a sensation on the PGA Tour—on the cover of the biggest sports magazine in the nation. Harvey made sure he saved his copy.

Jenkins, a Texan himself, wanted to capture why people were drawn toward Crenshaw. He noted the cherubic features and expressive face, the temperamental energy on the course leavened by the disarming good cheer away from it, the flowing move to the ball and the sound, organic mechanics Harvey had coaxed out of him when Crenshaw was first orienting his fingers around the grip. Jenkins also suggested that a certain mystique may have been at play: that Crenshaw, a stunning winner in his first attempt on the PGA Tour, portended a once-in-a-generation talent about which witnesses to his greatness would always tell stories.

"Writers adore instant heroes, as civilization knows, and now they had Crenshaw with his mod hair and smile like the nice young man who sacks your groceries, not to forget a long, powerful swing that looks as if an artist might have drawn it after studying the finest movements of Ben Hogan, Sam Snead and the Rolex GMT-Master. Already, Crenshaw seemed to be the best thing to happen to golf since beltless slacks," Jenkins wrote.

The story felt like testimony. Jenkins larded the four-page meditation on charisma with salutations from Crenshaw's peers. From Allen Miller, a contemporary of Crenshaw's on the amateur circuit:

> Ben beats you to death, but you can't resist liking him and respecting him. It's like he's representing us out here, our era. If he wins, it's like we win. The thing about him is, he almost roots for you to beat him — if you're good enough.

From Lee Trevino, who at the time had won four of his eventual six major championships:

> He's got the best grip, the best setup and the best swing I've ever seen.

From Johnny Miller, the reigning U.S. Open champion:

> His personality is too good to be true. We may never know it, but down inside of him there might be the cockiest killer there ever was.

The story ended with the observation that women adored him.

Back in Austin, one of Harvey's former players read the account. It gave him an idea.

William Penn — "Billy" when he was on the Longhorn team two decades earlier — now was an attorney at the Austin National Bank Building and president of Austin Country Club. He sat down to compose a letter to *Sports Illustrated* on his professional letterhead. "There is no golf personality of more current interest than Ben Crenshaw," Penn typed. "Nor is there any abler writer to portray him than Den Jenkins."

But Penn thought it was Harvey who warranted his own profile in *Sports Illustrated*. He suggested to the editors that "the world should take more note of Harvey Penick, although he could be the last to say so. This kind and gentle man . . . is one of a diminishing breed of complete club professionals. Harvey has and still could supervise the course maintenance. Should the need arise, and admittedly it doesn't much anymore, he could show you where the roll point is in your Schenectady putter and put in a new hickory shaft. But he can also tell you what's new in golf, although it wouldn't take nearly so long as a lost wax process club manufacturer might think it should. Most of all he can teach. He can really teach."

Penn neglected to mention that Harvey was now a traveling teacher. His retirement from his formal position at the club had given Harvey the time to spend summers in Colorado and portions of the winter in Mexico. Harvey conducted lessons for members during his month-long residence at Cherry Hills Country Club near Denver, where a former Texas professional was the director of golf. And Harvey traveled to Monterrey when the air got cold in Austin. He taught wealthy Mexican businessmen at the Club Campestre, in the foothills of the Sierra Madre Oriental. His notebook, now wearing at the edges, made both trips each year.

The letter from Penn to *Sports Illustrated* noted that Harvey had nothing new to add to the library of teaching methods, conceding "that they have, in the main, been written down before. As compared to many teachers of considerable reputation, his teaching lore is not so marketable in printed form — for all the world loves a sure-fire short-cut to excellence and I have never known Harvey to promise one." Penn raised yet another plea for what eventually became the *Little Red Book* and its successors. He listed the players Harvey had helped — the players whose names eventually filled the *Little Red Book*. Crenshaw and Kite. Ed White. Betsy Rawls, Kathy Whitworth, Sandra Palmer, "and a special mention for Morris Williams Jr." Penn concluded: "Harvey Penick would never see it this way, but the game of golf is in his debt and for a lot more than the countless unbilled lessons he has given to youngsters who simply wanted his help bad enough to ask for it."

There is no record of what the editors did with the letter, and no evidence that they replied to Penn. The Harvey Penick story, prepared for a mass audience beyond short articles in the boutique golf press, would not be told until the last years of his life.

Meanwhile, none of Harvey's players had won a men's major championship. Crenshaw came the closest in 1975, when he contended at the memorably hot and humid U.S. Open at Medinah until the seventy-first hole, where a mishit 2-iron failed to carry a water hazard. He finished with a share of third.

But Harvey's women continued to win at a furious pace.

In July, a month after Crenshaw lost the U.S. Open with that wayward shot at Medinah, the diminutive Sandra Palmer arrived in Northfield, New Jersey, at the peak of her form. Now thirty-four, she already had won the Colgate–Dinah Shore Winner's Circle that spring in California. She made regular appearances inside the top ten in other, less prestigious tournaments. But she had not yet won a U.S. Women's Open.

Palmer finished the first two rounds at Atlantic City Country Club, taxed by raking winds, at 152, five shots astray of the leader, Judy Rankin of Midland, Harvey's friend and a future golf broadcaster. Palmer shot a 1-under 71 in the third round on Saturday to tie for the lead. An amateur named Nancy Lopez was a stroke behind. Defending champion Sandra Haynie, who spent her formative golf years in Austin and knew Harvey well, was behind by two.

The wind blew even harder in the final round Saturday afternoon. Palmer, who weighed barely a hundred pounds, struggled to anchor herself to the ground. She shot even-par 37 on the front nine. Other contenders plummeted. Her lead stretched to two.

Palmer wanted desperately to prove to herself that she could win the national championship of women's golf. There was a great deal at stake for her in her pursuit of validation.

She came from a poor, often broken family — a past she was ashamed to share with childhood friends. She met her father when she was six. He was a traveling salesman when her mother remarried him. When her parents sent her to live with a grandmother in Fort Worth, she experienced loneliness, insecurity, and emotional distress. She was reunited with her parents when they settled on a lake outside Bangor, Maine.

She took a bus to a rural middle school near Lake Lucerne with three grades in one room. Every day the bus passed a nine-hole golf course, which looked to Palmer like a place of calm serenity. One day she asked the driver to let her out there.

Though she was not built for it, Palmer decided to become a caddie at the course. She was small and thin and unendowed with the muscles required to carry golf bags. But the work strengthened her. "I found out I could make money by caddying on weekends, so I did," she said. "I carried two bags, and eventually I was making more money than my mother, who was working in a department store." She issued a standing request to get off the school bus at the golf course each afternoon after classes. The more time she spent there, the more she wanted to play. "It was just meant to be," Palmer said.

She played in her first tournament at the age of thirteen. She shot 98 with her wide, flat swing and Jackie Burke signature golf clubs. It was the highest score of the day, but Palmer saw her showing as a challenge, not a failure. She wanted to prove that she could shoot 97 the next time out.

When her parents divorced for the second time a year later, Palmer moved back to Texas. She played on her high school basketball team and practiced golf at a municipal course until Glen Garden Country Club, where Hogan and Nelson had sharpened their games, told her she was welcome to play there. She soon was good enough to contend at state tournaments.

Palmer won the West Texas Amateur four times. At North Texas State University — where she was runner-up in the 1961 national collegiate championship — she studied physical education, joined a sorority, made the cheerleading squad, became homecoming queen, and dated a boy who ultimately made her choose between him and golf. "I've always wondered," she said years later, "what if we'd gotten married? Would I be a principal's wife? I can't picture myself wearing white gloves and going to teas."

She never went to teas. But she did go to Austin to see Harvey.

Palmer taught gym and biology for a year at Sam Houston High School in Arlington. On weekends she surrounded herself with golf by practicing, playing, or, when the LPGA had a tournament nearby, watching. "I was not a great player," she said. "I was not very big. I didn't have any training, really. But I always had that fire and determination." On one of her weekend trips to watch the LPGA, Palmer met Rawls, who thought her new friend needed the right person to harness her burn to get better. Rawls called Harvey. She told him about the consuming passion she saw in Palmer to give her life definition through golf. She was small, Rawls told her teacher, but full of conviction.

Send her down, Harvey told Rawls.

Palmer drove to Austin Country Club to meet the semiretired professional. They exchanged greetings. Then Harvey said, "Let me see your hands on the club."

Harvey and Palmer spent every weekend together for a year except during summer break, when Palmer lived with Harvey and Helen on Penick Circle off of Riverside Drive. Harvey spent considerable time on her putting and wedge shots; he knew a player of her small size needed to compensate for a lack of distance.

He made her walk when she played, hauling her big red leather golf bag up and down the Perry Maxwell holes to build her endurance. Harvey had Palmer hit a lot of balls on the range. He wanted to build her golf muscles. He also wanted her to know that he believed in her thoroughly.

Palmer felt like a daughter to the Penicks, who offered the unconditional stability she never had as a child. "It was the greatest thing that ever happened to me," Palmer said. Harvey and Helen gave her something she could count on. "They were so embracing," she said.

After Palmer won the Texas Women's Amateur in 1963, she decided that she could be a better golfer than public school teacher and turned professional in 1964. She shot 78 in her first tournament round, looked at the leaderboard, and saw many scores in the 60s, including a 64.

A sense of inadequacy washed over her that day. She distanced herself from other players, but veterans on the tour coaxed her into their circles. Betsy Rawls, Mickey Wright, and Kathy Whitworth—with their common fondness for Harvey—sought to include Palmer, to help her navigate this new world she had chosen. "I stayed to myself, wouldn't let people get close to me," Palmer said later, with many years of hindsight. "I was kind of mean. In fact I was a bitch. I was such a perfectionist that I got irritated with myself and I took it out on other people. [Then] I started putting the blame where it belongs."

She also learned to invest herself completely in how Harvey was shaping her. His insistence, for example, on practicing her short shots led her to practice pitch shots from long rough for a month before the 1975 U.S. Women's Open.

At the nine-hole turn in the final round that Saturday at Atlantic City Country Club, when she held the lead by two, Palmer tapped an inner calm. She played the tenth through fourteenth holes in one stroke under par, while her chasers fell to the pressure and the wind and the clear impression that Palmer would make no mistakes. She coasted to a four-shot victory. She had won the trophy she most wanted to win.

"Now that I've won the Open I want to do it again," Palmer told reporters. "Just to prove to myself it was no fluke."

She had that chance a year later. Palmer shot rounds of 70-74-73-75 at Rolling Green Golf Club in Springfield, Pennsylvania, to tie JoAnne Gunderson Carner at 8 over par. The two convened the next morning for an eighteen-hole playoff to settle the 1976 U.S. Women's Open.

The pairing seemed almost comical in its contrast of appearances and styles. The petite Palmer, a former college cheerleader and homecoming queen, had no hope of matching the length or booming personality of Carner, a raspy-voiced aggressor on the golf course who traveled the tour with her husband in an Airstream and stood six inches taller than Palmer. It was a familiar setting for the two. Palmer had lost a playoff to Carner in February, at the Orange Blossom Classic in St. Petersburg, Florida.

"Big mama," Palmer said that morning at Rolling Green, "I'm going to beat you this time."

"No you're not, you little shrimp," Carner replied.

Only one of them could be right. It was Carner, by two. Neither woman won another U.S. Women's Open Championship.

Half a continent away, Harvey monitored the careers of his women and of Kite and Crenshaw from newspaper accounts and, when he could, television. In his semiretirement, Harvey no longer managed membership issues, scheduled tee times, cataloged inventory, or ran the shop at Austin Country Club. He had more time to watch his boys, who by the summer of 1978 had won six titles between them on the PGA Tour.

Kite and Crenshaw both qualified that season for the Open Championship at St. Andrews. Kite had played the Old Course once, as a member of the 1971 Walker Cup team that played the amateurs from Great Britain and Ireland. Crenshaw had never seen the most famous golf course in the world — a course that later would have a profound and enduring influence on his golf-course design interests.

"I was just fascinated," Crenshaw said of his impressions of St. Andrews when he arrived in Scotland that July. "It's basically a very flat golf course from some perspectives. But when you get out and play it, it's anything but flat. It's just a sea of very minute and interesting undulations. I still marvel at them."

Since his sensational debut at the 1973 Texas Open, Crenshaw had won four other tournaments, most recently the Colonial Invitational in Fort Worth the season before. Kite had won once, in 1976. But both were playing sharp golf that summer. And Crenshaw had enjoyed a fleeting brush with success at the Open Championship in 1977, when he tied for third on the stunning cliffs of Turnberry on the southwest coast of Scotland. Kite and Crenshaw expected to be in good form at St. Andrews. So did Harvey. He always did.

Harvey never saw Scotland. He never traveled the Ayrshire coast on the train that stops at Prestwick, where Willie Park of Musselburgh won the red Morocco belt awarded to the first Open Championship winner in 1860, or at Troon, home of Royal Troon Golf Club. He never walked Carnoustie or Muirfield. Harvey never saw England. All he knew of Liverpool or Birkdale or Lytham & St. Annes was what he read in the newspapers or saw on his TV. He never made the short stroll down Golf Place to see the Old Course for himself. But he paid close attention to the happenings there in July 1978.

Crenshaw, then twenty-six, opened his first Open Championship at St. Andrews with a 70. Kite, twenty-eight, shot 72. Both played the second round in 69 strokes; Crenshaw shared the lead with Isao Aoki of Japan and Seve Ballesteros of Spain. Kite was tied for seventh.

"My confidence was up," Crenshaw said. "I was in great position. I'd done some nice things there at St. Andrews."

But he listed on Friday. (Until 1980, the Open Championship finished on Saturday.) Crenshaw produced a 73, a round he remembered in 2010 as "a little loose." He left the course that evening in 1978 in a tie for third, a shot behind leaders Peter Oosterhuis and Tom Watson. Kite, who shot 72 in the third round, remained in a tie for seventh. Each round at the Old Course taught him something new about its vagaries. "It's a learning experience every time you go there," Kite said in 2010. "You have to refresh your memory as to where all the hazards are, because they're not out there for you to see."

As Jack Nicklaus and Simon Owen dueled for the lead the next day, Crenshaw played the front nine in a discouraging thirty-nine shots, drifting down the hand-operated leaderboards positioned around the ancient links. Kite, meanwhile, drove the green on No. 12, a par-4, and made birdie. It occurred to him that he could win.

But Kite missed birdie putts of fifteen feet on the thirteenth and fourteenth holes, losing strokes that he needed badly to catch or pass Nicklaus, Owen, and a surging Raymond Floyd. "At St. Andrews, you don't get the ball close to the hole very often," Kite recalled. "The greens are so huge, the bounces are so erratic, that you don't always feel like you have total control. That particular day, I had a number of putts that were in the fifteen-to-twenty-foot range, and I didn't make any of them." He gave luck its chances. But luck was elusive that day.

Crenshaw rallied on the inward nine, playing home in thirty-two strokes for a final-round 71. Kite finished at 70. The pair spent the remainder of the championship on the steps of the Royal and Ancient Clubhouse, wondering if their four-round total of 5-under-par 283 would be good enough.

It wasn't. Nicklaus shot 69 and beat Harvey's boys by two.

The result left Harvey disappointed but not discouraged. Kite and Crenshaw were young; they would have other chances. Harvey hoped he would see them win a major championship. He trusted his stewardship had prepared them for the trials of winning on a Sunday at a major.

A year later, in the late summer of 1979, the new Texas Golf Hall of Fame named Harvey to its second induction class. With an aching back—he had injured it in a fall from a golf cart—Harvey declined an invitation to play in a pro-am scheduled as part of the ceremony at Texas National Golf Club in Willis.

But he was there to accept the honor, which was presented by his old friend Hardy Loudermilk, the man who had sent Kathy Whitworth to him from Jal, New Mexico. Harvey was enshrined with some other people who had been important in his life. The class included Jack Burke Jr., Don January, and Betty Jameson. The old caddie-turned-pro could barely believe he deserved any kind of fame, especially the kind that put him in this kind of company.

Beyond his purview, a contingent of Austin Country Club members was agitating for change.

The club was in a state of churn. Many members wanted to move to the more prosperous west side of Austin, where eight of every ten members lived. The newer country clubs, including Onion Creek, had been pulling new members from the Austin Country Club rolls. The membership, once full at 650, had shrunk to 500.

"We had a strong club from the standpoint of golf," said club president Bill Gainer, Morris Williams Jr.'s high school friend. "But it was becoming less of a social gathering point."

But even as one constituency at the club pressed for relocation, other members resisted. An early vote on whether to move to a planned subdivision on 1,300 hilly acres on Lake Austin, west of downtown, failed, but club officials later contacted the developer and floated the idea again. This time they stipulated that the club would maintain complete control over its business operation and would hire the new course architect. The club had three in mind, including Pete Dye, a former high school state champion in Ohio and prolific course architect who had designed the Stadium Course at TPC Sawgrass in Florida and Harbour Town Golf Links in South Carolina.

But another issue divided club membership as it braced for the inevitable move.

The golf landscape in Texas had changed considerably by the early 1980s from what it had been during Harvey's career as a head professional. Clubs such as River Oaks in Houston, Colonial in Fort Worth, Brook Hollow in Dallas, and Oak Hills in San Antonio had head professionals with high profiles who worked aggressively to promote both their own place in Texas golf and the reputation of their club. Austin Country Club, meanwhile, had Tinsley Penick, as docile and mild-mannered as his father but lacking his reputation as a teacher of champions. The modest and humble son of Harvey knew how to run a shop and serve a golf membership. But he understood little about the emerging role of a golf professional as an ambassador for his club beyond its city limits.

Some at Austin Country Club wanted him gone. They shortsightedly wanted a brand name.

Important members put up strong resistance. Charlie Crenshaw, Ben's father and a longtime and influential member of the club, articulated his concerns in a one-page letter, dated February 19, 1982, to the new president, Bill Gainer. "There has never been a club in the history of golf that owed as much to one man as the Country Club owes to

Harvey," the letter began. It noted that Austin Country Club "is standing on a foundation built largely by him."

Crenshaw continued: "His son, Tinsley, is carrying on the tradition and I certainly hope that his services will be retained now and in the future." He had heard of the pressure to fire Tinsley Penick, "but I trust that this will not materialize with any kind of real force." He ended with a plea. "Please do all you can to preserve the Penick heritage in the Austin Country Club."

Crenshaw's plea resonated. The call to terminate Harvey's son went quietly away.

Harvey continued to teach on the range, at a physical and metaphorical distance from the controversy. He was unaware that his son's job had been at stake. Members kept it from him out of respect.

For Harvey, now seventy-eight, the country club retained the rhythm it had always had, with the exception of the seasonal jobs he took in Denver and Monterrey, Mexico. He spent mornings at the first tee of the country club, cross-checking starting times in a ledger on his lap and noting which cart went out with which group. "Have a nice round," he would tell members. "Try not to take any mulligans. Keep the carts on the paths and out of the rough. That's from the board of directors. And keep the balls out of the rough. That's from Harvey."

He watched the shots soar into the sky. The best shots, the ones that drew slightly against the right-to-left cant of the yonder fairway, stirred in him a melancholic yearning. He sometimes wished he could play still. He sometimes longed for the anticipation that accompanied that slow walk to the first tee, when a career round might be at hand. But he could not play. He could only wish to. Sometimes that was enough, because it had to be.

And as always, he maintained his Scribbletex notebook, which he kept in the same rolltop desk, for a destiny not yet in place.

The Penick name survived another year at Austin Country Club.

Then came the spring of 1984.

Crenshaw arrived at Augusta National Golf Club at the summit of his form. He felt energized, gathered, and poised. He had made the cut in his nine previous starts that season, finishing inside the top fifteen in five of them. On the Sunday before his thirteenth Masters Tournament, Crenshaw had shot a final-round 67 at the Greater Greensboro Open, where he tied for third. He arrived in eastern Georgia the next week with fresh memories of the Masters the year before, when he shot 70-68. He and Kite had shared second place, just as they had done at St. Andrews in 1978. Both of them left the 1983 Masters determined to return and win in 1984.

When he opened the 1984 tournament with a 5-under-par 67, his best first round during his favorite week on the schedule, Crenshaw seemed to have dislodged every splinter of doubt from the wreckage of two seasons before.

In 1982, his tenth season on the PGA Tour, Crenshaw had fallen to eighty-third on the earnings list. He missed seven cuts and, most alarmingly, failed again to win a major championship. He was thirty years old, broken and adrift. He thought too much—about the length of his backswing, about the looseness of it, about the opinions of other people, about everything Harvey always had warned him against. In August, Crenshaw shot 73-76 at the 1982 PGA Championship at Southern Hills to ensure another early flight home. "It was the worst golf you can imagine," he said. "I didn't have any idea what was happening." Unintentionally, Crenshaw had forgotten who he was and who he was supposed to be.

He sought clarity where he knew he could count on it: from Harvey.

Harvey was now teaching only about twenty lessons a week at the country club. But he always had time for Crenshaw. After the missed cut at Southern Hills, Crenshaw closeted his clubs, uninterested in playing again until he and Harvey had convened on the practice range.

Harvey started where he always started. He asked to see Crenshaw's grip. He wanted to examine Crenshaw's feet, his alignment, his ball position, and his stance. Harvey knew how to help Crenshaw find his best self. It had nothing to do with his swing in motion. It had everything to do with his body at rest. Harvey wanted to see the Crenshaw

Harvey learned golf as a caddie. He joined two of his brothers at Austin Country Club in 1912, when he was eight years old, and became a fine player.

Harvey served Austin Country Club from 1912 until his death in 1995, first as a caddie, then as shop assistant, and finally as head professional. He retired in 1971, but retained the title "professional emeritus."

Ben Crenshaw (right) and Tom Kite (left) met at Austin Country Club on a monumental Saturday in 1963, when Kite was thirteen years old and Crenshaw was eleven. Both worked with Harvey throughout their careers.

Harvey was more than an instructor. He also served as greenskeeper and clubmaker at Austin Country Club.

Harvey presents his son, Tinsley, with a trophy after a junior golf tournament at Austin Country Club. In 1971 Tinsley succeeded his father as head professional.

Harvey was a public figure in Austin. Texas governor Allan Shivers sits with Harvey at a banquet honoring his thirtieth anniversary at Austin Country Club.

Harvey (far right) played an exhibition in late 1950 with (from left) Morris Williams Jr., Alice Bauer, and Betsy Rawls.

Harvey helps reigning 1963 Women's Texas State Amateur Champion Sandra Palmer of Fort Worth with her face angle at Austin Country Club in this photo dated May 2, 1964. Palmer went on to win nineteen tournaments on the LPGA Tour, including two major championships. Harvey gave her the stability she never knew as a child. "It was the greatest thing that ever happened to me," Palmer said.

Harvey left Austin as a young man only to compete and, in his later years, teach. He participated in a PGA seminar in February 1978 in Sacramento, California.

Even former U.S. presidents came to see Harvey. Gerald Ford spent a rainy day at Austin Country Club in the mid-1980s.

Harvey first placed a golf club in Ben Crenshaw's hands when Crenshaw was in elementary school. They became lifelong friends and collaborators.

A mutual friend introduced Kathy Whitworth to Harvey in 1957, when Whitworth was seventeen. He became her confidant and primary instructor, and a significant reason she won eighty-eight times on the LPGA Tour. "I still marvel at how all this started, how lucky I was," Whitworth said in 2013.

Tom Kite won the 1992 U.S. Open on a blustery Sunday at Pebble Beach. He later credited his early lessons at Austin Country Club, where Harvey would make him practice in the wind.

Harvey chose Bud Shrake, an Austin-based journalist, novelist, and screenwriter, to cowrite his *Little Red Book*. Its rousing success spawned three additional titles, two of them published after Harvey's death. "The fates had transpired to put me with Harvey," Shrake said in 2009.

Prolific author James Michener, who lived in Austin in his later years, arranged a visit with Harvey to talk about the *Little Red Book,* published in 1992.

Harvey signed his books and wrote notes to readers up until the week of his death. He kept stacks of books in his bedroom, waiting to be autographed, and insisted on hand-lettering each message. "He wanted to finish what he needed done," said his son, Tinsley.

Tom Kite, Harvey, and Ben Crenshaw reflect during a video shoot in 1993 at Austin Country Club.

Ben Crenshaw received word of Harvey's death on Sunday, April 2, 1995, during dinner with his wife, Julie, at Augusta National Golf Club, where Crenshaw was preparing for the Masters. Crenshaw flew back to Austin the following Wednesday to serve as a pallbearer at Harvey's funeral. "He was a total mess," friend Chuck Cook said of Crenshaw.

Ben Crenshaw (left) and Tom Kite (right) carry Harvey's casket at Memorial Park Cemetery in Austin on Wednesday, April 5, 1995. After the service, both flew to Augusta to play in the Masters. Crenshaw drove directly to Augusta National and rolled putts in silence on the practice green.

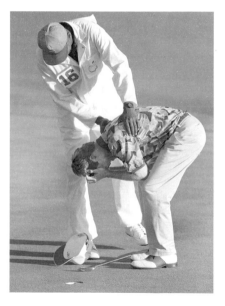

Longtime Augusta National caddie Carl Jackson holds Ben Crenshaw on the seventy-second and final hole of the Masters Tournament on April 9, 1995. Crenshaw had just won his second green jacket. "It was like someone put their hand on my shoulder and sort of guided me," Crenshaw said later.

Editorial cartoonist Drew Litton imagined a scene in heaven after Ben Crenshaw won his second Masters Tournament title in 1995.

Helen Penick, Harvey's widow, accepts a bouquet at a press conference announcing an LPGA tournament in her husband's name in 1998. Their son, Tinsley, looks on. "Harvey would be so pleased about this," Helen Penick said, "because he always did like the women."

Harvey on May 16, 1994, as he greeted golfers from his golf cart at Austin Country Club.

he knew, not the Crenshaw pretending to be what someone else expected him to be. "Just swing like Ben," Harvey told him.

It rained. They spent three hours together in the golf shop. It was as if it were twenty years ago. It occurred to Crenshaw that he should have come to Harvey much sooner, before things got this bad. They talked about Crenshaw's family. They talked about books. They talked about how to forget. "I told him to put this year behind him," Harvey said. He also reminded Crenshaw that Ben Hogan and Harry Vardon had long, fluid swings like his own. "Bobby Jones was every bit as long," he added.

Crenshaw perked up. References to Bobby Jones always got his attention. Crenshaw told Harvey about all the advice he was getting from well-meaning friends on the tour. They seemed like they wanted to help, but their advice turned into dissonant echoes in his mind. Every time he set out to start anew, he heard someone telling him to stand closer to the ball, or stand farther away. Turn less. Turn more. Feel your hands here at the top. Or here. Too long. Too short.

Harvey interrupted. "Ben," he said. "God gave you two ears. Let all that advice go in one ear and out the other."

Harvey understood what Crenshaw needed to hear. "Ben Hogan didn't have the prettiest swing in the world," he told Crenshaw. "But Ben Hogan knew his game better than anyone knew theirs."

"What Harvey was saying was, 'Get back to your game, play it, live by it, do not change it,'" Crenshaw said. "It hit home."

Crenshaw then played and lived his game—his true self, the one Harvey understood and conjured during their visit—on that first Thursday in April 1984 at the Masters. He missed only two fairways with the ten-degree, blond persimmon MacGregor M85 driver he'd bought in Houston. Metal drivers were common that week at Augusta National. They had been around since Ron Streck won in Houston with a new TaylorMade with a smoky tint. But the old MacGregor felt to Crenshaw like an extension of his hands. He made no bogeys in the first round of the '84 Masters and led by a shot at the end.

He played the second round in even-par 72. He holed an improbable bunker shot for birdie on the ninth hole and followed that with birdies on the tenth and eleventh. No one birdied ten and eleven, and especially not nine, ten, and eleven. Crenshaw made bogey with a missed four-foot putt on the eighteenth, "but that bunker shot at the ninth kept sticking in my mind," Crenshaw wrote years later. "I wasn't worried."

Rain shortened the third round. Crenshaw made a two-putt birdie on the par-5 thirteenth and left the grounds at 7 under par, two shots behind leader Mark Lye and a shot behind Kite. It was 1967 all over again at Morris Williams, but with a jacket at stake instead.

Crenshaw returned Sunday morning, completed his round with five consecutive fours, signed for a 2-under-par 70, and learned he would be playing the last round later that afternoon in the penultimate group with the chilly Englishman Nick Faldo.

The scene back home at Austin Country Club was electric. Kite now had a one-shot lead at the Masters. Crenshaw was two shots behind. The men who played a regular game on Sundays requested earlier tee times so they could huddle around the television in the grill for the final round. The city braced itself, and Harvey allowed himself to wonder:

Would this be the year one of his boys won his first major?

Crenshaw napped for ninety minutes before his final round. The rest energized him for the remainder of the day. He shot a 3-under-par 33 on the front, with birdies on the eighth and ninth holes. On the tenth, a tenuous drive left him with a long-iron approach. Crenshaw watched his ball stop sixty feet from the hole.

He and his loyal Augusta National caddie Carl Jackson walked down the hill. They skirted the famous, sharply edged bunker that Alister MacKenzie had planted in the fairway and up to the sinister green, which Perry Maxwell, designer of Austin Country Club on Riverside Drive, had moved fifty yards farther away in 1937. Crenshaw and Jackson analyzed the putt. "That putt goes up the hill, and then it makes a sharp turn to the left," said Tom Watson, who knew. He had won the Masters in 1977 and '81.

Crenshaw and Jackson calculated. They predicted a break of eight or nine feet to the left and a quickening pace before a slight rise at the cup. Neither man spoke. Both of them realized the precariousness of the moment. A bogey there? And then Amen Corner?

Jackson held the flagstick. Crenshaw hoped to give himself a second putt of no more than six feet, a credible chance at par. He convinced himself to trust his past: all those practice putts at the country club, with Harvey watching, reminding him to believe. Crenshaw tried not to try. And his putt did something that sent a volley through the pines.

It went in.

The birdie gave Crenshaw a two-shot lead over Kite. He made bogey at No. 11 and a birdie at No. 12, where Kite, playing in the group behind Crenshaw and Faldo, rinsed his tee shot in Rae's Creek. Crenshaw holed a long putt for par on the par-4 fourteenth. He birdied the par-5 fifteenth. He played the last three holes at par. He shot 68 that Sunday at Augusta National to beat Watson by two at 11-under-par 277.

Years later, Crenshaw reflected on that weekend in April 1984. "I knew I was capable," he said. "But you never *know*. You never *know* in golf. You never know when your time may come."

Seve Ballesteros helped Crenshaw into his first green jacket that afternoon.

"Welcome to our club," he told the winner.

Crenshaw spoke to reporters for about thirty minutes. He mentioned a clarifying visit that morning with Jackie Burke of Houston, who told him: "Think fairways and greens." He cited the colossal putt on the tenth green. He thanked his Masters caddie of eight years, Carl Jackson. He acknowledged Bobby Jones. Crenshaw also said this: "I wanted to win it for my friends. I have so many of them. And I have so many people to thank, people who stood by me, who talked with me, who pulled for me. I want to thank my father and teacher, Harvey Penick, who knows so much about the game, so much about people and about living."

Crenshaw stayed up late that night with friends. They drank. They played gin. They watched the highlights on television, relived the outlandish putt on the tenth, cheered the birdie at the fifteenth, rejoiced when the final putt fell, and it seemed like they were witnessing it and cheering it and bathing in it for the first time all over again. No one wanted to forget the moment when one of Harvey's boys won the Masters.

Crenshaw thought back to that Sunday on the flight home from Georgia. He remembered the walk up to Augusta National's eighteenth hole, a hill of such glory and torment. He wondered if he ever would feel that kind of joy again. He didn't know. He concluded that he might never live a sweeter moment again.

But he would.

His plane descended, gliding over the familiar wrinkles of Morris Williams Golf Course across the street from the Austin airport. As he walked down the Jetway, the new Masters champion expected to see a gathering of friends in the terminal, maybe from the country club. Instead, he saw Harvey.

His teacher, now seventy-four, was leaning on his cane. He held out his hand, palm up.

"Mighty proud of you," Harvey said.

Chapter Ten

HARVEY WAS INDUCTED into his second hall of fame in 1985. He was the only golfer that year in the Texas Sports Hall of Fame class, which included pitcher Nolan Ryan and five Texas-born football players. Joe Hornaday, the Austin newspaper reporter who had written many times about Harvey and his pupils, nominated him with a passionate letter to the induction committee. "For seven decades, Harvey Penick has been practicing the art of golf teaching like no one before," Hornaday wrote.

Austin Country Club had moved the year before to the residential development near Lake Austin, where Pete Dye designed a lavish course with six holes along the water. Tinsley and his wife Betty Ann helped Harvey and Helen move to a small townhouse near enough to the club that Harvey could take his personal golf cart to the course. There he parked in a spot designated for him and stationed himself in the shade of an oak. He minded the starter sheet and gave lessons from the seat of his cart.

Harvey no longer wrote often in his notebook. He showed it to no one. He barely gave it much thought anymore. He was eighty years old with less and less to do each day.

Fifty-six players were invited to Austin that spring to participate in the Legends of Golf Tournament at Onion Creek. The field included many players Harvey knew and admired, men he considered friends:

Arnold Palmer, Jack Burke Jr., Dow Finsterwald Jr., Jay and Lionel Hebert, Don January, Paul Runyan, Gene Sarazen, Sam Snead, and Harvie Ward.

But the appearance of two new contestants that year inspired Harvey to postpone all lesson appointments, arrange for a ride to Onion Creek, settle in his chair on the first tee, and wait for their arrival.

The tournament had invited Kathy Whitworth and Mickey Wright. Nothing could keep their teacher from being there when, in a sense, his two LPGA Hall of Fame players came home.

Wright, now fifty, had last played tournament golf five years earlier. The expectation of winning every time she played had begun to cripple her ability. She began suffering an adverse reaction to sunlight. Flying made her anxious. She also developed neuromas, abnormal growths in the nerve fibers in her feet, which made walking difficult, even in loosely tied sneakers. She endured two operations. The prohibition of carts on the LPGA Tour ensured her informal retirement from competition in 1969. But the Legends of Golf had no such regulation. At Onion Creek, Wright could ride.

She had won eighty-two tournaments in her career, most of them between 1957 and 1968, when she averaged nearly eight titles a year. She won four U.S. Women's Open championships. Only Betsy Rawls, another pupil of Harvey's, had won as many.

The only player with more was Wright's partner that week at Onion Creek.

Whitworth was forty-five years old in the spring of 1985, a six-time champion in the LPGA majors, still a regular competitor on the tour, and still a committed devotee of Harvey and his lessons. She traveled to Austin in part to see Harvey and in part to see Wright. But she also wanted to see how well she could play with the men.

No women had ever competed with the seniors. Babe Didrikson Zaharias famously had played in three PGA Tour tournaments in 1945. But the five-year-old Senior PGA Tour, still establishing its footing among the regular men's and women's tours, had never invited a woman to play. The addition of Whitworth and Wright brought a wave of attention that week to Austin, which was hailed for its spirit of inclusion. All Harvey wanted to do was see the two women he considered something close to daughters.

"When you or Mickey hit a good shot," he told Whitworth, "I get goose bumps."

Wright and Whitworth gave their teacher plenty to remember. They birdied four of the first six holes at Onion Creek. They shot 65 in the first round, four shots under par and three behind the leaders, Billy Casper and Gay Brewer. "I'm just following Mickey," Whitworth chirped, happy to be in Austin, to have seen Harvey, to be playing with Palmer and Sarazen and Snead. "Isn't Mickey great? It's like old times, almost." Whitworth made five birdies on Thursday. She chipped in for one of them on the par-5 eighteenth hole. "I felt so nervous," Wright acknowledged after the round. "Like a teenager who never held a golf club — scared to death. I don't think I've ever been that scared." She and Whitworth started the second round in a tie for sixth place among the twenty-eight teams.

They faltered on the second day, finishing with a 72. "You don't recapture the magic," said Wright, who had started practicing in December and played her first full round in five years on February 14, her birthday. She even traveled to Austin a week before the tournament to prepare. But, she said, "you don't go back twenty years. I knew that before I came here. I thought, 'I've got four months to catch up for five years.' And I don't know [that] there's a way to do that." They shot 69-69 on the weekend, ending the tournament at 3 under par and eighteen shots behind January and Gene Littler. But in three of the four rounds, the women beat the men they played with.

The experience left Wright in a reflective mood. She had loved playing with her friend, and she had felt that welcome rush of adrenaline when her 7-iron stopped four feet from the hole at the par-3 seventeenth hole in the third round. She smiled when she remembered her approach at the par-4 sixteenth colliding with the flagstick. But Wright also accepted the inevitable consequences of a hasty return to competitive golf after so many years away from it. "Quitting a sport is like quitting cigarettes," she said. "It's not easy. You don't want to start something again that's so hard quitting. That's kind of how I feel about golf."

A week later, Whitworth rejoined the LPGA Tour. She won the United Virginia Bank Classic. It was her eighty-eighth official victory. It also was her last.

Whitworth began to cull her schedule soon after. She wanted to do more teaching, to share what she had learned from Harvey three decades before at the country club. When he found out about her plans, Harvey invited her back to Austin, where he told her: "There are some things you need to know."

The dynamic had changed. Harvey shared different ideas with his longtime pupil, ones that had more to do with teaching than learning. He advised Whitworth to think like a beginner again. He wanted her to remember what had resonated when she lay on the bed in that motel room in Austin, pantomiming her grip. He asked her to think about how he went about encouraging students to make commitments like that. "As a player, you didn't need to know that," he told her. But teachers did. Whitworth marveled at Harvey's range as a teacher. How could one man teach players one way and teachers in another?

Harvey was the honorary starter at the last Legends of Golf Tournament at Onion Creek, this one in 1989. Don January and his partner that year, Sam Snead, shook Harvey's fragile hand before their rounds.

It had been years since January had seen Harvey. They knew one another from the Labor Day tournament at the country club, which January had won in 1954. January had chased the West Texas pro-am circuit with Morris Williams Jr. in the early 1950s, gunning from town to town for Friday qualifying, Friday night barbecue dinners and dances, thirty-six holes of better-ball play on Saturday, and then again on Sunday. Like Williams, January had enlisted in the air force. When he returned from the service, he needed someone he trusted to ascertain his readiness for the tour. So he called Harvey.

January had been living in Lampasas, about an hour northwest of Austin, and practicing at Hancock Park, the municipal course his father managed. January had played little golf in the air force. He went six months without playing a competitive round. When he'd arrived at the country club that day in 1955, January complained to Harvey that he felt uncertain of his swing—a swing that had helped Bill Maxwell and Joe Conrad and his other North Texas State teammates win four NCAA championships.

Harvey watched January on the putting green. He watched him hit a half-dozen balls each with a short iron, a middle iron, and a long iron. He asked the slender Texan to swing a driver.

Fifty-nine years later, January recalled: "He never said a word." But when January asked Harvey that day if he was ready to play with Hogan and Nelson and Snead, Harvey had an answer. "Go," Harvey told him.

"It gave me a hell of a lot of confidence," said January, who won ten times on the PGA Tour and twenty-two titles on the Champions Tour, including a Legends of Golf trophy in Austin. When he saw Harvey at Onion Creek all those years after the one-word affirmation, January felt a keen sense of gratitude.

It wasn't merely for the encouragement in 1955. Harvey had formally endorsed January's promotion to professional golf. He was one of the required two registered professionals, along with Tod Menefee of San Antonio Country Club, who had signed January's application to join the Texas section of the PGA.

Harvey was beginning to feel vulnerably old at the close of the 1980s. The pain in his back was so severe that it kept him from standing straight, and he resembled an ambulatory question mark, rarely proceeding at a pace faster than a shuffle. Barely able to look up, he learned to remember shoes—he recognized people from the color of their saddles or the pattern of their oxfords. His condition rarely allowed him to spend a comfortable day on the range, where he longed to be because it was all he knew. He wished he could be the man he once was: strong, durable, tireless, able to stand in the sun for as long as it took to watch a student, new or old, swing the bucket or the weed cutter.

But he was not that man anymore in 1990. He was tired now. His back ached. He sometimes was disoriented. The first indication that Harvey was becoming too frail to teach came in November 1990. His wife Helen wrote to the country club, suggesting that her husband might not be able to continue his lessons.

Louis R. Brill, the president of the club's board of directors, replied to Helen Penick in a letter dated November 20. "As you well can imagine, we are all very sad to hear that it's possible he may not be able to return to us," Brill wrote. "Obviously, the Austin Country Club will not be the same without him — in many ways Austin Country Club is Harvey Penick." Brill informed Helen that the board voted on November 9 to extend "an indefinite salary continuation plan for Mr. Penick. This means that Mr. Penick will continue to receive a monthly salary even though he may be unable to return to work."

Harvey was admitted to St. David's Hospital in Austin, where doctors discovered he had cancer in his prostate. His frustration with old age deepened into a sense of hopelessness. His search for purpose seemed futile. When his family visited Harvey at St. David's, they encountered a man who seemed ready to surrender. "Every day when I left the hospital, I thought it was for the last time," said his son, Tinsley.

Harvey looked like he was going to die.

His spirits brightened in late 1989 when he learned that he had been named Teacher of the Year by the PGA of America. He wrote Patrick Reilly, the president of the organization, and told him the announcement was the best moment of his life in golf since the day he became the head professional at Austin Country Club in 1923. "My teaching methods have been mostly a result of conversations and observations with my peers in the PGA," Harvey explained in his letter to Reilly, "and while fundamentals of the golf swing have changed very little over the years, the new understanding of muscle involvement, the new appreciation of psychological factors and the new methods of presenting ideas are constantly being updated and revised and I will continue to learn. When I stop learning, I will stop teaching."

Harvey knew that he would not attend the ceremony in his honor. "I now teach from a golf cart," he wrote. "Please know that I would be with you if it were humanly possible, and I pray that in some way my fellow members of the PGA realize they made an old man feel almost young again and very happy." Harvey mailed the envelope with melancholic pride.

The idea for a golf book returned in March of the next year. A lawyer in Houston who had taken a lesson from Harvey recently had encouraged Tinsley to consider putting together a collection of his father's most treasured truths for publication. The lawyer, Harris Greenwood, a friend of Harvey's since the late 1950s, even suggested a title: *Keep It Simple.*

"Golf needs a book by Harvey Penick," Greenwood wrote to Tinsley on March 21, 1990. "The book needs to have all of his tips, advice and opinions on the game and some of the game's players." Remarkably, Greenwood grasped the central feature of Harvey's appeal and lore long before the *Little Red Book.* "Many of the stories that you will get have probably been so embellished over the years that they actually bear little resemblance to the truth," Greenwood wrote. "But I think that part of Harvey's story is pure mythology. There are so many people who love your dad and would want to contribute and help in this project that you would be absolutely flooded with material if you will only ask."

Greenwood thanked Tinsley for his consideration. He wondered if Harvey might enjoy a reunion of his University of Texas players someday. He said he regretted not visiting Harvey more often.

"It made me feel almost like it was 1959 to have that lesson," Greenwood wrote.

Tinsley considered the idea, but he was worried that his ailing father would not live to see it come to fruition. A reunion might be good for him. So might a book project about his life in golf. His first concern, however, was doing whatever it took to get Harvey well. After that, anything was possible.

Harvey rallied and went home from the hospital. His longtime friend and teaching understudy, Barbara Puett, recognized that Harvey needed extra care: "We knew he needed someone there all the time," Puett said. So she organized a campaign to raise money. She sent a letter to his former players at Texas and others he had helped over the years, often at no charge. "It's time to pay for your lessons," the letter said. Kite, Crenshaw, and Davis Love III, whose father played for Harvey at Texas, donated $5,000 apiece. The campaign raised more than $60,000. Soon Harvey had his own nurse.

Most of his women were now retired. Crenshaw and Kite continued to win on the PGA Tour, but only Crenshaw had won a major championship, the Masters in 1984. It began to look like Harvey's boys would only have one. Nevertheless, Harvey was immensely proud of both of them. He knew they expected more. So had he. But they were good men with good families and good reputations in a game that valued honor and dignity. What else could Harvey ask of them? What more could he want?

The spring of 1991 became a season of tender reflection for the old teacher of golf.

Harvey had turned eighty-six in October. He had survived cancer. He had imprinted his gentle lessons on so many successful players, from the women who formed the LPGA to Crenshaw and Kite, now two of the most admired players on the men's tour. He had done what he could do. Harvey now was becoming acutely aware of time—time gone by and time remaining. He began to think about the encouragement he'd received in years past to write a book, to share for posterity what he knew about golf.

In the past, Harvey had entertained the possibility of writing a book but had always talked himself out of it. He found it difficult to identify with an occupation as intimidating as that of author. He considered himself a conduit—a modest steward of a game he had loved since he was a boy with a bag of clubs on his back, with little regard for compensation and even less for self-promotion. But his acceptance of his mortality had changed him. Harvey began to also accept that his defining contribution to golf would occupy him until the end of his life.

So one fateful morning in the spring of 1991, Harvey asked his nurse to take him to the club. She helped him into his golf cart on Fawn Creek Path, crossed Westlake Drive, and turned right on Long Champ. They whirred down the shaded street, flanked by million-dollar mansions with European sedans in the driveways, past the sixteenth green surrounded by a grove of live oaks, and up to the familiar iron gates. The guard waved them through.

The nurse parked Harvey under the old tree that had sheltered him on so many mornings and afternoons from the piercing Central Texas sun. He watched squirrels flit at the wheels of his cart. He noticed a noisy, belligerent grackle hopping from branch to branch over his head. For a little while, he reconsidered his decision, but by that hour he surely had convinced himself of its rightness. He had come to feel that he had been selfishly hoarding in the old red Scribbletex notebook a body of knowledge that belonged to everyone who played golf, not just to him and his children. He entertained the possibility that he had been allowed to study golf for eighty years so that he might spread what he had learned to anyone who wanted to know. As Harvey would write later: "This gift had not been given to me to keep secret."

Harvey summoned Tinsley, who was in the shop.

He told his son what he wanted to do.

Tinsley could barely contain his joy. He returned to the shop, foraged through his desk for a telephone number, picked up the receiver, and dialed. A big, brassy voice answered the ring. Tinsley spoke briefly, explaining what his father had shared moments before. It involved a visit, Tinsley said. Now, if possible.

Bud Shrake said he would be there as soon as he could.

Chapter Eleven

BUD SHRAKE LIVED in a quiet writer's lair deep in the woods. His house on Wildcat Hollow, in an undeveloped area of West Austin, stood on a steep slope that fell toward Lake Austin and was tangled with Hill Country underbrush and blooming prickly pear cactus. It was near enough to the city that he could be anywhere—a favorite bar, a new restaurant, Lions Municipal Golf Course, Austin Country Club—in minutes. He even could see the skyline of the city on leafless winter days. It was the perfect retreat for writing, which was the only vocation Shrake had ever cared to pursue.

It also was a lovely location for extracurricular activities, from staying up to see the sunrise to swearing, playing cards, drinking tequila, smoking weed, cutting cocaine, and filling the den with ribbons of cigarette smoke and laughter from ribald jokes. The cabin on the slope on Wildcat Hollow was close to all that mattered to Shrake—and just remote enough that he and his considerable band of friends could hide in the oaks in the company of roadrunners and coyotes and a thousand glinting stars.

Shrake had bought the two-acre lot and built the house in 1971, using the $100,000 fee he'd just earned from selling a movie script. It was his last true and proper home—the destination he'd spent twenty raucous, rowdy, and frequently dangerous years careening toward. He had always seemed destined for Austin. The city embraced volatile, effusive, agitating, long-haired, freethinking castaways like Shrake. He of all people had never seemed destined, until that spring morning in 1991 at Austin Country Club, to align his fortunes with a man like Harvey Penick.

Edwin Shrake became Bud because he didn't want his father's name. He and his brother Bruce, six years younger, endured a ragged upbringing complicated by an alcoholic father in 1930s-era Fort Worth. Indeed, said Bruce Shrake, "I didn't have a drink until I was a sophomore in college, because I didn't want to be my dad." The senior Edwin Shrake, a dashing and wealthy accountant and cattle trader who was an early member at Colonial and Glen Garden Country Clubs, darkened under the influence of spirits. He assaulted his wife. He gambled. He threatened his sons with words and fists and sullen moods. His drunken rages left Shrake scrambling for a baseball bat or croquet mallet as protection. The family teetered on emotional disintegration. The patriarch's corrosive addiction to alcohol left the once-prosperous family nearly bankrupt in the early 1940s. At the tender age of eleven, Bud Shrake, still in elementary school, was forced to go to work at a grocery store to help the family survive.

Golf was a salve for some of the raw psychic wounds. The Shrake boys and their father joined an informal golf league associated with Travis Avenue Baptist Church, where their mother was a devoted member. "My dad wasn't a great golfer—he shot in the seventies—but he was good enough to play in tournaments," Bud Shrake said. "I loved the game, but I had no talent for it." The Shrake brothers learned the game at Glen Garden Country Club, where Ben Hogan and Byron Nelson had caddied two decades before. The symmetry of his and Harvey's experiences—that he was chasing a ball down the same corridors that had trained two of the greatest American players of a generation that included Harvey and was learning to read breaks on the same greens that had captured the imaginations of two friends of Harvey's who had played with him in Austin—eluded Shrake for the next fifty years.

Standing six feet six inches tall, long-boned and lanky, with a regal nose and a finely tuned ear for turns of phrase, Shrake joined the newspaper staff as a freshman at Paschal High School, where he met Dan Jenkins, a cantankerous junior with an acerbic wit and similar interests in sports. Jenkins played on the golf team. Shrake played football until he stepped on a teammate's finger in practice and severed it, an experience traumatic enough to convince Shrake that it was better to observe the game from a safe distance than to participate in it. Jenkins and Shrake joined the journalism club and wrote columns for the *Paschal Pantherette*. They acted in school plays. The two friends also frequented The Pig Stand and Herb Massey's café after classes, burning through cigarettes and contemplating their sparkling futures in American letters. The proper adults who frowned with disapproval had no clue that they were looking at two boys who would one day write memorably and famously for the greatest sports magazine in the United States.

Before he lost to Morris Williams Jr. at Colonial in the presence of Ben Hogan, and before he profiled Ben Crenshaw early in his long career at *Sports Illustrated,* Jenkins earned a job his senior year at the *Fort Worth Press,* the smaller but spunkier afternoon newspaper whose sports section was under the stewardship of Blackie Sherrod. After reading a parody that Jenkins had written for the *Pantherette,* Sherrod hired him for $25 a week, starting as soon as he graduated from high school.

Jenkins covered games at night for the *Press,* attended classes at TCU in the morning, joined the student newspaper in between, and played for the golf team. Shrake, meanwhile, matriculated in 1949, scored 178 on an IQ test, and considered an offer to attend Yale University. Financially limited, Shrake elected to join his old friend at TCU until he could save enough money to leave Fort Worth for the University of Texas, which he did after his freshman year. Shrake moved to Austin to enroll in prelaw. He majored in government. He rarely thought anymore about writing. But his sophomore year at Texas drained his savings, and when he returned to Fort Worth for his junior year at TCU,

Jenkins presented an idea to help his friend replenish both his meager finances and his ambivalent writer's spirit.

Jenkins recommended Shrake to Blackie Sherrod, who invited the rudderless Shrake to the *Press* newsroom, situated behind the New Jim Hotel on East Fifth, where prostitutes loitered. The building smelled bad. It was noisy and dirty. Shrake felt connected to it the moment he arrived. "I looked around at all the people, and the state editor was over there eating a can of sardines at his desk at six o'clock in the morning, and the bowling writer was back there drunk and had set fire to the wastebasket, and the one-legged city editor was threatening people with his crutch," Shrake said. "All of a sudden I walked into a world I knew I belonged to."

Sherrod offered Shrake a part-time job in the summer of 1951. A budding golf writer now, Jenkins went off to report from his first U.S. Open, the one that Hogan won at Oakland Hills. Shrake remained in Fort Worth, learning his new craft. Sherrod liked his work well enough to offer him a full-time position that fall, as Shrake prepared for his junior year of college. The transition to staff reporter worked a welcome act of magic on Shrake, who changed his major to English and declared again that he wanted to write. He told reporters at the newspaper that he planned to publish his first novel by the age of twenty-three. Nothing seemed to be in his way.

"Everybody had this sense of urgency and excitement, and right then I thought, 'This is what I want,'" Shrake said.

The bold journalistic climate at the *Press* encouraged creativity and risk. Sports journalism in the 1950s was shedding the hagiographic influence of established sportswriters such as Grantland Rice and developing a bolder, more skeptical, even cynical, style. Fort Worth was a perfect laboratory for Jenkins and Shrake. The *Press* was an afternoon newspaper valued for its florid voice and plucky news judgment, a counterbalance to the establishment morning newspaper, the *Fort Worth Star-Telegram*. Sherrod wanted his writers to trump the *Star-Telegram* in terms of style, not necessarily substance. His sports section "came to function as the equivalent of a college creative writing program—with a dash of boot camp thrown in." Staff writers formed an informal book club. They reviewed each other, competed with each other, critiqued each other. At bars and on trains to Texas League baseball games, they debated and celebrated the craft of writing.

The next decade brought a mix of crushing disappointments and tremendous triumphs for Shrake and Jenkins. Jenkins rose to sports editor of the *Press* when Sherrod moved thirty miles west to lead the sports section of the *Dallas Times Herald*. Before Sherrod left, back in August 1954, Jenkins had spotted a new magazine on his desk with Eddie Mathews of the Milwaukee Braves on the cover. "What's that?" Jenkins asked Sherrod. "The new weekly sports magazine from Time Inc.," Sherrod replied. Jenkins knew at that moment that he wanted to be a part of this new magazine called *Sports Illustrated*.

When a sports position opened in 1958 at the *Dallas Times Herald*, Sherrod called Shrake to see if he was interested. Shrake deliberated with Jenkins, who told him: "Sports pages are where the readers are. If you want to get noticed, writing sports is the way to do it." Shrake agreed. He made the pivotal decision to immerse himself again in games and the lives of the people who played them.

Shrake was twenty-six years old when he joined his old editor in Dallas. He was there when the city and its other daily newspaper, the right-leaning *Dallas Morning News,* promoted a radical shift toward intolerance. He was there when Edwin Walker, a disgraced army general, bought a mansion in a fancy neighborhood, established a political base influenced by the John Birch Society, and contemplated a run for Texas governor. Shrake was in Dallas when Lyndon Baines Johnson, the senator from Johnson City, joined John F. Kennedy on the Democratic ticket in the 1960 presidential election. He was there when a mob at a campaign stop spit on Johnson and his wife Lady Bird.

He was also there when Lamar Hunt, the son of a billionaire Dallas oilman, petitioned the National Football League for permission to launch an expansion team in Dallas. The league denied the request, but Hunt brought enough money to the idea to subvert the NFL entirely.

Hunt announced in the summer of '59 the formation of the American Football League and its first team, the Dallas Texans. Soon after, the NFL granted another wealthy businessman, Clint Murchison, an expansion license to create the Dallas Cowboys. The *Times Herald* assigned Shrake to cover the upstart Cowboys. The newspaper needed another reporter for the new Texans beat. Sherrod found one in Gary Cartwright, who worked for Jenkins in Fort Worth.

Shrake and Cartwright sat at adjoining desks in the newsroom and were neighbors at an apartment complex near Southern Methodist University. Just like Shrake and Jenkins back at Paschal High, they became instant friends, and their bond endured for the rest of Shrake's life. Decades later, when both men lived in Austin, Cartwright would write lovingly in *Texas Monthly* magazine about Shrake and the final—and certainly the most popular and the most lucrative—literary project of his career: the improbable collaboration between the garrulous, hard-living, cosmopolitan author of books and screenplays and a gentle old teacher of golf named Harvey.

Shrake's marriage began to splinter. He rarely was at home long enough for his wife, Joyce, and their two young sons. But his reputation in journalistic circles was growing as his voice and authority matured. One of Shrake's columns for the *Times Herald* in 1961 was included in the annual *Best Sports Stories* anthology. The *Dallas Morning News* hired him that fall to become its lead sports columnist. Shrake also, finally, began writing fiction. He published a novel, *Blood Reckoning*, in 1962, the year he and Joyce, who kept the children, finalized their inevitable divorce.

Shrake sold a television script, dabbled in the short-story form, and attended lavish parties with the moneyed elite of Dallas. In the 1960s, he was becoming a brand. Harvey, meanwhile, was nearing the conclusion of his career as the varsity golf coach at the University of Texas and would retire as the head professional at Austin Country Club a decade later. He was still delighted when Rawls, Whitworth, Wright, and his other favorite women stopped by Austin to see him for a quick check of their grip and ball position. Harvey was still grieving the death of Morris Williams Jr. He also was quietly hopeful about the distinctly different new boys, Kite and Crenshaw, who just kept making one another better. Three hours to the north, Shrake was about to get farther away from Austin than he ever had been.

Shrake wanted to start a second novel, and he felt certain he wanted to write it in Europe. He asked the *Morning News* to grant him a leave of absence, though he knew, with the deep and permanent roots he'd put down in Dallas and Fort Worth, that he would return to Texas. Instead of granting him a leave, the newspaper instead allowed him to move to Spain in return for a consistent flow of stories from the continent. When he failed to provide those stories, he essentially doomed any prospect of extending his posting as the newspaper's only foreign correspondent. But he did finish his second book, *But Not for Love,* making the sabbatical, from his perspective, a success. He also traveled to Paris and Frankfurt, broadening his world.

When Shrake returned to Dallas in 1963, he was restored to his old position as the lead sports columnist for the *Morning News,* writing six columns a week. He drove a white Cadillac and shared an apartment with Cartwright, his old friend from the *Times Herald.* The two of them closed the bars every night and invited everyone in the room back to the apartment to share a nightcap. "On any given night the living room would be full of famous athletes, coaches, billionaires, nightclub acts, artists, hoodlums, drunks, writers," Cartwright said. When they were sober enough, Shrake and Cartwright traveled frequently to Austin, where they spent weekend nights with the writers Larry McMurtry and Billy Brammer at Scholz Garten. In 1963 they did whatever they could to escape Dallas, if only briefly.

Shrake burned through bags of marijuana. He wrote in feverish fits, wired on amphetamines. He dated a stripper named Jada, who motored around downtown in a mink coat and worked at a nightclub owned by Jack Ruby. Cartwright, Shrake, and other B-list literati spent many nights of excess at Ruby's club, watching Jada snap her G-string for dollar bills. The owner made sure the local celebrities cocktailed at no charge. No one knew when to stop. "We had boundless energy and a lot of speed," Shrake recalled. In a quieter moment, Shrake met Ann Richards, a tireless political activist who, despite the conservative climate of the city, helped to found the Dallas Committee for Peaceful Integration. Decades later, Richards became governor of Texas. She also spent the last years of her life in a committed, romantic relationship with Shrake.

By late 1963, *Sports Illustrated* was a magazine that mattered. Managing editor André Laguerre had brought Jenkins to New York the year before, to write about college football. He now wanted to expand the magazine's coverage of the AFL and NFL. The magazine needed more writers — trained and polished journalists capable of taking fresh angles and writing with panache. Laguerre installed Roy Terrell as assistant managing editor, a position responsible for identifying emerging talent, and Terrell listened to his staff. "I told [Terrell] that Bud Shrake was the best sportswriter in the country who wasn't already working for us," Jenkins said. "I didn't mention that he'd been my best friend since Paschal."

Terrell contacted Shrake in January 1964 to gauge his interest, which was considerable. Shrake flew to New York to meet Laguerre, who conducted the interview over cocktails. Shrake charmed the editor with his bonhomie and skill with words. Two weeks later, Laguerre offered Shrake a job. He took it.

Shrake's first impression of the culture at *SI* validated his decision to accept the job. The elevator delivered him to the twentieth floor of the Time & Life Building, where he encountered a group of people playing hockey in the hall with a tennis ball. Staffers worked hard and recreated harder, often recessing for three-hour lunches in the dim lights of the Three Gs, lubricated by martinis and Scotch. The magazine dispatched Shrake to the Bahamas, where he wrote about a backgammon tournament. He also profiled the enigmatic Buffalo Bills fullback Cookie Gilchrist, who was challenging the racial bigotry that simmered in professional football.

Because he had published two works of fiction, Shrake enjoyed great latitude at *SI*. Only one of his ideas in his fourteen-year career there was rejected. It was not the one he pitched early in 1965, when he cajoled Laguerre into sending him back to Texas to write about the Hill Country. "There was no direct connection to sports, but a mention of fishing or rodeo would make it close enough to get in our magazine," Shrake wrote in an anthology of his work, *Land of the Permanent Wave*. "Lyndon Johnson had been president for nearly two years. He was making the Hill Country famous. André agreed to the idea, and I took off for Austin."

He returned with the notion of crafting a long, fondly rendered portrayal of the limestone-encrusted expanse west of the Balcones Escarpment around Johnson City, spliced by the Pedernales River. The essay ventured into historical reflection, geology, anthropology, folklore, climatology, and ecology and succinctly summarized the settling of Austin. "The Colorado River flows through the city and catches its lights in dark water," he wrote. "To the west in the hills above Lake Austin, it is possible to live in splendid isolation in homes that cling to the cliffs like those of Sausalito or the French Riviera, and yet be able to drive downtown in fifteen minutes." It was clear that Shrake felt a visceral calling to Central Texas. It seemed just as certain he would surrender to it.

Shrake embraced other opportunities in his new, cosmopolitan life at *SI*. He befriended George Plimpton, Norman Mailer, and Willie Morris. He frequented Toots Shor's, P. J. Clarke's, and Elaine's, the establishment at East Eighty-Eighth and Second Avenue that doubled as a cultural salon for the New York literary scene. There was Tennessee Williams in the corner, along with William Styron. Over there were Kurt Vonnegut, Terry Southern, Gay Talese, and David Halberstam. The new company Shrake kept in Manhattan inspired him to push boundaries. He lived fast and hard on the edge. He talked of writing another novel. He tried LSD.

"This is a wonderful city," Shrake wrote to a friend in October 1964. "True, it may be filthy, noisy, expensive and overcrowded, but there is such sport to be seen in the streets. Queers, pimps, cops, thieves, whores, toe-freaks, blackjacketed motorcycle faggots, behind every lamppost is a guy with his dingus out." He later added: "I believe that is what they call the hustle and bustle of a great city." He signed the letter "Odysseus." "On the way to the 3 G's Bar in the evenings I stop and look at the ice skaters gliding around and listen to the music and the blades scraping. If it weren't for that, I would have gone mad. Some say I already have."

Shrake turned thirty-four in 1966. He loved and hated New York, depending on the hour. The long, liquid nights at Elaine's filled him with a greater sense of status and belonging. At the same time, Shrake never denied the allure of Texas, a return that beckoned when New York seemed claustrophobic and chaotic. He played golf infrequently, occasionally joining Jenkins and others from the magazine at the annual "5:42 P.M. Open," an outing at Winged Foot Golf Club in Westchester County for the Manhattan regulars at Toots Shor's.

Shrake's life stabilized somewhat when he met Charlene Sedlmayr, whom everyone called Doatsy, a fact-checker at *SI*. "She is beautiful, twenty-three, straw-blond, from Long Island, flies a plane, has just been initiated into the mysteries of our dark circle and took to them like a mountain goat, and is obviously insane," Shrake wrote to a friend. She was, in other words, a perfect companion for Shrake. They married at the end of the year.

Shrake expanded his literary canvas between his assignments for *SI*. He finished his third novel, *Blessed McGill*, in 1967. The book explored the adventures of a Reconstruction-era Catholic frontiersman who died a martyr in the American Southwest. The book received tepid critical praise. His friends, including George Plimpton, loved it.

The editors at the magazine, meanwhile, agreed to allow correspondents to live wherever they chose, so long as they could travel easily to story destinations. Shrake leaped at the chance to get closer to his friends (besides Jenkins in New York) and his home. He considered a move to Santa Fe, but he needed to be near a major airport. Fort Worth held no appeal, and Shrake had no interest in living in Dallas again. Austin, however, intrigued him immensely. His sophomore year at the

University of Texas and his forays into the Hill Country with Cartwright and other companions had convinced him that he belonged there someday. Now was that time.

Bud and Doatsy Shrake moved to Austin in 1968. The city now was home to 234,375 residents — nearly twice as populous as when he arrived on the UT campus in the early 1950s. The university and the state government drew smart, liberally educated people to the city — the sort of neighbors Shrake wanted to have. Shrake felt a particular kinship with the counterculture of Austin, the people drawn there by an emerging drug and music scene.

The couple bought a house in West Austin near Bee Creek, across the Colorado River from Lions Municipal Golf Course, where Harvey and his brother Tom shared both history and legacy. In 1969 Shrake pitched his editor at *Sports Illustrated* on a reported essay set in the Big Thicket region of East Texas. "He wanted to focus on the area's deforestation at the hands of the timber industry, and as such the article would complement the numerous conservation-minded features *Sports Illustrated* had published over the years," Steven Davis wrote in *Texas Literary Outlaws,* his 2004 book about Shrake, Jenkins, Cartwright, and other Texas writers. Laguerre approved the project. But by the time he finished the story a Texas lumber company had assumed significant ownership of Time Inc., which published *SI.* Management spiked the piece. It was the only piece of Shrake's ever rejected by the magazine.

Shrake still maintained an apartment in New York and would meet Willie Morris, the editor of *Harper's Magazine,* over highballs at Elaine's when he was in the city. "The Land of the Permanent Wave," refashioned for *Harper's,* appeared in the February 1970 issue. Instead of documenting the destruction of the Thicket, the piece chronicled Shrake's reporting experience in East Texas, where his long hair and hippie clothes drew hard glares from the suspicious citizenry, hotel rooms were denied to him because he looked different, restaurants refused to serve him, and the local police kept a persistent, paranoid eye on him. Morris later cited "The Permanent Wave" as one of his favorite pieces of journalism. "To me few finer magazine essays have ever been written," Morris said.

Shrake had little time for golf when he was home. He was writing constantly, getting stoned, drinking at hippie outposts such as the Vulcan Gas Company, and entertaining the idea of writing a movie script. But had he been reading the Austin newspapers, he would have learned that George Hannon and the University of Texas Longhorns had won their first national championship in men's golf in the spring of 1971. He would have known about Tom Kite and Ben Crenshaw, who credited Harvey for every measure of their still-unrealized successes. He would have understood that the old head professional at Austin Country Club, the quiet man who spoke in parables and cultivated champions, was teaching golf in a way that crossed boundaries of age, gender, ability, generations, even time itself. Shrake might have been curious enough to go meet Harvey had he not been so busy as one of the most celebrated writers in a city that nurtured artists of every kind — from those who traded in words to those who examined grips.

Shrake was thirty-nine years old in 1970. He was eager to stretch his wings again, so he asked the editors at *Sports Illustrated* for a leave of absence to write another book. The magazine granted him four months. In January 1971, Shrake and his wife left for London.

London appealed to Shrake because he thought he could write in solitude there, with no distractions. He had just come off the most prolific two years of his career, completing two novels, two screenplays, the Big Thicket essay for *Harper's*, his meditation on the Texas Hill Country, and a portfolio of other strong journalism for *SI*. He had settled into a productive cycle, spending the football season in an apartment in New York, where he could be close to the Time & Life Building, and the rest of the year in Austin.

"I really liked going back and forth," Shrake said. "I'd come to Austin and it was great at first, getting so laid back. People in Austin really weren't doing much of anything — a lot of them didn't even have jobs. But I'd get so lazy here that I had to go back to New York to recharge my batteries. In New York it was always work, work, accomplish, accomplish."

In London, Shrake found a flat with a view of an herb garden and, in the distance, the River Thames. He wrote every morning. He and his wife rolled joints in the afternoons and took long walks through the city. He later remembered the experience of writing in London as "a very pleasant period of my life." He finished the novel, *Strange Peaches,* and returned to Austin to build a new house on the edge of the growing city. Shrake had plenty of money at the time. Having just sold a movie, he used the proceeds to buy those two acres on the side of a hill in West Austin and build the house above the lake.

During construction, Shrake and some friends descended on Durango, Mexico, for the filming of the movie *Kid Blue,* which featured Dennis Hopper of *Easy Rider* fame in the lead role as a Fort Worth train robber seeking redemption. The entourage bound for Durango included Cartwright, Shrake's friend from their newspaper days in Dallas, and Peter Gent, a former Dallas Cowboys wide receiver who had just begun work on his own book, the seminal inside-the-NFL novel *North Dallas Forty.* The men spent three months in Mexico living every minute as if it were their last. They ingested psychedelic mushrooms on crackers. They took LSD. They crushed the stimulant Dexedrine and flambéed it in brandy. "The longer we were in Durango, the crazier it got," Cartwright said. Astonishingly, they survived.

Shrake returned to Austin to a new house but a marriage in crisis and hurtling toward divorce. He sought comfort at the Armadillo World Headquarters, an eclectic concert hall in a converted National Guard armory across the street from the municipal auditorium. Shrake befriended Jerry Jeff Walker, Willie Nelson, and other musicians at the Armadillo. The novel he wrote in London, *Strange Peaches,* was published in 1972, and his friends at the Armadillo embraced it as a brilliant, ironic, and caustically realistic examination of Dallas in the days leading up to the Kennedy assassination. The *New York Times* review said that "this big novel, two parts anger to one part humor, is fast and surefire," and suggested that "Edwin Shrake's narrative technique has been amply dosed with Dexedrine." *Time* magazine asserted that Shrake "captures superbly the feeling of combustible chaos that climaxed in the Kennedy assassination." Other reviewers hailed *Strange Peaches* as one of the most finely rendered works of fiction since World War II. The commercial marketplace, however, seemed to disagree. The book fell flat among readers, "but commercial failure was hardly new to [Shrake], and he began to take a certain pride in being a cult favorite — a stranger to the best-seller lists but well respected among a small coterie of peers and critics."

Shrake continued to push boundaries and reason. He lived life on a dangerous plane of existential disregard, hopped on speed, snorting cocaine, inviting risk. Hunter S. Thompson, the counterculture journalist responsible for writing *Fear and Loathing in Las Vegas,* came to Austin for a drug-fueled bender with Shrake and his friends. It lasted for forty consecutive hours. Other nights out ended sooner but not without similar debauchery. Shrake bounced merrily from the Armadillo to the Raw Deal to the Soap Creek Saloon, gathering enthusiastic commitments from his many friends to convene after last call at the cabin in the woods, where he kept his weed under the floorboards. Poker games materialized. Music and song ensued. Smoke curled in every room. Laughter rolled through the cedars, down to the lake. There was no tomorrow for the unstoppable Edwin "Bud" Shrake — except that there was, and it often unfurled precisely like the night before.

His work, meanwhile, demonstrated his uncanny aptitude for balancing competent journalistic production with great personal excess. The editors at *Sports Illustrated* assigned him longer and more deeply reported stories, including the Joe Frazier–George Foreman fight in Kingston, Jamaica, in 1973 and profiles of Dallas Cowboys coach Tom Landry, Buffalo Bills halfback O. J. Simpson, professional bull rider Larry Mahan, a community college dance team called the Kilgore Rangerettes, and a languid canoe trip down the Rio Grande River in Big Bend National Park.

But the mood at the magazine was beginning to shift. The spirit of boundless possibility and, in the opinion of some, the loose management of its stable of writers were on the cusp of extinction. Shrake soon faced an important choice.

The magazine replaced Laguerre in the fall of 1974 with Roy Terrell, the assistant managing editor who had hired Shrake. Terrell ran a tighter, leaner, and more disciplined operation than Laguerre had. He sought more control over his writers' out-of-town expense accounts and demanded faster stories and firmer deadlines. He erased the long-standing *SI* ritual of planning stories with the assistance of endless cocktails during a long lunch. The new policies alienated some on the magazine's staff. Shrake found himself caring less and less about his work for *SI*.

He missed the atmosphere that Laguerre had created. In his nearly fourteen-year stewardship at *SI*, Laguerre had led the magazine to an unforeseen level of prosperity. Advertising revenue climbed from $11.9 million to $72.2 million. Circulation rose from 900,000 to 2.25 million. More than that, Laguerre had proved that literary excellence mattered to thoughtful readers of sports. The professional ambition and bonhomie that Shrake had shared with the spirited Jenkins, Roy Blount Jr., Curry Kirkpatrick, Mark Kram, Tex Maule, Jack Olsen, and others seemed to melt after Laguerre left the Time & Life Building. An essential part of Shrake seemed to vanish with it.

Shrake was ready to evolve. He wrote a novel in Hawaii with Jenkins. A studio hired the two to turn it into a movie that was never made. Another studio retained Shrake to adapt the screenplay for *Nightwing*, a popular novel by Martin Cruz Smith. Shrake wrote one draft of the screenplay before he was fired. But as interest from Hollywood continued to come his way, Shrake learned to accept the fickleness of the movie business. He was tired of roaming the world to watch and write about sports. He wanted to stay at his home in the woods of West Austin and write about what interested him, not readers of a weekly magazine.

Late in 1978, when Shrake was forty-eight, *SI* assigned him to write about a junior rodeo. He refused. He then requested a leave of absence for a year, so he could spend more time on films. The magazine refused. The stalemate ended when Shrake quit.

He never held another formal job. Shortly after his resignation, Shrake again surrendered to the fiction impulse. "I was going to write a Texas book about Texas history that was so long and so thick that nobody could ever finish reading it but everybody would have to buy it," he said. He selected as the backdrop the Comanche raids in 1842 that stemmed from the anti–Native American policies advanced by Mirabeau Lamar, the president of the Republic of Texas. Shrake found an apartment in San Antonio to rent, making sure it had an inspiring view of the Alamo. But then a summoning to California complicated the plan: Steve McQueen wanted to meet with Shrake to talk about writing a movie. The long, thick book about the Comanches and Lamar never got published.

Shrake flew to Los Angeles in a pair of Levi Strauss jeans and a cowboy hat. McQueen explained that another screenwriter had started the project, based on the nineteenth-century Old West outlaw Tom Horn, but that the draft fell short of his expectations. They began their collaboration that afternoon. The picture, *Tom Horn,* was McQueen's second-to-last movie. It was released in 1980, the same year Shrake and Willie Nelson, who knew one another from the Armadillo in Austin, met to discuss the possibility of doing a feature film based loosely on Nelson's life. "The story involved a country songwriter getting fucked by Nashville who moves home to Texas and figures out how to fuck Nashville back and come out on top," Shrake said. "The movie was going to be about greed and power and loyalty and love." They decided to call the film *Songwriter.* Kris Kristofferson starred alongside Nelson. It arrived in theaters in 1984.

"I notice it's been described as a surreal version of Willie's life story, which it sort of is," Shrake said, "but it's sort of like my life story, too, and everybody else's who's tried to make a living in show business."

Songwriter gave Shrake the creative nudge he'd sought when he left *Sports Illustrated.* The film seemed to him authentic, uncompromised, even allegorical. But physically Shrake felt drained. He nearly fainted during one of his rare rounds of golf. Every hour felt to him like the morning after a bender with Hunter S. Thompson. The abuse he leveled at his body through cigarettes, drugs, and alcohol had compromised his health to the point that a friend recommended he see a doctor right away. Shrake was diagnosed with diabetes and liver damage the year *Songwriter* was released. The physician told him he needed to change immediately or expect to be dead in nine months.

"Even then, I actually had to think about it," he said. "I thought I needed the speed for energy and the whiskey for dreaming." He would find out that a good night's sleep accomplished all of that and more, and he would become even more productive later in sobriety. "In a way I wish I'd changed sooner," he said. "But on the other hand, maybe I wouldn't have been ready for it sooner."

Like any addict committed to recovery, Shrake needed a new pursuit, a beneficial and healthy distraction to complement his realization that he would have to change or die.

He found that salvation in golf.

He spent long hours on the golf course with his friends Darrell Royal, the retired head football coach at the University of Texas, and Nelson, who had purchased a nine-hole golf course near his studio in the cedar-dotted hills of Spicewood, west of Austin. The game touched Shrake in a way it never had before. He played every day. He sometimes finished fifty-four holes before sundown. He often met a bunch of musicians and writers after lunch at Nelson's course, a minimally maintained swatch of Hill Country known lovingly as Pedernales Country Club, where, according to the scorecard no one paid attention to, "when another player is shooting, no player should talk, whistle, hum, clink coins or pass gas"; where "excessive displays of affection are discouraged" and "penalized five strokes"; where "no more than twelve [are allowed] in your foursome"; where "gambling is forbidden . . . unless you're stuck or you need a legal deduction for charitable or educational expenses"; and where the rules forbade "bikinis, mini-skirts, skimpy see-through, or sexually exploitive attire. Except on women."

It was perfect.

The group typically included Ray Benson, who relocated his Western swing band, Asleep at the Wheel, to Austin in the early 1970s from California. "All of us had been golfers in previous lives," Benson said. "But with the advent of the sixties, we all turned away because of the social implications. It was a rich white man's sport. We weren't rich. Even though we respected the game, it was counter to the counterculture we were creating." The golf scene in Austin, however, carried a different vibration. Unifying rather than divisive, golf in Austin was a vibrant expression of Austin itself: contrary, inclusive, egalitarian, delightfully off-center. "I love the way P. G. Wodehouse put it," said Shrake, citing his favorite quotation. "'Some people say that golf is a microcosm of life, but just the opposite is true. Life is a microcosm of golf.'" Wodehouse would have felt at home in Austin.

After relocating a third time, Austin Country Club was now miles closer to Shrake's cabin in the hills, and as a bit of a celebrity, he never had to work very hard for an invitation to play there. Shrake often stopped to shake the delicate hand of the old man folded into his golf cart, wearing a U.S. Open bucket hat or, if it was autumn, a wool ivy.

Shrake also continued to write. He lived project to project. He finished a novel on his Smith Corona Skyriter called *Night Never Falls,* which examined a foreign correspondent's experience witnessing the defeat of the French in Vietnam at Dien Bien Phu. As his first creative work since he quit his vices, writing the book was the strongest test of will Shrake had ever attempted. He said he wanted to see if he could write without whiskey and speed. He could.

He later collaborated with Willie Nelson and former University of Oklahoma football coach Barry Switzer on their autobiographies. Both books appeared on best-seller lists, earning Shrake enough money to move along to the next project — and to tilt at the windmills of better golf. Shrake filled his library at home with instructional manuals. He certainly was not reading them for pleasure as he struggled with the numb tone and boring voice of the boutique genre. He might have wondered why these books routinely seemed so inelegantly written, but wanting to improve his game, he plowed through them anyway.

"Bud read every single golf instruction book," said Benson. "Bud read it, digested it, and tried it."

Shrake also found love again, in 1989. He courted Ann Richards, his old friend from Dallas before his move to New York, who had risen in local politics since her divorce from her husband. A Democrat, Richards had served two terms as a popular Travis County commissioner. Texas voters elected her state treasurer in 1982, when she became the first woman in a top state office in fifty years. The national Democratic Party appreciated her tough, uncompromising brand of governance, and its leaders saw her as a new face and strong voice for the organization. Richards gave the keynote speech at the Democratic convention in 1988 in Atlanta and playfully scolded Vice President George H. W. Bush about his wealth. "He was born with a silver foot in his mouth," she said. The audience howled, and the clip made the rounds on the television news programs. Richards, it was clear that night, was a woman with a formidable future.

Richards and Shrake shared a profound kinship beyond romance. She, too, had made a choice between mortality and addiction. She underwent treatment for alcoholism in 1980, an experience that became a campaign issue for her in 1990, when she decided to run for governor of Texas. She won the Democratic nomination in a testy three-candidate race, enduring the innuendos of Attorney General Jim Mattox that she had engaged in substance abuse after rehabilitation. Richards survived the claims. On November 6, 1990, she defeated Republican Clayton Williams to become the first woman elected governor of Texas since Miriam Ferguson in 1932.

Shrake accompanied her to parties, receptions, and formal state dinners. He danced with his girlfriend the governor at official balls. He smartly refused to insert himself in politics, telling reporters that she never asked for his advice and he never offered it. They never gave much thought to marriage. She traveled regularly, and Shrake preferred to stay home, writing in the cabin, trying to play better golf, learning to thrive without drug or drink. "This is the only relationship

I've ever had in my life that was completely guilt-free," Richards once remarked. "Each of us is totally free to live our lives and do the things we want to do without the other feeling that it intrudes or takes up space."

The relationship fit. Shrake and Richards spent evenings at the movies, not running up bar tabs. Their companionship functioned on a quiet level of maturity, sincerity, and mutual respect that Shrake had never achieved in his past relationships. He had found, at the age of fifty-eight, his eternal ballast.

Then one morning in 1991 he answered his telephone.

When Shrake heard the voice of Tinsley Penick, he thought Harvey was asking to see him to talk about his younger brother Bruce, who had attempted but failed to qualify for the Texas golf team as a freshman and sophomore in the mid-1950s. Many years later, Bruce Shrake, a member at Champions Golf Club in Houston, had contracted a devastating hitch in his golf swing that rendered him completely unable to bring the club to the ball. So he had taken the only action that made sense. He drove to Austin to see Harvey.

The lesson had been brief. Harvey watched the younger Shrake assemble his grip, align his feet, adjust his hips, address the ball, and lift the club up, over his shoulders. But nothing happened after that. There was no swing down. There was no clipping of grass. There was no swinging of buckets. There was nothing after Bruce Shrake reached the top of his swing and froze, like a child caught stealing from the brownie jar.

Harvey had seen a lot of staggering faults in a golf swing. But he had never seen anything like that. Shrake waited for Harvey to speak, prepared to hear a simple string of words that would thaw his paralyzing hitch.

"Well," Harvey said after much deliberation, "don't do that anymore."

But Tinsley was not calling about Bruce. Would Shrake be willing to meet with Harvey? His father had something on his mind.

Shrake arrived at the club to find Harvey in his cart. He saw a briefcase in his lap.

"I want to show you something that nobody except Tinsley has ever read," the old man said.

He snapped open the latch.

"Here."

Chapter Twelve

SHRAKE TOOK THE red Scribbletex notebook back to the cabin in the woods. As he thumbed through the pages, he detected a poetic meter in the way Harvey used language. The words on the pages seemed that day to take life inside Shrake's mind.

"I said, yeah, I could do this, and all of a sudden I felt like I had been called upon to do this for some reason," Shrake recalled in 2009. "The fates had transpired to put me with Harvey."

He wrote in longhand a two-page proposal for a book. He called his assistant, Jo Ellen Gent, from her office downstairs. He asked her to stop whatever she was doing to type the proposal and put it in the mail.

Shrake called Esther Newberg, his agent in New York, and revealed his idea about Harvey Penick and his Scribbletex notebook. He told her about taking dead aim and swinging buckets and weed cutters, about taking one pill, not the whole bottle, and about clipping tees. He described Harvey's friendships with Ben Crenshaw and Tom Kite and Betsy Rawls and Kathy Whitworth. Shrake tried to explain that being in Harvey's presence felt like being a part of the Tao of golf, like being there at the beginning.

"Who's going to buy that?" Newberg demanded.

The proposal arrived a couple of days later. As she read it, Newberg began to see the same potential in the book idea that Shrake had seen the morning he met Harvey at the club. "It was charming," she said.

"Bud had such a way of summing things up." She called Charles Hayward, the president of the adult trade division at Simon & Schuster. He asked her to send the two-page pitch.

Hayward took it to Jeff Neuman, a senior editor and the director of sports books at the publishing house. "If this guy is who Bud says he is, this could be something," Hayward said. Neuman read Shrake's idea in his office on the fourteenth floor at Rockefeller Center. He admired Shrake from his career at *Sports Illustrated.* He knew of Harvey from stories he'd read about Crenshaw and Kite. Neuman understood golf books. He also understood that this one was different.

Simon & Schuster had a history in golf books. It had published Hogan's *Five Lessons: The Modern Fundamentals of Golf,* as well as *Golf My Way* by Jack Nicklaus, a copy of which Nicklaus had sent to Harvey with the inscription, "Golf needs you." Those were excellent books, standards in the genre, timeless. But the two-page pitch Neuman read that day struck him as something that golf needed right now. "It's like the antidote to how-to books," Neuman said. This one was about "loving and understanding what you do."

He told Hayward to buy it.

Hayward called Newberg. "I'll give you $75,000," he said.

For a two-page pitch? The agent was stunned. She also sensed Hayward's interest. She could hear it in his voice. She requested a larger advance. The two negotiated a $90,000 contract. Newberg called Shrake in Austin to tell him to start writing the *Little Red Book.*

What happened next remains a matter of lore and florid speculation: there are many versions of who said what, what figures were bandied, when it happened, even where. Gary Cartwright, writing in the December 1993 issue of *Texas Monthly* magazine, provides the most detailed account of how Shrake informed Harvey that their book had been sold. Cartwright wrote that Shrake called Helen, who shared their conversation with Harvey.

"Maybe something got lost in the translation, but Shrake got the impression that Harvey was strangely noncommittal about the deal," Cartwright wrote. Shrake returned the next day to the country club, where he found Harvey. "In a voice so soft and feeble that Bud could hardly hear it, Harvey confessed that he'd been awake all night worrying about the proposal," Cartwright wrote. He quoted Harvey: "With all my medical bills and everything, I'm not sure I can afford to pay ninety thousand dollars."

Bud explained to Harvey that the advance would be coming to him.

Harvey had to ask Bud to repeat what he just heard. He wanted to make sure he understood that a famous publishing house in New York City was really going to give him a lot of money, more than he had ever held in his bank accounts, more than he had ever imagined having, for a book based on all those notes he'd written in the Scribbletex he'd kept in a rolltop desk.

Bud typed a short letter to Harvey in June. He wanted to explain, in the simplest of terms, everything Harvey needed to know about writing his first book. He informed Harvey that he would get $45,000 of the advance; Shrake absorbed his agent's commission, earning $36,000 as his share. Shrake promised Harvey 60 percent of the book's earnings. He told him he would do all of the writing. "Your job will be to let me interview you on tape," Shrake wrote. Harvey's obligations ended there.

They signed the contract on July 18, committing to a range of 50,000 to 75,000 words to be delivered by November 1. The formalities were over. Now it was time to work.

Shrake and Harvey agreed to meet on Mondays, when the club was closed. They conducted their visits at Harvey's house on Fawn Creek Path, across a busy street from the fourteenth tee. Shrake brought a small, clip-on microphone for those days when Harvey's voice was too weak to project. The Scribbletex notebook served as a kind of map. Discussing each entry, Harvey would elaborate and tell stories that Shrake had never heard, sharing memories he had not thought of in years. The process was like following a trail that included diversions but always led to a clearing. For much of that summer of '91, Harvey sat in his velour chair near the sliding-glass doors that allowed a view of the oaks and a burbling creek and told Shrake what he had learned from his eight decades of watching men and women propel golf balls. The most popular sports book in the history of the genre was a work of extraction.

The first interview took place on June 24. The first words Harvey spoke for the book addressed the grip. It was a fitting commencement for the project on that summer day in West Austin. For Harvey, golf was grounded in the tactile connection between player and club. Everything flowed from the hands.

"Why is the grip so important?" Shrake asked.

"Well, it controls everything," Harvey replied. "When a pupil compensates for a bad grip, he gets bad aim. If you make a mistake going back, to offset a bad grip, you've got to make a mistake going down, to offset that one."

So evolved the potent magic of the *Little Red Book*. From the moment their collaboration began, the conversations between Harvey and Shrake were layered in meaning — exemplifying Shrake's favorite quote about life and golf from Wodehouse. Until the *Little Red Book*, golf instruction had been written literally, procedurally, mechanically, and often too narrowly. Golf books had propounded theories but done little to engage the reader along any other dimension.

Harvey, by contrast, described his ideas in ways that could be extrapolated. A poor grip in golf produced necessary but disastrous compensations, which led to problems in other areas of the swing, which often produced a bad shot or, worse, a bad habit. Too many bad habits and bad shots resulted in bad golf. What was he really saying? What did he really mean in a larger sense? That a faulty foundation required faulty measures, which could lead to bigger problems? Maybe it could. Maybe golf was a microcosm.

"If you get a grip that fits you, leave it alone," Harvey said.

"How can you tell if you've got a grip that fits you?" Shrake said.

Harvey paused. "The way the ball flies," he answered simply.

Shrake also began to consider the executorial demands of the book with Harvey. The original Scribbletex, after all, was a charmingly primitive receptacle of theories and observations maintained by a man with an impressive grasp of golf but only modest aptitude as a writer. Thumbing through the fifty-page notebook, sprinkled with names and telephone numbers and sentence fragments and misused punctuation, Shrake wondered how to extract the authentic voice of the man he was interviewing from scraps of passages with no sign of a narrative pulse.

He studied the words for the answer.

Strong grips: must use more loft on woods. also prefer smaller heads.

Ben — Vardon or overlap:
Tom — Interlock — Nicklaus
Betty Hicks — Full finger Alice Ritzman
Best help: Hold a yard stick in both hands or ping pong bat: as to hit with it.

New pupils:
Not much ability: chipping first
Emphasize (not to help ball up)

When pupil misses a shot they should not be embarrassed: I am supposed to be teacher: and one to be embarrassed.

Young players grow so fast. We have to watch them or they will lose their good natural swing.

John Bredemus once called me a "wise, old Owl."

I like to call it Guide their learning instead of teaching: Especially after the pupil becomes a good player.

This much was clear on that June morning in '91: there was power in Harvey's words, but they needed something to hold them together.

They had function, but needed form. Shrake understood that he would be "writing in another person's voice."

Shrake cast around in every direction in that early interview. He mentioned Hogan. He wanted to know what Harvey thought of *Five Lessons*. Harvey noted that Hogan fought a fierce hook before adopting a weaker grip, a modest adjustment that changed Hogan's career. "I feel like Hogan is a self-made man," Harvey said. He told Shrake that someone from Austin recently had played in the member-guest tournament at Shady Oaks Country Club, where Hogan spent his retirement smoking cigarettes in the dining room that overlooked the eighteenth green and, every so often, carting out to a private spot on the course to hit shots that no one could see. Hogan was playing cards at Shady Oaks that day when he learned that someone in the member-guest was from Austin. Hogan found the man. "You tell Harvey I've got a loop in my swing," Hogan told him. "I'm going to come for some help." But he never did.

Harvey told Shrake about his years as the head coach at Texas. He affirmed what he had told many others. "Boys would come from all over the state," Harvey told him. "The local pros helped these boys. I took thirty-two years of knowledge from these golf pros all over the state."

Shrake asked Harvey if he had known Bobby Jones, the great amateur from Atlanta. Harvey kept a picture of Jones in his shop for many years because he wanted golfers to see that Jones finished his swing with his elbows in front of his body. Harvey said that he copied Jones's putting stroke. Harvey saw him once, he said, at the 1928 U.S. Open at Olympia Fields in Chicago, when he played a practice round with the eventual champion, Johnny Farrell. But then Harvey stopped. What he was about to say next was to be left out of the book, he said.

"Jones and another fellow passed by on a par-three hole," Harvey explained. "He stopped to watch us. I hit a spoon shot up within about two feet of the hole. And he says, 'Fine shot.'"

The answer to the question was no. Harvey did not know Jones. But

Jones knew Harvey once hit a fine shot at the '28 U.S. Open. And Harvey did not want that in his book, because the book was about helping others, not about him, not about building his image among readers of the book, and not about Bobby Jones once seeing him hit a spoon shot to two feet.

Tinsley arrived. He shouted a greeting to his father from across the room. Shrake asked Harvey what he could tell about a player's swing by simply looking at the face of his golf club.

"There's his seven-iron," Tinsley said. He gave Shrake's club to Harvey.

"Turn that light on," Harvey said.

Harvey examined Shrake's 7-iron. "Has it been cleaned since?" he said.

"I cleaned the grooves," Shrake said.

Harvey studied the club. He turned it in his hands until the light caught it just so.

"He's been meeting the ball with the blade a little open," he said finally. "You see these marks right here? See, they're going up thataway. That's the sand and the dirt between the ball and the club. It's hitting this way." Harvey dragged a finger across the clubface, tracing its collision with the ball. "You follow that?"

Harvey then spoke the words he repeated often for the remainder of his life. He said them in interviews. He said them at book signings. He said them whenever people came to him to congratulate him on his new fame as a best-selling author at the age of eighty-seven. He said them to Shrake that day:

"This is something that you can use for sure."

Harvey had something else he wanted to say to Shrake: "I have probably seen more golf shots than anybody that ever lived. Caddying. Watching. Giving lessons. Coaching. Being the starter. Too many of them were my own." Harvey wanted to make sure Shrake heard the next part, because he took a lot of pride in why he had seen all those shots: "I can't imagine anybody seeing more, working seven days a week."

Harvey had given his life to golf. He wanted to make sure Shrake knew that.

In July, Harvey and Shrake discussed the final preparations of the *Little Red Book*. Harvey sat in his chair by the deck, paging through his Scribbletex, being careful not to overlook anything.

"Be sure and try to get a hold of Ben," Harvey told Shrake. "Ask him if he'll write a little foreword, a couple of paragraphs. I think we might do it today. He might be in town."

"I'm sure he'll do it," Shrake said.

Crenshaw did. Shrake also solicited remarks from Kite, Mickey Wright, Betsy Rawls, Mary Lena Faulk, Dave Marr, and Byron Nelson. "Harvey Penick is one of the great teachers in the history of golf," Nelson wrote. The *Little Red Book* had the blessings of some of the greatest players of their generation.

The two men spent most of that July day visiting familiar themes. They discussed how professional golf had changed since the 1920s, when Harvey was entering opens in San Antonio, Houston, Harlingen, and elsewhere. Men in suit jackets and women in long dresses came to watch, but only out of curiosity, and certainly not in great numbers. "But it's changed now," Harvey observed. He had recently watched the PGA Tour tournament in Memphis and marveled at the crowds that lined the curling zoysia fairways at TPC Southwind. There were thousands of people out there. They wore Titleist hats and Callaway shirts and golf shoes. *Golf shoes!*

"I used to think of it as a participating sport," Harvey told Shrake. "It's a spectator sport. You see those big crowds?"

The interview that day followed no logical order. Shrake darted from subject to subject, asking Harvey about the day he met young Crenshaw and how to accept failure on the course ("It's hard," Harvey managed) and the highest fee that he ever charged for lessons ($25). Shrake inquired about Harvey's thoughts on etiquette. He pushed for memories and probed for details. He pried out of Harvey reluctant criticisms of Nicklaus (the left heel, which Nicklaus lifted at the top) and Hogan (the length of his swing). They discussed golfers who played cards well. (Doug Sanders, Lloyd Mangrum, Bill Mehlhorn, and Tommy Armour, Harvey said, dating himself considerably.) Then Shrake asked Harvey for his opinion of the condition of modern golf instruction in 1991.

"I see things written that I can't even believe," Harvey said.

He added: "Anything I say in this book has been tried and tested, with success."

Shrake sensed a rare moment in the room. Typically a man of rigorous humility, Harvey rarely spoke about his portfolio of ideas with such conviction. He was confident, of course. But he also was modest, content to define his methods as suggestions, not prescriptions. Yet here he was, on this hot July day in Austin, speaking in absolutes.

Shrake knew a story opportunity when he saw one. He asked Harvey: Could you help a student right here, in your house, on the carpet? "I sure can," Harvey replied, assuming it was a question of fact, not a request for a lesson.

The interviews for the book with Shrake gave Harvey joy and purpose. He felt relevant again. He mattered. The questions gave him new angles on golf to think about and allowed him to revisit what he thought were the best years of his life.

When Shrake asked him to rank his pupils, Harvey seemed weary of the topic but prepared to confront it again. He said people always asked him to do that, but it was difficult. It seemed unfair. In mentioning certain players, Harvey knew he would be leaving out others, and he did not want to hurt anyone's feelings. But he knew readers of his book would be curious.

"Ed White," he said finally. "He hit the ball as well as anybody ever did. Freddie Haas played him in the finals. Said he was the best player he ever saw.

"Then Morris Williams came along. Everybody thought he couldn't be beat. He had such a fine character.

"Then came along Tom Kite and Ben Crenshaw. They have proven they are fine golfers, but also fine citizens."

Shrake asked Harvey about his own career as a player.

"I played in an awful lot of tournaments," Harvey said. "But I felt like I was playing as much for what I learned in association with my fellow pros."

Two months into their collaboration, Shrake could begin to predict the way Harvey would articulate his thoughts. Harvey preferred not to talk about himself. He liked to talk about success, not failure, especially when the conversation turned to one of his pupils. He also made great efforts to draw parallels between golf and character. Shrake noticed that Harvey spent as much time praising morals and ethics as he did celebrating skill and technique and that he also never assumed he had an answer to every question. Shrake was beginning to understand that their book would transcend golf instruction.

"You think golf teaches you anything about how to live your life?" he asked Harvey.

"I, in a roundabout way, somehow tried to teach that," Harvey replied. "That golf and life are similar. There's nothing fair in either one. And we shouldn't expect it."

Shrake wrote the manuscript at his corner desk in the woods of West Austin. He sat at a high-backed chair covered in brown leather, surrounded by the vestiges of his career in writing. Framed dust jackets from his books hung on the dark, paneled walls, which were cluttered with newspaper clippings, pennants, and campaign bumper stickers. Photographs of Shrake with his story subjects and golf partners leaned against books on the shelves, which wrapped around the room. Shrake had an easel set up in the room so that he could paint between chapters. He wrote in the soft illumination of one lamp. Gazing through a pair of long, narrow windows that opened to the woods, he searched his own voice for Harvey's.

He knew he wanted to organize the book in short chapters. He told friends he wanted the reading experience to "be like eating peanuts. You read two or three chapters and you can't stop." The tone of the prose came to Shrake as he listened to the tapes of his interviews with

Harvey. He soon was poking away at his typewriter, day turning to night.

When he finished, Shrake made sure Harvey read and approved what he had composed, which Harvey did by marking with faint pencil above every word, the way fact-checkers used to do at *Sports Illustrated.* Shrake was mindful of not misleading readers. He needed the book to be a true reflection of Harvey's ideas. "It scared me to think of golfers reading this book and taking away a piece of bad instruction that somehow came from me and not Harvey."

When he finished, Shrake felt sure he had just written one of the most important books of his career. "What Harvey had to say was so important that it had to be preserved for all golfers, everywhere, for all the ages," he said. "It happened to fall on me to make it happen."

Shrake submitted the manuscript in the fall. "It needed very, very little work," said Jeff Neuman, the editor at Simon & Schuster. "The voice was great right away. It had that friendly, wise, folksy feel of someone who had never heard the word 'writerly.' And that's such a rare thing to capture." Neuman rearranged some of the chapters to encourage a stronger sense of randomness to the passages and load the book with a charming element of surprise. He changed little else. At a positioning meeting with sales and marketing staff, someone in the room noted the association with another Little Red Book—the one written by Mao Tse-tung. "I said that wouldn't be bad, because that was a pretty big seller," Neuman wrote in 2015. "We came out of the meeting with the book called *Harvey Penick's Little Red Book,* and it never changed."

The designers and editors at Simon & Schuster considered options for presentation. They agreed on a new size. Smaller than the standard eight inches tall by five inches wide, it became known in the industry as the "Harvey trim." It was, after all, the *little* red book. They wanted the design to make a nostalgic, antique impression. The jacket artists created a cover with gold lettering and an oval image of a golfer in plus-fours, accompanied by his caddie, in the style of a cameo. They decided the book would contain no illustrations. "We didn't want to give the impression that this is what you must do," Neuman said. "It just felt right."

Neuman met with the publisher's sales team and told them: "Do not think of this as a new book. This is simply the classic golf book that has not been published yet."

The surprising appeal of the book rippled through the offices at Simon & Schuster.

Neuman and the others who had read parts of it were seduced by Harvey's aphorisms and the chat-over-coffee manner in which Shrake had rendered them. In ways Harvey surely never imagined, the *Little Red Book* seemed to be about everything else as much as it was about golf. It was a sports book about life.

"It was simple, but it wasn't simplistic," Esther Newberg recalled. "It was just so unexpected. He [Harvey] wanted to leave a legacy. But he didn't have any idea it would change his life so."

Shrake knew he needed early publicity to build momentum. He wanted to send complimentary copies of the *Little Red Book* to notable figures in journalism, sports, and the literary industry. He borrowed a list of names that his friend Dan Jenkins had used in the summer of 1991 for his novel *You Gotta Play Hurt*. It was a roster of elites. Jenkins would not have had it any other way. Shrake wouldn't either.

The publisher sent the book to Dave Anderson at the *New York Times*, Mitch Albom at the *Detroit Free Press*, Ben Bradlee at the *Washington Post*, Tom Brokaw at NBC, Howard Cosell, John Feinstein, Jim Murray at the *Los Angeles Times*, George Plimpton, Dan Rather at CBS, Liz Smith at *Newsday*, and Jack Whitaker at ABC. "Jack Whitaker did an essay on [the *Little Red Book*] on ABC-TV yesterday," Shrake wrote to Neuman. "We owe him a love letter."

Jenkins mailed President George H. W. Bush a copy of the *Little Red Book* in May. He included a typewritten letter from his home in Ponte Vedra Beach, Florida. Jenkins told the president it was "the best instruction book you will ever read" and "pure uncomplicated pleasure." He referred to Harvey as "a Texas legend."

A week later Bush replied directly to Harvey and Shrake on presidential letterhead. He noted that he, and not an assistant, had typed the note. Bush playfully disparaged his own golf game, suggesting that not even the *Little Red Book* could correct the faults in his swing. Bush wrote that he regretted how little time he was able to devote to his game, given his responsibilities as commander in chief. He concluded his letter with a simple acknowledgment of how much he loved the game and thanked Harvey and Shrake for their contribution to golf.

Harvey would cherish that letter. He liked every shred of correspondence from people who found joy in the *Little Red Book* — and the books that followed — but a piece of paper with the seal of the President of the United States at the top carried a certain sense of accomplishment and wonder.

Harvey fetched a sheet of paper — Austin Country Club letterhead, to be sure — to compose his reply. He tried to keep the pen steady in his hand so that what he wrote didn't look like nervous scribble.

"Dear Mr. President," he wrote carefully.

> I hope you will enjoy reading my "Little Red Book" when you have the time.
>
> I've got to tell you, Mr. President, that I am having a hard time trying to put into words the high honor and true joy your letter has brought to this old caddy. It would have been nice to think that I might have been half as good a teacher as you have been a leader of our country, and I do mean that.
>
> Now about your golf game: May I suggest that you are over-analyzing your swing? Why don't you try using your good natural athletic ability and just swinging the club like a bucket of water: nice and easy, without spilling. Get the lowest point of your swing level with the ball: then let your head follow thru on up with a good balanced follow thru.
>
> Don't give up a good swing to hold your head steady: straight left arm etc. etc. etc.

Also remember to take dead aim: both in your golf and your coming election.

"My best regards," he finished. "Harvey Penick."

In early June, the *Little Red Book* rose to number one in the nonfiction category on the *New York Times* best-seller list. Harvey and Shrake were thrilled. Harvey no longer was just a grown-up caddie and golf teacher with a letter from the President of the United States.

He was a famous author. It said so right there in the most trusted newspaper in the world.

Golf Digest had published a color portrait of Harvey on the cover of its May issue. The light illuminated the right half of his face, accentuating his considerable wrinkles in a way that suggested prophecy. He wore a dark tie and a cardigan for the picture, which captured his hand resting on his Scribbletex, the tabs poking out from the pages, like hints. Inside, the magazine excerpted passages from the *Little Red Book*. It included an introduction from Kite. Harvey was now the biggest name in golf.

More letters arrived. Harvey could barely keep pace, but he read them all.

Dinah Shore sent a card. Ernest L. Ransome III, the chairman of the board at Pine Valley Golf Club, wrote to tell Harvey his book was "the best and most informative book I have ever read on the subject of golf." J. D. Montgomerie, the secretary at Royal Troon Golf Club in Scotland, mailed a letter to tell Harvey that he had shared the book with his promising son Colin.

Jim McLean, a fellow teacher of touring professionals, shipped five books to Harvey for him to sign, including one for the vice president, Dan Quayle. Harvey's old friend Byron Nelson, long retired at his ranch in Roanoke, addressed a letter to Harvey and Helen in his neat cursive. "What a great thing for golfers, the Little Red Book," Nelson told them. "I am proud to count you as one of my friends."

Billy Graham, the Southern Baptist minister and celebrated evangelist, found biblical inspiration in the pages Harvey and Shrake wrote. "I think of you and the positive outlook on life that you have and I think of the Scripture verse, 'With long life I will satisfy thee.'"

The words buoyed Harvey. Mail from faraway states and foreign countries he had never visited waited for him in bundles at Austin Country Club. The *Little Red Book* was a fixture on the best-seller lists. Harvey was about to turn eighty-eight, but even though his back ached, his eyesight was getting worse, and his hearing continued to fade, in many respects he had never felt better. His association with Shrake, christened under the oak tree at the club, had given Harvey an identity and his life a meaning that he never considered possible. He wanted to live forever.

More letters arrived.

"The Little Red Book is wonderful!" wrote Betsy Rawls. She told Harvey how the chapters brought back "many fond memories" and added: "The world of golf is much better from your having published your red book entries."

From Charles Crenshaw, Harvey's longtime friend and advocate, who had been in Colorado for a month:

Today I'm back, and I really want to thank you from the bottom of my heart for the loveliest gift I've ever received. At last, the world can see what a great man and teacher you are. You have been a dear and wonderful friend to me and my whole family, especially Ben, for more than a half century. And we all feel the warmest glow of friendship for you now and always.

From Jeff Neuman, the editor at Simon & Schuster:

There are many books I've published that have sold well, a few that I have truly loved, and hardly any that I felt were a privilege to be involved with. Yours is in the second and third categories, and I have no doubt it will be in the first as well. Don't let Bud Shrake know I said this, but in my heart that's the least important of the three.

And from Shrake, quickly written on gray paper:

> I believe the Little Red Book will sell briskly all through the summer and will really take off when people start buying Christmas gifts. So keep your writing fingers in good condition, Harvey. You have many more thousands of autographs to sign.

It was a short note that Shrake wrote in a hurry. He even forgot to date it.

But as prophecy it was timeless.

PART III

THE FAME

Chapter Thirteen

THE SUMMER OF 1992 brought a new season of simmering concern
for Tom Kite. He'd won fifteen titles in twenty years, but he'd failed to
shake one annoying distinction. In seventy-one starts, Kite had never
won a major championship.

That bothered him. He regarded his tour career so far as a qualified success. He'd competed on six Ryder Cup teams, won the Vardon
Trophy twice, finished in the top ten more than a hundred times. He'd
earned millions in prize money. But he was forty-two years old now.
Many of his peers had their majors. All he had was the disappointment
of finishing two Masters (1983, 1986) and that 1978 Open Championship at St. Andrews in second place. "I began to wonder if the whispers
on and off the course, that I didn't have what it takes to win the big
one, were correct," he wrote years later.

Harvey sympathized. He sometimes wondered why the cosmos
seemed to collude against his longtime student and friend. Harvey was
among the few people who truly appreciated what the lack of a major
championship meant to Kite, a driven man with a colossal work ethic
but a fraction of the athletic ability of someone like Crenshaw. Golf
never came easily to Kite. But he worked so hard at the game that he
seemed to bend its will in his favor. Crenshaw won with ambivalent
grace. Kite won with rabid commitment. Harvey loved and admired

them both. Their differences simply proved to their teacher that golf was a game for everyone.

Longtime *Los Angeles Times* columnist Jim Murray once wrote of Kite:

> He was the "other" player out of the University of Texas. Ben Crenshaw was the star. Kite and Crenshaw were NCAA co-champions in 1972, but Crenshaw won it two other years. Crenshaw was supposed to be the next Ben Hogan. Kite was supposed to finish 10th or 20th, go for the fat part of the green, make money and leave the legends to Ben. It has never worked that way.

A new year in 1992 brought new promise. Kite lost the Bob Hope in January in a playoff, but he shot a final-round 63 to get there. He tied for seventh at the Doral and eighth at the Nestlé. He tied for third in Greensboro in April. He won the BellSouth Classic in May.

But the triumph on Mother's Day in Atlanta came too late for the Masters, which Kite missed that spring for the first time since 1975. Winless in a full-field start since Memphis in the summer of 1990, Kite had ten top-ten finishes at Augusta, including two ties for second place. But none of it was enough to warrant an invitation in '92. He was hurt. He was mad. Kite refused to even watch the Masters on television. Instead, he cut trees in his yard, practiced at the club, and spent most of Sunday afternoon avoiding the CBS telecast of Fred Couples winning his first major.

He returned home after the jacket ceremony. "Who won?" he asked his wife Christy.

"Freddie," she said.

"Good," Tom said. "Good for Freddie. He deserved it."

Kite and his wife traveled to Baltimore the week before the U.S. Open that summer to watch their ten-year-old daughter, Stephanie, compete in the Olympic gymnastics trials. He practiced at Caves Valley Golf Club in nearby Owings Mills, Maryland, where an old friend,

Dennis Satyshur, was the head professional. He sat through an Orioles game at Camden Yards.

"He didn't put any pressure on himself," Christy Kite said.

Nevertheless, a past failure at the national championship still haunted Kite. He had led by three shots early in the final round of the 1989 U.S. Open at Oak Hill in Rochester, New York. He made a bad swing on the fifth tee, sprayed his ball into a stream to the right of the fairway, and made a triple-bogey on the hole. "When I saw that triple go up on the leaderboard," said eventual winner Curtis Strange, "I felt like I'd just make three birdies." Kite suffered a double-bogey on No. 13. He doubled the fifteenth too.

He signed his scorecard, which registered seventy-eight swings that Sunday, five strokes behind Strange. His disintegration silenced an entire room back in Austin, where an ABC television crew insisted on documenting the afternoon with Harvey and Kite's father, who sat wordlessly. Harvey watched numbly. He knew Kite had more tenacity and drive than anyone in golf. He wondered if tenacity and drive would ever be enough. "It was just awful," Tom Kite Sr. said of the day. "You have no idea how awful. Here I am watching Tom blow a three-shot lead on one hole. You can't express your emotions. You don't want to talk."

Neither did his son. But he had to. He had to explain how he'd lost the U.S. Open with a triple and two doubles and a ball in the water. He told reporters he thought he had seemed like a model composite of a national open champion: consistent, ever prepared, a competent putter, and exacting with all thirteen other clubs, especially his wedges. But the U.S. Open also vexed him. So Kite told the only truth he knew with conviction.

"It's a cruel game sometimes," he said after the final round, which sank him into a tie for ninth place. "But I'm not going to curl up and die because of one round of golf. I'll come back and contend in some more majors. I promise you."

The Kites arrived in California for the ninety-second U.S. Open at

Pebble Beach Golf Links. They checked into the Vagabond's House Inn, where they often stayed for the national pro-am on the regular tour schedule. It always felt good to come back to Pebble. Kite had made the two-round cut in the two previous U.S. Opens there, in 1972 and '82. He was eager to hear the wind and the surf, to see the Del Monte Forest and 17-Mile Drive and Carmel-by-the-Sea, to walk the finest string of holes he had ever seen.

"I think it's the best golf course in the world," Kite said.

"It's a great blend of God and man," said Tom Watson, who won there in '82.

The championship began on a misty Thursday morning, gloomy and still on the California coast. Ten former winners — including Jack Nicklaus, the champion at Pebble in '72 — joined the field of fifty-two exempt players. The golf media that year numbered 1,568 from nineteen nations. They were there to follow, among other story lines, the professional debut of Phil Mickelson. Mickelson wisely said before his round: "It's funny how, in the U.S. Open, you make birdies when you least expect it."

Kite and his brass Bulls Eye putter opened with a 1-under 71. But Gil Morgan, an optometrist from Wewoka, Oklahoma, seared the field with a 6-under 66, a shot clear of Strange, two better than Andy Dillard, and three ahead of Tom Lehman. Kite played a patient and smart round of golf, just right for the U.S. Open. "When you win a tournament, you win on Sunday," he reflected two decades later. "All the other stuff, it puts you in position."

He kept his position on Friday under similarly gray skies. Kite shot even-par 72, rising up the leaderboard as others in the field succumbed to the quickening greens, the growing rough, and the pressure to play the weekend. But nothing seemed to bother Morgan. He shot 3-under 69, the only player to stack two rounds in the 60s. "Gil was lighting it up," Kite said. "Nobody thought it was going to be anybody's week but Gil's."

It appeared so through seven holes Saturday. Morgan made history through half of the third round. He birdied No. 3 with a 9-iron to twenty-five feet and a successful birdie putt, becoming the first player to reach 10 under par in the ninety-two incarnations of the U.S. Open. Morgan birdied the sixth, a par-5, from two bunkers and a pitch to ten feet—he was now 11 under. He birdied the minuscule par-3 seventh, a lobe on the Monterey Bay, with a wedge and a putt from three paces—now 12 under. "It looked like we were playing for second," said Ian Woosnam, the Welshman who'd won the Masters in '91.

Kite, meanwhile, forged through the third round with a 2-under 70. He was playing sound, cautious, and fundamental championship golf—the style that suited him.

"We're all trying to win the golf tournament and achieve a little greatness," he said.

But beyond his purview, circumstances changed. Mark Brooks, himself a former Texas Longhorn, mentioned during the week the tonal shift of Pebble after the opening seven holes. Veterans knew that the best scores were available early in the course but that the demands amplified on the eighth, where the seaside holes tested patience and nerve. "When you step on the eighth tee," Brooks said, "you've got a lot of work to get to the house."

Morgan stumbled behind Kite that Saturday with a sloppy double-bogey on the eighth, a bogey on the ninth, a double on the tenth, and bogeys on the next two holes. When he made a third double-bogey on the fourteenth, a par-5, the untouchable Morgan had misplayed nine shots in seven holes. His lead crumbled to one. Kite, Woosnam, and Brooks were a shot behind Morgan at the conclusion of play. Two strokes back were Joey Sindelar, Nick Faldo, and Gary Hallberg. Five other players, including Tom Lehman and Payne Stewart, trailed by three.

They seemed to be playing for first again.

Like Kite in '89, Morgan fumbled for answers. He called his play "yucky." He called his round "dumb." He called his performance "pretty embarrassing at times." Morgan recognized that in a matter of three hours he had gone from holding a seven-shot lead to allowing twenty-seven players to crawl to within five of him. "It was a long day, and I'm glad it's over," Morgan said. "The pressure of being that far out front may have kept me too uneasy. It seemed to drift away. I don't really understand it myself."

Kite understood. But after his round, he didn't want to address the theme of major-championship collapse, whether Morgan's or his own at Oak Hill. A reporter asked Kite what he had learned from his own catastrophe three years before. It was a fair question. Kite returned a fair, but curt, answer. "I prefer not to comment," he said. "I've got to try to play golf tomorrow and win the tournament. I think the thing I need to do is to dwell on the positive and not the negative."

Back in Austin, those who read those words knew they were hearing the voice of Harvey.

In his rounds of 71-72-70, Kite found a lot to appreciate. He improved his putting each day, from 30 in the first round to 28 in the second to 25 on Saturday. That kind of progress always pleased Harvey, who insisted throughout his life that a good putter is a match for anyone and a bad putter is a match for no one. Kite's driving through fifty-four holes was unimpressive — twenty-seven fairways out of a possible forty-two — but his ability to snatch par with a single putt portended great things. Only one question remained: would 1992 be different from 1989?

Kite noticed other factors coming into play Saturday as he made his way through the course. "The wind has turned 180 degrees on us," he said. "It's a hard old golf course, and it's difficult to keep it going."

He had no idea how true that would be.

The Kites and his parents went out to dinner that evening, which was so pleasant they took a stroll through the streets of Carmel. "We just love the little town," Christy Kite said. Walking past art galleries and clothing boutiques, they came across a couple they knew from Austin, Lance and Haley Hughes, who had spent the third round at the green of the par-5 fourteenth hole.

Lance Hughes mentioned to Kite that the 565-yard fourteenth seemed to play easier for players who tried to reach the green in two shots. Few of them actually succeeded, but the notoriously pitched green was best attacked with a short chip or pitch, Hughes explained, because longer shots failed to hold. Kite seemed intrigued by the idea. "Tom had been playing there for years, but he'd never thought of going for it in two," Christy Kite said.

On the morning of the final round, two hours ahead of the time in California, Riverbend Baptist Church in Austin, where the Kites were members, began to fill. The pastor, Gerald Mann, told his congregation: "I don't know if God is into golf. But I am praying for Tom Kite to win the Open, and I want you to pray for him, too. If you don't want to pray for Tommy, I suggest you go someplace where they don't pray for winners."

Near the country club, Harvey and Helen settled into their living room chairs for the broadcast.

Kite woke to a nip in the air and a breeze bustling from the Pacific. He stepped outside, long before he planned to go to the course, and absorbed the moment. With the atmosphere seeming to build, he somehow could tell the day would be different from the three before. And he remembered Harvey. He thought about those rare, rainy days in Austin, when other kids stayed home to trade baseball cards or watch cartoons, when Harvey insisted Kite learn to play in the wind and the rain and the mud and the chill. Kite was thankful for Harvey, especially now.

Kite knew he was ready that morning.

He fit a bright red Hogan sweater over his head and drove to Pebble Beach. The practice range at Pebble Beach lay some distance from the ocean, protected from the coastal winds. By the time Kite arrived there with his caddie, Mike Carrick, much of the field was on the course, playing in frisky but manageable huffs from the bay.

Kite felt the wind even on the range as he rehearsed his swing, which seemed comfortably familiar and reliable, like stepping into slippers. Proceeding through his bag, his turn felt uninhibited, his swings fluid, his release precise, his shots crisp and true. He and Carrick moved to the practice putting green as his starting time approached. "Even then, it was blowing," Kite said. "The early starters got a lot of their rounds in before it got up to full peak."

Kite drew Brooks in a final-round Texas pairing. They would be the second-to-last to play.

"It was gut check time," he said.

Morgan and Woosnam, who shot 69 in the third round, completed the last pairing.

"It's going to be a hard day," Morgan said gravely.

The sun appeared for the first time as the leaders were summoned to the tee. Kite birdied the first hole. An errant drive at the short par-4 fourth hole produced a double-bogey, but Morgan, playing behind Kite, mismanaged the same hole, with the same result. Kite slammed home a twenty-foot birdie putt on the sixth. The winds swirled. Flagsticks quivered. When Morgan reached the sixth green, on a promontory over the coastline, his U.S. Open crashed to a fitful end. He took another double-bogey.

Then the winds intensified. Gales later clocked at up to forty-five miles an hour scraped the exposed peninsula, parching the tiny Pebble Beach greens, snapping their yellow flags, and scattering golf shots en route. Players later claimed that Sunday afternoon in '92 was the hardest stretch of U.S. Open golf they'd ever played. Bob Estes, who played collegiately at Texas, remembered where he was when the gusts peaked. He was hitting his approach at the third hole, a par-4 of 400 yards. Estes swung an 8-iron from 150 yards, and when his ball reached the peak of its flight, the air atomized. "All of a sudden, the wind just slammed it," Estes said. His shot fell twenty hopeless yards short of the green. "It wasn't even the same golf course."

The field flailed. Many players later criticized the USGA for its oversight of the course, especially the deteriorating greens, which turned an alarming shade of blue. Twenty players, three of them former U.S. Open champions, were on their way to scores in the 80s. Some players thought hole positions were ridiculous. "The course was out of control," barked one of them, Payne Stewart, who shot 81. "If the USGA knew the sun was coming out and the wind was coming up, why did they put the pin placements where they did?"

Couples, who played the first and second rounds with Kite, said bluntly: "It was brutal. It wasn't really golf. You could shoot anything." Scores would range from 70 to 88. There were no 60s that Sunday at Pebble.

Kite made the climb to the top of the seventh tee after his birdie at the sixth. The iconic, 107-yard seventh — enveloped by menacing bunkers, the bay whitecapping on three sides, so disarming in appearance that Woosnam had disparagingly called it a "practice hole" earlier in the week — needed only a sand wedge from Kite on Saturday. On Sunday it required a 6-iron. Nick Price had swung a 9-iron there earlier. "It was getting more and more difficult by the minute," said Price, who tied for fourth after a final-round 1-under 71. "It was the kind of wind that, if you pulled it, it would go forever."

But Kite's shot did not. His ball hopped over the green and into a nest of rough, steps away from the cliff. Brooks walked over to assess the predicament Kite faced. "He probably had a fifty-fifty chance to get up and down," Brooks said later.

The wind rushed across the bay in startling fits. It was becoming unbearable on the exposed peninsula. A reporter following Kite asked Rick Roza, a volunteer marshal on the seventh hole, when it had blown the hardest that day.

"Right now," Roza replied.

But the wind actually helped Kite to buttress his lob shot, which parachuted to the green. Its pace quickened as it tumbled toward the hole. "Hit the stick!" begged Carrick, Kite's caddie.

It did. And then it vanished.

The air detonated. Kite rubbed his hands in a gesture of expectant relief, certain that he'd turned a potential bogey into a divine birdie. Almost simultaneously, ten holes ahead and on the north side of Stillwater Cove, Colin Montgomerie had finished at even par for the championship with a birdie on the eighteenth. "I holed about a four-footer, left to right, in a howling gale," Montgomerie recalled. Jack Nicklaus, who missed the cut, famously approached the Scotsman and extended his hand. "Congratulations on winning your first U.S. Open championship," Nicklaus told him. The leaderboard then registered Kite's stunning birdie at the seventh.

"I had the entire golf course left," Kite said later, trying to describe his state of mind as he entered the most difficult stretch at Pebble, the eighth through the eighteenth. "It turned out to be a big shot, but there were so many big shots left to play."

There were. Not all of them were good. Kite made bogey after a blind pitch from the hazard under the cliff at the ninth. He erased the lost shot on the twelfth with a birdie putt from thirty-five feet. After a par on the next hole, Kite ripped his drive at the par-5 fourteenth and remembered his conversation the night before on the streets of Carmel. He unsheathed his 3-wood. He took his stance—and took dead aim at the green.

His ball finished in dense grass, but near enough to the hole to loft it up to the hole. Kite made birdie. He led Montgomerie by five and 1988 PGA Championship winner Jeff Sluman by four. He had four holes to play.

"We'll just sit here and watch," said Sluman, who birdied the eighteenth to finish at minus 1.

It was tense. It was complicated. It was not without doubt. Kite mismanaged the sixteenth and seventeenth, losing two shots to par after missing both greens in regulation. His lead shrunk to two. He inhaled deeply on the tee of the eighteenth, the invigorating par-5 that hugs the coastline, and aimed away from the frothy bay.

Francis McComas, the painter from Tasmania, called the Monterey Peninsula "the greatest meeting of land and sea in the world." He might indeed have been describing the final hole at Pebble Beach—more than a quarter-mile of crosscut rye grass, exploding surf, rugged seawall, and, on that Sunday afternoon in June 1992, Tom Kite's vindication for 1989 at Oak Hill in the form of a sterling silver trophy.

Kite endeavored to ignore all but his ball. He executed the next five shots with the precision that Harvey had always admired in his calculating, inquisitive pupil. Kite drove safely, slightly beyond the iconic twin cypress trees in the crescent fairway. He placed his second shot in wedge range for his third. His birdie putt teased the hole.

Kite smiled widely as he won the ninety-second U.S. Open Championship with a short, sure putt for an even-par 72 — on a day when the average score was 77.3 — and a four-round aggregate score of 3-under-par 285, two shots clear of Sluman. Kite thrust his hands above his head. He looked for Christy, who met him on the green. They shared a long embrace, one of the most heartfelt the world of sports had ever seen. Back home in Austin, his old teacher sat in his living room, blocks from the country club, and blinked tears.

Harvey felt so happy for Kite. He remembered the crushing disappointments at Oak Hill, at St. Andrews in 1978, at the Masters in 1983 and '86. He thought about how hard Kite worked, how close he had come before, and how unfairly but gamely he had carried the reputation of a player who could win the good tournaments but not the great championships. He now had seen Ben and Tom win their majors.

"I feel very uplifted and proud," he told a reporter by telephone. "I always thought this day would come. I always thought Tom could do it."

"We watched every stroke," Helen said, adding, "Harvey's been longing for this to happen."

Kite sat for the post-round press conference with a rising sense of validation. He had always imagined this moment, what it would be like to answer questions about how he did it, not how he failed to. "How do you describe the emotions I'm going through right now?" he said. "I don't know. We're talking about dreams that have been around many, many years. And there are an awful lot of dreams left."

Hours later, as he drove to the airport, Kite spoke with John Maher, a columnist for the *Austin American-Statesman*. Kite told Maher he knew he had a chance to win that week. But he'd told no one, out of fear of looking foolish. Maher asked Kite about Sunday morning, when he felt the freshening wind. "I really relish those days when the wind blows," Kite told him. "I dream of days like those. Some of my best wins have come in bad weather. It all goes back to when I was a boy. Harvey Penick would make us practice on those kinds of days."

A wire-service reporter reached George Hannon, Harvey's successor at Texas and the man who coached Kite. "I don't cry very often," Hannon said, "but it was very emotional. He wanted the major so badly."

The Kites flew Sunday night to St. Louis, where Tom had committed to a corporate outing Monday at Bellerive Country Club. That morning Christy Kite borrowed a canvas bag from her sister, who lived in St. Louis, to protect the U.S. Open trophy on its journey to Austin. Before she left, Tom, who was going on to Westchester to play the Buick Classic, asked her to deliver the trophy to Harvey as soon as possible.

"Looking back, I don't know why we didn't wait," Christy Kite said. "But he said, 'Take this down to the club and give it to Harvey. Go put it in Harvey's lap.'"

Harvey, now eighty-seven, still spent about three hours a day at Austin Country Club.

Christy Kite found him there on the Tuesday morning after her husband won the national championship. He was parked in his golf cart in the shade of an oak near the sixteenth green, his favorite spot. Harvey seemed surprised by her sudden appearance.

She said nothing as she approached. She placed the enormous trophy in his lap, as Tom wanted her to do. Harvey beamed. His eyes blurred. He was holding the most important emblem of excellence in American golf.

"Tom said a big piece of this trophy belongs to you," Christy Kite told Harvey.

Harvey had no words. He thought about the fair-skinned boy who appeared at the club that morning many years earlier with his fancy bag and a burn to be the best. He thought about their hours on the range together. He remembered Kite's questions, but more than that he remembered his insatiable need for answers. He recalled the moment Kite left Austin for the PGA Tour. His mind returned to that

Sunday afternoon two days before as he watched his inquisitive pupil raise his arms in California on Father's Day.

Harvey wanted to say something to someone. To Kite. To Francis Ouimet. To Bobby Jones, Walter Hagen, John Bredemus, Horton Smith, or Jack Burke Sr. To Morris Williams Jr., Hogan, or Nelson. But no one was there.

So instead, he wept.

Chapter Fourteen

THE REMARKABLE SUMMER of '92 sustained Harvey with strength and purpose. The *Little Red Book* sold briskly. Letters arrived in stacks. When Harvey felt well enough to go to the club, members brought their friends to his cart so they could shake the hand of a celebrity. Harvey signed hundreds of books. Shrake offered to procure a stamp molded with his signature, but Harvey refused. He wanted to do it the right way.

A month after Kite's triumph at Pebble Beach, Crenshaw won the Western Open, giving him his sixteenth PGA Tour title and Harvey another trophy to admire. Harvey watched every shot on his television near the club. "He's crippled, and he can't hear, but his mind is mighty brilliant," Helen Penick told a reporter from Dallas. Then Harvey got on the phone. "You can't believe how I feel about those boys," he said of Kite and Crenshaw. "I don't have the words."

A few weeks later, Harvey opened a letter from Esther Newberg, Shrake's agent at International Creative Management. The publisher intended to print 50,000 additional books. Harvey could barely believe what he was hearing.

The September 21 issue of *People* magazine featured a cover photograph of Princess Grace, with a posthumous photo essay inside. The magazine that week also included stories on a retreat in New Jersey for

HIV-positive families, a controversial veterinarian in Texas who bred primates for research, retiring Miss America chaperone Ellie Ross, Harry Truman, Garry Shandling, celebrity TV weatherman Bryan Norcross, fired and disgraced State Department analyst Felix Bloch, the First Cat "Socks," and Superman. And there, on page 140, was a half-page picture of Harvey in a bucket hat and a seven-paragraph celebration of the *Little Red Book*. "Lore of the Links," the magazine called it. Harvey was quoted: "What it says about playing golf has stood the test of time." What being in *People* said about Harvey was even more meaningful. He was a crossover talent: a folksy, celebrity golf teacher with a transcendent appeal. Harvey Penick, the grown-up caddie, was a worldwide maker of news and object of fascination.

James Michener, the Pulitzer Prize–winning novelist then living in Austin, called Shrake one evening and asked him to arrange a visit with Harvey. Shrake dialed the Penick house, and Helen answered. Shrake told her to tell Harvey that the author of more than forty books, including one that had won the biggest prize in fiction in 1948, wanted to meet Harvey in the morning at the country club.

Helen cupped the receiver and told Harvey of the plans.

"James Michener, the writer?" Shrake heard Harvey's voice inquire through the muffled telephone.

"Yes, Harvey," Helen Penick replied. "He doesn't want a golf lesson. He just wants to meet you."

"But he's a famous man. Why, he's a very famous writer."

"Don't you want to meet him?"

"Well, sure, I'd like to meet him, but I don't know what I would have to talk about with a famous man like James Michener."

The two authors met the next morning at 11:30. They sat in Harvey's golf cart and talked about writing and books. Harvey cherished that visit, as he did the time Ernie Banks, the ebullient former Hall of Fame baseball player for the Chicago Cubs, traveled to the country club for a golf lesson. A representative for Michael Jordan, the basketball player, sent word of Jordan's interest in taking a lesson with Harvey. Letters of similar interest arrived from all over the world. Everyone wanted his or her moment with Harvey Penick. Everyone wanted a swatch of his good and common sense.

Those close to him wondered how the attention would affect the modest old gentleman from Austin. They were thrilled for him, but they also were concerned about the hot glare of fame and attendant stress on his health. Yet Harvey responded with youthful aplomb. All the attention was like the medicine he needed.

"The book has given Harvey new life," Helen Penick said. "He used to sit in his chair and sleep because he couldn't hear. Now he signs books. Billy Graham sent Harvey a wonderful letter of thanks after he received a copy. He quoted scripture from the Bible about an old man who helped others by sharing his knowledge. This year has enriched our lives."

On October 4, the *Little Red Book* became the number-one advice book on the *New York Times* best-seller list. It had been on the list for twelve weeks. John Garrity, a journalist with *Sports Illustrated,* interviewed Harvey about the sensation his first book had become. "You just wouldn't believe that a grown caddie could get so much out of life," Harvey marveled to him.

Shrake spent a lot of time with Harvey as the first north winds of fall blew through Central Texas. They sat in Harvey's living room, or sometimes on the deck, as Shrake dealt copies of the *Little Red Book* for Harvey to sign.

On bad days, it took as long as ten minutes for Harvey to address just one book. Shrake noticed that Harvey often included the inscription, "To my pupil and friend." Shrake asked him why he wrote those words.

"If they read my book, they're my pupil," Harvey replied. "And if they play golf, they're my friend."

Shrake pondered that idea for weeks. It made perfect sense, of course. It spoke to the core of Harvey Penick—of his earliest ideas about golf at the old Austin Country Club, of his earnest concern for the welfare of the game and the people who played it, of his devotion.

Late that year Shrake was on the telephone with Jeff Neuman, their Simon & Schuster editor. Shrake mentioned his conversation with Harvey.

"There," Neuman said, "is the title for our sequel."

Harvey and Shrake signed their new contract on January 26, 1993. It included a royalty schedule identical to the one for the first book: 10 percent on the first 5,000 books, 12 percent on the second 5,000, and 15 percent on the 10,001th copy and beyond. The advance: a stunning $500,000. Harvey Penick, an eighty-eight-year-old golf teacher who rarely charged more than $20 for a lesson, had just signed his name for a half-million dollars.

Simon & Schuster announced the new book a month later. The *Little Red Book* had spent thirty-two weeks on the *New York Times* bestseller list, twelve of them at the top. There were 450,000 copies in circulation, making it "the best selling hardcover sports book of all time," read a news release from Simon & Schuster. It had passed *Season on the Brink* by John Feinstein, *Men at Work* by George Will, and *Bo Knows Bo* by Bo Jackson and Dick Schaap. The new book, jacketed in green, would "pick up where THE LITTLE RED BOOK left off, with the same mix of simple wisdom, sound golfing instruction, and good common sense that has made THE LITTLE RED BOOK such a phenomenal success," the publisher trumpeted.

That book, meanwhile, was being printed in languages Harvey had never heard, in nations he had never seen. It had been serialized in the United Kingdom in the *Sunday Telegraph* and *Golf Weekly*. It had readers in Australia, Italy, Japan, Poland, and even Thailand.

The old caddie was a famous man wherever golf was played, which was everywhere.

Shrake and Harvey convened early in the winter of '93, conducting their recorded conversations about golf and life in the sunlight strobing through the sliding-glass doors of Harvey's living room. They talked about the success of the first book, and how the second book could do just as well. "I'm glad to see it making that money," Harvey told Shrake. "And I'm so proud that golf has made such strides. It's unbelievable. I get letters every day from people."

"That's wonderful," Shrake said.

"I tell you," Harvey said. "The best part of golf is the association of golf."

Golf Digest, which had published the early excerpt from the first book in May 1992, was planning to devote its December 1993 issue to the second book. But Harvey was a brand now, the modest and charming teacher who provided a counterbalance to what had become for other teachers — but didn't need to be — the complicated business of teaching the golf swing. To satisfy the raging interest of its market, the magazine wanted to harness Harvey's energy in its pages again.

The editor of *Golf Digest* offered Harvey an appointment for 1994 as a member of its "professional advisory staff," with his name appearing on the masthead. Harvey would write ten one-page instruction pieces of five hundred words each, with ideas approved in advance, and be paid $2,000 for each article. *Golf Digest* would retain world periodical rights; Harvey would agree to write for no other publication. Jerry Tarde, the editor, hoped to announce the agreement to readers in the issue excerpting the green book.

The summer before, Golfsmith International, an Austin retail company, founded the Harvey Penick Golf Academy and began planning a series of instructional sessions based on the *Little Red Book.* The company, which did most of its club-component business through catalogs, hired Bryan Gathright, a Texan living in Colorado, to create the academy at its new forty-acre corporate headquarters and practice range along Interstate 35 north of downtown.

Carl Paul and his wife Barbara had founded Golfsmith in 1967. They operated their component business from their home in New Jersey until Carl's brother Frank joined the growing company. Golfsmith moved to Austin in the early 1970s, and in 1975 the brothers opened their first store. When the company attached Harvey's name to its new academy venture, Golfsmith and its four hundred employees were selling $80 million worth of golf equipment a year. The company also conscripted Harvey to design a line of clubs.

Gathright left a job as the director of a junior golf tournament in Aspen to join the venture. He was happy to go back in Texas. He'd grown up in Teague, a small town east of Waco, and been childhood friends with Dale Morgan, a highly regarded golf professional from nearby Fairfield who supervised the golf division of a private club in Austin. He'd been captivated by Harvey's book. Gathright moved to Austin in January 1993, met Harvey, and concluded that he had just encountered a man so singularly committed to his craft that "I didn't know if he chose golf or golf chose him." The two of them convened at least weekly for the next seven months. Gathright wanted to make sure the Harvey Penick Golf Academy taught golf the way Harvey taught golf.

Gathright supplied his academy instructors with a teaching manual derived from the lessons in Harvey's books. The manual included quotations from Harvey:

The day I stop learning is the day I will quit teaching.

It's the simple things that last.

The prettiest swing in the world won't do any good unless you can hit a spot.

A good putter is a match for anyone. A bad putter is a match for no one.

The woods are full of long hitters.

The teacher who makes the fewest mistakes is the best teacher.

The thirty-one-page manual cited the books, including page numbers. It became the bible for the Harvey Penick Golf Academy.

The academy opened on July 15, 1993. Participants paid $598 for a hotel room, transportation, three days of instruction with professionals trained by Gathright, and their own copies of the *Little Red Book,* which they were expected to memorize. At its peak, the academy employed twenty-two instructors and hummed at full capacity — twenty to thirty participants from the United States and beyond — for twenty-six days a month.

The agreement between Golfsmith and Harvey stipulated no personal appearances. Harvey was in the building one day, examining the golf clubs the company made with his name on them, when someone informed him that an academy session was under way outside.

"Well," Harvey said, "can I go and say hello to my students?"

Other emerging obligations pulled at Harvey, who was delighted to meet them. He spent most of his days in a wheelchair, his old body folded into place like a crumpled straw, but his mind and heart seemed as full of life as they were when he was playing the Texas Open in the 1920s.

A production company from Dallas pitched the idea of a video to complement the lessons in the *Little Red Book.* For the occasion, Harvey selected a dark tartan cardigan with dark brown trousers and a navy ivy cap stitched with the Austin Country Club crest. At the end of the day of filming, the crew had finished its work, but fortunately did not pack up the cameras before catching the following scene:

Kite, Crenshaw, and Harvey remained on the range. An upstart wind brushed the tops of the live oaks. No one really cared to leave.

Kite sat on the base of the Hogan golf staff bag lying on the turf. Crenshaw leaned against the fender of cart number 59 with Harvey folded inside, alarmingly thin, holding the handle of the weed cutter in his sinewy hands, his long underwear visible under the cuffs of his brown trousers. They talked about golf swings and Tommy Armour III. Harvey explained again, because it mattered a lot to him, how a teacher must listen. He said he learned much from his former players, who came to the University of Texas and shared their experiences with their early teachers, the head professionals in Midland and Houston and Waco and Dallas. Harvey, Crenshaw, and Kite talked about the importance of simplicity in the golf swing and the teaching of it. They invoked dead aim.

Crenshaw offhandedly mentioned to Harvey an ache in his right thumb. That turned the conversation toward the grip, which brightened Harvey's eyes like flares. Harvey suddenly had an idea. He asked Crenshaw to take a club and assume his stance, someplace where the teacher could get a good view of his old friend. Then he asked Crenshaw to take a few swings.

"Let me know what the balls do," Harvey told Kite.

Crenshaw swung.

"Where was that ball?"

Crenshaw swung again.

"Was that good or bad or medium, Ben?"

Crenshaw scraped another ball between his feet. He fired.

Harvey asked Crenshaw to adjust his hands on the club. They discussed the boys from West Texas who came to Harvey to play at Texas, right-to-left slingers, like Billy Munn from Midland, whose four-knuckle grips propelled shots that carved the wind like skinner blades.

Another one, Harvey told Crenshaw.

"Which way did it fall?"

"Perfect shot," Kite said.

"That's what it sounded like," Harvey said. He examined the marks in the grass Crenshaw had made with the iron, like the dollar bills Walter Benson Jr. used to leave at Lions.

"I study the divots," Harvey said.

Kite hit some shots too. But it was getting late. The air began to cool, and the tartan cardigan Harvey wore was barely keeping him warm enough. They had been there an extra hour, remembering players, remembering tournaments and putts that had won or lost them, laughing some, meddling with grips, watching swings, decorating the range with divots.

It was Lions Municipal Golf Course before urethane-covered golf balls and titanium drivers and 7,500-yard golf courses.

It was the 1960s again at the Perry Maxwell course on Riverside.

It was persimmon and balata and teaching golf through stories.

It was the 1970s, when Kite and Crenshaw were winning national championships for Texas.

It was the 1980s, when the players returned home between PGA Tour starts.

It was just like it used to be. Except it wasn't. And Harvey had broken his rule, the one he had gently but firmly enforced for thirty years.

He'd granted Kite and Crenshaw a shared lesson.

With the publication of the green book, interest in Harvey burst beyond the golf magazines and sports pages. He was the vintage rags-to-riches trope: a former hardscrabble caddie, now a famous celebrity. He was the classic late-bloomer story: high school graduate turned best-selling author at the age of eighty-seven. He was the mystic-poet: conduit of wisdom, with no regard for attention, doing what he did for the love of it. He also was the anti-Texan, a slayer of stereotypes: meek, modest, grateful, graceful, amused by the fuss over his simple books. Harvey represented a wholesome theme suited for any medium. Especially TV.

Day One, an ABC newsmagazine on the air from 1993 to 1995, sent correspondent Michel McQueen to meet Harvey at the country club. The advance team arranged interviews with Kite, Crenshaw, Shrake, Sandra Palmer, and Tinsley Penick. A former reporter for the *Washington Post* and White House correspondent for the *Wall Street Journal,* McQueen served as a participant-reporter. The story was called "The Old Pro."

Cameras filmed Harvey as he sat in his cart with an afghan over his lap, thumbing through the Scribbletex and wishing players good fortune in their rounds. An unidentified man wandered over and asked Harvey, awkwardly and self-consciously, for strokes on the back nine. Harvey misunderstood the question. Another unidentified man described for the camera the power of Harvey's optimistic belief that he could help anyone play better golf if they committed to it. "Harvey

Penick's number-one lesson," McQueen intoned. "Love of the game comes first."

McQueen repeated the now-familiar lore preceding the publication of the books: that Harvey had intended to save his notebook for his son, that not even his most loyal pupils had seen it. "But failing health changed his mind," McQueen said gravely.

Shrake: "I had a chilling feeling that there was something really special there, that I had been called over here to perform some kind of a duty. And the duty was, I think, to preserve Harvey Penick's words and teachings, for everybody, forever."

Tinsley Penick: "Three years ago he was in the hospital. He had a fractured spine, many other ailments. He was depressed, disorientated. I'd go by to see him every day, as would other people, thinking this is the last time I'm going to see this man. And to go from that point to where he is now is unexplainable. It's as much of a miracle as anything I've experienced."

Crenshaw: "The book is filled with so many other things, other than golf. It's a way to live. It's a very nice approach to life. Harvey just leads by example."

McQueen: "What is almost as amazing about Harvey Penick is that the wisdom he has bestowed on all those weekend duffers is the same advice he has given to some of the greatest players on the professional circuit today."

Palmer: "I kind of think he's a saint."

McQueen and *Day One* further unspooled the hagiography through an anecdote Kite shared on the broadcast. Kite revealed that Harvey had agreed to give lessons to a paroled felon who had confessed to his crime and apologized. That admission was all Harvey needed to hear. But certain officials at Austin Country Club objected, Kite said. "The board of directors threw a tizzy."

Harvey insisted that his new pupil deserved the grace offered by golf.

"The board of directors relented," Kite said.

McQueen, a beginner at golf, procured an iron and met Harvey on the range for a made-for-TV lesson. Her first effort plinked the metal wheel of his electric cart. "Harvey, I almost hit you!" McQueen said, aghast. Her next ball hopped a few feet away. She looked horrified.

"Get your hands pointed at your left leg," Harvey said.

McQueen adjusted.

"A little more."

McQueen complied.

The broadcast neglected to report how many takes it required, but McQueen eventually produced an actual golf shot. The ball leaped up and away.

"Look at that!" Harvey exalted.

He clapped feebly. He was thrilled. Harvey was getting better at these interviews, more comfortable as a public figure whose growing reach extended beyond Austin, beyond even golf. He knew what journalists wanted now, and he could oblige. But he clearly felt most at ease when he helped McQueen experience her first real golf shot, which seemed spontaneous and improvised and organic, unlike the scripted questions of a formal one-on-one. Harvey told McQueen that he hoped she would take up the game. She smiled tenderly.

"What is life if you don't have friends?" he asked her.

"Now," he said, nodding at McQueen, "make it two times in a row."

Texas Monthly staff writer Gary Cartwright, who had known Shrake since their boom years at newspapers in Dallas and Fort Worth, pitched a profile of Harvey and his rise from the caddie yard. The magazine commissioned noted Austin photographer Michael O'Brien to make the accompanying portraits. O'Brien scouted locations one autumn day at the country club. He found two settings he liked: the cart barn and, appropriately, the practice range. He arranged to meet Harvey and Shrake on an October afternoon in 1993 for the picture.

Harvey arrived in an unpretentious navy sweater from Ballybunion Golf Club in Ireland over a knotted red tie. He wore one of his smart ivy caps in gray tweed, his best brown shoes, and an expression that suggested to O'Brien sincere flattery. He offered O'Brien his hand.

"He said he couldn't imagine any magazine paying this much attention to him," the photographer said. With his back pain worsening by the week, Harvey could stand for just a few minutes at a time. O'Brien arranged him and Shrake on a wooden bench, with the range behind them, illuminated by a strobe. He scattered a garden of red-striped golf balls at their feet.

O'Brien snapped seventy-five frames that afternoon with a Hasselblad camera and eighty-millimeter Zeiss lens. He later selected an image that struck him as emblematic of the friendship between the two men. Harvey sits nobly with his hands in his lap, his lips pursed, his head high, his diminutive frame shrinking into the slats of the bench. Shrake, sturdy and tall, leans forward slightly in a cardinal red sweater. Neither man smiles. They project honor and dignity. "The circumstances of life have brought them together," O'Brien said. The composition endures as a study in quiet pride.

Many years later, the photograph became part of the permanent collection at the National Portrait Gallery in Washington, DC. The golf teacher and his unlikely collaborator would reside forever and together with presidents, philosophers, statesmen, authors, artists, musicians, inventors, composers, poets, civil rights activists, four-star generals, and the founding fathers of the United States.

In December, subscribers to *Golf Digest* magazine received an edition whose cover was bathed in green. A diffuse, watercolor portrait of Harvey, wearing a bucket hat and a tie under his ACC sweater, occupied half of the page. "Exclusive: Harvey Penick's NEW Little Green Book," it announced in bold white letters. The ten-page feature, written by Harvey as a member of the magazine's professional advisory staff, supplied readers with a casserole of new observations, stylistically identical to those in the first book. The Harvey Penick brand continued to grow.

Jeff Neuman traveled to Austin from New York in the spring of 1994. He, Harvey, and Shrake discussed a possible third book, maybe even a fourth.

The first and second books had been written for anyone who played

golf. The idea for the third was that Harvey had much to offer two particular audiences: women and older players.

Shrake had been thinking about the idea for some time. After Neuman left, he composed a one-page letter to his agent, which he sent
overnight on May 16, 1994. In it, he proposed the title *Harvey Penick's
Little Blue Book: Learnings and Teachings for Women, Seasoned Citizens . . . and Other Lovers of the Game.*

Shrake clearly was calculating the project from a marketing angle as
much as from a writing angle. "I sense from hanging out around golfers of all sorts that we need to make a little space between the second
and third Harvey," he wrote to Esther Newberg. "The Green book and
the Red book should keep feeding off each other. I don't see how a person can read one and not eventually read the other. Harvey Penick has
many devoted readers, but a Blue Book this Christmas would be too
much, too soon, I believe."

Shrake and Harvey agreed to write two more books of 50,000 to
60,000 words each. The third book would be written for women. The
fourth and final book would be for seniors. Simon & Schuster committed to an astounding advance of $2 million, payable in six install-
ments of $333,333 each from signing on June 23 through publication.
The manuscripts were scheduled for delivery in December 1994 and
August 1995.

The two collaborators began planning their visits again.

"At the age of ninety he is as busy as he has ever been in his life,"
Shrake wrote to his agent in May 1994. "Despite his crippling pain, he
loves to teach and feel needed. He is gaining strength, and once again
you can hear his voice clearly on the practice range."

Shrake interviewed others that fall as well. He spoke in September to
Mary Lena Faulk, Betty Jameson, Sandra Palmer, and Mickey Wright,
then hurriedly wove together the stories due in December to Simon &
Schuster. Then it would be time to start on the fourth and final project.

Shrake told Wright on September 16 that the events of the last three years had given Harvey something close to a new identity. "What a great feeling it is to feel wanted," Shrake said. "He had sort of been, more or less, discarded by the world for so long. He goes out now to Golfsmith and gives lectures once a week and he tells me he feels like Bob Hope. They laugh at every word he says."

"Isn't that wonderful," Wright said. "It couldn't happen to a nicer man."

Rick Rogers, a lawyer who had taken golf lessons from Harvey since the 1960s, gave the *Little Red Book* to Mark Allen Doty, the pastor of the First United Methodist Church in Corpus Christi, Texas, where Rogers lived. Doty used the book in one of his sermons. Facing his congregation one Sunday morning, he admitted that he had never played golf, that the appeal of the game eluded him. But Harvey and his message, he said, gave him a new way to think about something that did matter to him: the beatitudes in the Gospel of Matthew.

"The power of Harvey Penick's *Little Red Book* is that it tells us not only how to play the game of golf successfully, but it also reveals something about the nature of the man who is doing the advising," Doty said that morning in church. "The same holds true with respect to the Sermon on the Mount. It not only tells Christians how to live but emphasizes the importance of Jesus."

Doty called Harvey a "master teacher." He noted that his "drawing power is the same as all great teachers — for they really teach themselves."

By the end of the year, the *Little Red Book* had sold 800,000 copies.

The green book, *And If You Play Golf, You Are My Friend,* sold 400,000 in its first month in stores.

Harvey continued to make regular appearances at his Golfsmith academy. But his worsening health curtailed his personal lessons, which provided the close-quarters interactions he considered most rewarding.

Harvey's last authentic lesson, with a bag of balls on the green grass of a practice range, where he could divine meaning from the depth and direction of a divot — the kind he believed in most — took place a year before he died.

Billy Munn, who played for Harvey at Texas in the mid-1960s, was on the fifth hole at Midland Country Club in April 1994 with two friends. One of them was George Tucker, who had won a national championship under Harvey's successor, George Hannon, at Texas. The other was Al Boudreaux, a five-handicapper who could play like a fifteen- and who, on that day in April, executed a shot so poorly that he declared to Munn and Tucker that he was abandoning the game forever. Munn called Harvey later that day.

His old coach told Munn to bring his friend to Austin. Munn, Tucker, and a reluctant Boudreaux boarded a flight the next morning. They arrived to sun and a seasonal springtime breeze from the southeast. They rented a car and drove to Harvey's home, expecting nothing more than an examination of Boudreaux's grip and perhaps a cursory evaluation of his posture. When they arrived, however, Harvey, now eighty-nine years old and ailing, was wearing his golf hat. "Let's go to the course," he told his visitors from Midland.

Munn and Tucker lifted Harvey from his chair. "We literally carried him and put him on the golf cart," Tucker recalled. They whirred over to Austin Country Club and helped Harvey to the practice range, where he watched Tucker swing a fairway wood and casually suggested that he adjust the position of his head. Then he motioned for Boudreaux.

Harvey and Boudreaux spent an hour together. They worked on alignment and aim. Munn and Tucker kept waiting for Harvey to end the lesson, but the old teacher seemed to want it to last as long as it could. "He couldn't see," Munn said. "But he could hear. He could hear those shots. He didn't have to see them." Occasionally, Harvey asked Munn or Tucker where a particular shot flew. *Where'd that one go? How about that one?* Soon, Harvey's nurse appeared. She informed him that he needed to break for lunch. Harvey declined. "This is doing more nourishment for my soul than food ever would," Harvey told her. "I'm going to watch some more."

And he did.

Nineteen years later, Boudreaux, Munn, and Tucker sat around a table, dipping tortilla chips in tomato salsa at a Tex-Mex restaurant in Midland, where they still lived and played golf at Midland Country Club. They reminisced about their visit with Harvey with laughter and silent nods. They remembered how, in their next round together after the lesson, Tucker shot a 4-under-par 32 on the front side. "I was the opponent," Munn said. Boudreaux played the best golf of his life for the next six months. He did not abandon the game.

Harvey did not abandon him that morning in Austin. "He was seventy-five and healthy that day," Boudreaux said. "I know right here" — Boudreaux tapped his chest — "that that day was as good for him as it was for me."

Chapter Fifteen

HARVEY AND SHRAKE continued their visits for the third and fourth books through the summer of 1994, but Shrake could tell that his friend was struggling. Harvey turned ninety in October. Simon & Schuster sent a magnum bottle of champagne as a gift. No one opened it. Harvey wanted badly to infuse the next two books with the same wisdom and humor that had so charmed his readers since 1992. But he often found it hard to simply rise from his bed in the morning.

He rarely left his home on Fawn Creek Path. Excursions, such as they were, required immense coordination between his full-time nurse, whomever Harvey was planning to visit, and someone to drive him there. In one of his last appearances in public, Harvey arrived at his Golfsmith academy on an October afternoon to robust applause from the gathering of thirty men and women in golf shirts of 1990s-vintage primary colors and bold stripes. He doffed his cap as his nurse rolled his wheelchair past a bag of golf clubs bearing his name to the front of the Penick Room on the ground floor of the company head-quarters in North Austin. On the yellow walls hung through-the-years portraits of Harvey and his famous players. A bronze bust of Harvey sat in the corner on a marble column. Harvey paid no attention to these relics.

He sat with his head cocked slightly to the left, swallowing often to clear his throat. He wore a purple plaid shirt, loose and bunched at the cuffs. It was buttoned to the top. A navy vest hung on his small, bony shoulders, like a tent draped mid-assembly on its poles, and liver spots speckled his face. He listened now through hearing aids secured under wings of white, wispy hair. Harvey's infirmities seemed to diminish a bit when he came to his golf schools to tell the stories from his books, both to people who had read them and to people who would hear them for the first time.

Harvey was under his physician's directions to not be away from home for more than two hours. He often violated that order when he went to his schools, which gave him the rare opportunity to go outside, to be in the presence of golf. "He tried to come to every school that we had," recalled Jim Hopkins, one of the veteran instructors at the academy and the proprietor of the namesake school after it left the property outside Golfsmith. Harvey insisted, even in failing health, on keeping appointments.

The applause settled that October day. Harvey held his hat in his fragile lap and peered through gold wire-framed glasses.

"If you play golf, you're my friend," he managed.

Crenshaw announced cheerily that Harvey had just turned ninety. "I went to visit him on his birthday the other day," Crenshaw said. "The first thing I said to him was, 'Harvey, congratulations. You broke ninety.'" Crenshaw laughed. Harvey laughed. Everyone laughed. The room carried a sense of moment: of Harvey's birthday, of the success of the books, of the confluence of knowledge and the thirst for it, of the connection between hickory-shafted golf on sand greens and the majesty of the game at that moment in 1994.

"I tell you, we ran a good time out there," Harvey said, reflecting on a memory his mind had retrieved. He looked at Crenshaw, who waited for Harvey to finish the thought. "I get goose pimples out there when they hit a good shot," his teacher said. "That's the truth."

Crenshaw had just concluded his twenty-first season on the PGA Tour. He had won his eighteenth tournament, the Freeport-McMoRan

Classic in New Orleans, in April. He later tied for eighteenth place in the Masters and ninth in the PGA Championship, and he had just finished with a final-round 65 in the Texas Open, where he shared eighth. Crenshaw had made twenty cuts, sixteen of them in a row. Now he was forty-two. And the baffling revolution of his brilliance, forever orbiting its own mystifying sun, appeared to restore itself that autumn of '94 to a position of hopeful light.

What, Crenshaw had to wonder, might the spring of 1995 hold?

At Golfsmith that day, Crenshaw and Harvey volleyed stories for more than thirty minutes. Harvey recited his chronicled experiences with Titanic Thompson, Herman Keiser, and Jimmy Demaret. The participants leaned in to better hear Harvey's soupy drawl. "Have we talked about Joe Kirkwood?" Harvey queried the room.

Kirkwood, an Australian trick-shot specialist in the 1920s and '30s who toured the world with Walter Hagen and played that exhibition match in 1924 with Harvey at the old Austin Country Club, could stack three golf balls and strike only the middle ball with his club. He could drive a golf ball from a tee in the mouth of a woman lying between his feet. He could hit a ball from the face of a watch without scratching the crystal. Harvey especially liked it when Kirkwood plopped a sand-bunker shot backwards like a boomerang, over his head and onto the green.

"Joe Kirkwood was the best trick-shot artist I ever saw," Harvey wrote in his first book — in the same chapter where he mentioned that he used to entertain baseball fans between doubleheader games at the old park in Austin.

When I walked out to home plate, the crowd took one look at me in my plus-fours knickers and plaid socks and started booing. They quieted down some when I started hitting curves to the right and to the left. Then I placed one ball on top of another with a bit of putty. I hit the bottom ball 125 yards with a seven-iron, and the top ball popped into the air so I could catch it in my hand. Almost any good player can do this trick, but the people in the stands didn't know that.

Another story: "I had a rubber hose, the kind you put air in your car tires with. It had a grip on one end and a three-wood head on the other. I hit a few shots with that rubber hose, and people started cheering."

Harvey missed Joe Kirkwood. He once told him, "You're the only man who ever held a club right to suit me." Harvey missed a lot of the men from that era, charismatic figures in cashmere cardigans and wool trousers, the personification of golf when golf was still a novelty in Texas. He missed the stage-show dimension of golf, the feats of co-ordination and concentration that no one really tried anymore, not with so much money at stake in tournament golf.

Harvey regretted that. Now golf was all about swing planes and shoulder positions and coil and a draftsman's preoccupation with utility and angles. "Hitting trick shots is a dying art," Harvey wrote in his book. Resignation seeped from his words.

"[Kirkwood] turned out to be a good friend," Harvey said that afternoon at Golfsmith. "You can't believe what he could do with that golf ball."

Sensing that Harvey was already beginning to tire, Crenshaw solicited questions to draw the gathering to a close. A man rose and asked Harvey how to calm the anxiety of playing the first shot of a round. Harvey asked someone nearby to repeat the question into the hearing aid in his left ear. He steeled himself, then straightened slightly in his wheelchair. "That man hasn't read my books," Harvey said with neither accusation nor blame. He seemed emboldened by the query. "Take dead aim and hit that golf ball," he said. "Forget everything else there is. Take ten seconds, five seconds, before you hit that ball. Then take dead aim at that golf ball and hit it."

The answer burdened the air. The man who asked the question appeared to wait for more, but Harvey had nothing more to contribute. What more was there? Even now, when Harvey was ninety years old and would be dead in six months, he resisted the opportunity to complicate the truth when the truth was as obvious as three short words: take dead aim.

The man sat down.

"Any questions? I've probably used up all of my time," Harvey said.

Another participant raised his hand. "You and Harvey obviously have such a special relationship," the man said to Crenshaw. "What do you think made him such a great teacher of golf?"

"I'll say this," Crenshaw replied. "I've seen a lot of teaching and I've read a lot about teaching. He has spent a lifetime learning what, and how, to say to a lot of people. He does not want the game to be complex. There's so much knowledge in that head there. He's seen so many shots. But the key thing is his heart."

Harvey smiled weakly.

The two of them — the teacher and the pupil — shared a few light anecdotes, trying to illuminate in some new way what had happened between them since that day at Austin Country Club when Charlie Crenshaw brought his six-year-old son to meet Harvey and Harvey took the Crenshaw boy outside for his introduction to golf.

"He teaches like an old Scot," Crenshaw continued, "the Scottish immigrant pro who came over at the turn of the century. They didn't say very much. They taught the grip, and they taught the stance. They didn't say many things. But what they said was meaningful."

Crenshaw glanced at Harvey. "I've enjoyed it," Harvey said.

Sports Illustrated observed Harvey's birthday that year with a short article in the October 31 issue. Tim Rosaforte, who later became an on-air talent at the Golf Channel, told his readers: "Helen [Penick[realized that a second career, as an author, had given her ailing husband a reason to live." Many of Harvey's friends and family members had also noticed that the books had given Harvey purpose and an identity. They gave him a reason to rise in the morning despite his aching back, his failing eyesight, and his muffled hearing. Harvey never wanted to be a celebrity. He never thought it possible. But then he *was* one, and he was as happy as he had been in a very long time.

"There's not one person who saw my dad five years ago who thought he'd be around now," said Tinsley Penick, who remained the head professional at the club. "Every spring I'd say, 'God, this old man's seen another spring.' You think in the winter that he'll never make it, and he just keeps going."

Harvey loved being the elderly emerging author of books that people loved and having the opportunity to answer letters and to sign his name on the frontispiece of a handsome book bearing his name. Simply knowing that people from far away found wisdom and joy in the words he had kept to himself for so long delighted him. The popularity of the books validated his decision that morning under the oaks at Austin Country Club.

"I could never have imagined anything like this," Harvey said. "I was a C student in school. It was hard for me to read a page. But they've been sold all over — in every country."

The books held more curative power than any bottle of medicine on Harvey's nightstand. But there was only so much he could will himself to do. Harvey lingered through the holidays and into the early weekends of the 1995 season on the PGA Tour, which he viewed as a more hopeful sign of spring than even the first winds from the south and the first blooms of the bluebonnets on the quiet roads in the hills. He tried to concentrate on his new books. He tried to tell himself that people were counting on him. And then he got sick.

Harvey contracted pneumonia in March 1995. He and Shrake continued to work on the next book, but Harvey seemed to accept that he might not live to sign a copy.

Harvey provided Shrake with three shoeboxes of papers and asked him to rummage through the garage to see what else might be there. The two collaborators read letters from older players who'd written to Harvey after they'd read the red and green books.

"Harvey's purpose in making his final book was to entertain and enlighten seasoned players," Shrake wrote, "reveal to them his beliefs, and encourage them to continue their romance with the most mysterious, most cerebral, most frustrating and supremely satisfying of all games that can be played by one person alone." Harvey had to read the letters with a magnifying glass.

He wrote his last note on March 3. That night, a Friday, Harvey's lungs became so congested that he had difficulty breathing, and an ambulance was summoned to take him to St. David's Hospital. He spent a week there. Then he went home and spent his final days of relative mobility in his wheelchair, parked on the deck outside, where he read his mail with his magnifying glass and signed books stacked nearby.

Three weeks before he died, Harvey asked to be placed in his bed.

He weighed eighty-four pounds. One morning Shrake walked into his bedroom and found Harvey struggling to write in his notebook. The old teacher shook his head. "I can't do it anymore," he told Shrake, who recalled the story in his foreword to the fourth book. Shrake looked at the notebook that morning on Fawn Creek Path to see what Harvey had written. The page was nothing but scribbles and circles and scrawls, like graffiti. "I know what I'm trying to say," Harvey told Shrake, "but this pen won't say it."

Shrake knew his friend and book partner was beginning to die.

Harvey no longer left his bed at all. He barely ate. He often was lucid enough to hear about the latest marketing deal related to the books, the most recent royalty payments from the publisher, or the status of other projects, such as the new *Little Red Golf Letter,* a monthly newsletter published by Belvoir Publications in Greenwich, Connecticut. He could page through the latest Golfsmith catalog, for instance, and see the new clubs that Tom Wishon, the company's club designer, had created with Harvey in mind. The cover of the newest catalog included an image of Harvey and the caption "A Lifetime in the Making."

Inside were nineteen pages of pictures and specifications for the 1995 line of clubs, shafts, grips, and ferrules. There was the Harvey Penick Master Cavity line of irons. The Harvey Penick Classic Player. The Harvey Penick Classic Lady. The Master metal wood and the Classic Player persimmon wood and the Weed Cutter—a nod to his favorite teaching tool—fairway wood. Harvey could only look at these pictures of golf equipment. His deteriorating body no longer permitted him to grip them, to feel their weight in his hands, to give them a good waggle or two. "Harvey is still hanging on," Shrake wrote on March 27 to his editor in New York. "But the Little Red Light is getting close."

Crenshaw had tied for forty-second place that month at the Nestlé Invitational. After missing the cut a week later at the Players Championship, he flew home before the Freeport-McMoRan, the tournament he'd won the year before in New Orleans, and took his family — his wife Julie and his daughters Katherine and Claire — to Cisco's on East Sixth Street, his favorite Tex-Mex restaurant for Sunday brunch. There the Crenshaws met Scotty Sayers, his longtime friend from Austin High School and now his business partner and agent. Sayers came with his own daughters and wife. It was an ordinary gathering of old friends who had known each other since childhood. Nothing suggested the consequences of that Sunday in March.

The Crenshaws left the restaurant to go see Harvey. They stopped to pick up flowers on the way. When they arrived, they found Shrake in the living room with Helen. "You'd better hurry," Shrake told Crenshaw. Crenshaw walked to the bedroom. Julie and her daughters waited with Helen and Shrake.

"A few minutes later," Shrake said, "I was surprised to see Harvey roll over on one elbow and hear him loudly and distinctly say, 'Go get the putter,' to begin the last lesson with Ben."

Harvey had Ben fetch a hickory-shafted Gene Sarazen putter from the garage. Harvey asked to see Crenshaw's stroke. He reminded him to keep his hands ahead of the ball. He also told Crenshaw to keep his faith. "All you need to do is trust," Harvey said.

Crenshaw kissed Harvey before he left. He flew to New Orleans the next day.

He played with Davis Love III in the first two rounds of the Freeport-McMoRan. Love opened with rounds of 68-69, but Crenshaw shot 73-74 to miss the cut by four. "His game was all over the place," Love said. The little lesson with Harvey, with the Sarazen putter on the carpet of his bedroom, failed to save Crenshaw on the fast and sloping greens of English Turn Golf & Country Club. "Even his vaunted putting game was ill," Love wrote. "He was so frustrated with his flat stick that he started putting with an iron on the last three or four holes."

Love assumed Crenshaw was concerned about Harvey back in Austin. "Ben was distracted," Love concluded.

On Saturday afternoon, as Crenshaw packed for his week in Augusta, Love shot 66 in New Orleans. He needed to win to join Crenshaw at the Masters, a tournament he had played five times since his debut in 1988, once finishing, in 1992, as high as a tie for twenty-fifth.

Harvey spent the last week of his life sleeping fitfully, fighting for breath. But he insisted on signing more books. "He wanted to finish what he needed done," said his son, Tinsley.

He also wanted to see the first Sunday in April, when the country club had scheduled a midafternoon event to reveal a statue in his and Tom Kite's honor. His illness weakened him so gravely the night before, however, that his wife wondered if he would live through the night. "I can't die tonight," Harvey told Helen. "I want that ceremony tomorrow to be joyous, not mournful."

It was joyous indeed. More than five hundred people assembled on the lawn at Austin Country Club for the long-planned unveiling of a statue that had stood in shrouded sentry over the golf course since the middle of March. Club member Don Davis, a lawyer and accomplished sculptor, had arranged with one of the club's golf professionals, Jackson Bradley, to build a bronze casting in honor of Harvey and Kite, who had demurred equally. "Mr. Penick said, 'No, I don't deserve to have anything done,'" Davis said that spring. "Tom said, 'No, I don't deserve to be mentioned in the same breath as Mr. Penick.'"

Both Harvey and Kite had nonetheless agreed to meet with Davis, who started his project by collecting more than one hundred photographs of his subjects. The artist interviewed Harvey and Kite, took measurements of their dimensions: height, waist, inseam, outseam, the widths of their shoulders, the lengths of their arms, the shape of their hands, the texture and thickness of their hair. He mapped their faces with a caliper. Harvey surely respected the precision that Davis brought to his tribute to the man who had contributed so much to golf in Austin and in Texas.

Davis molded Harvey's and Kite's heads at his studio in Aspen,

Colorado, and made their bodies in Austin. He cast the sculpture at Deep in the Heart Foundry in Bastrop, out in the lost pines of Central Texas east of the capital. In October, when Davis was satisfied with his progress, he asked Helen Penick to examine his work to ascertain its accuracy and authenticity. "She walked up to it and said, 'Well, hello honey,'" Davis said.

Contented, Davis shipped the life-sized, 1,500-pound creation to Davenport Ranch (where the club had moved in 1984) about five weeks before the ceremony. Harvey was very sick and getting no better. Tinsley Penick wanted to take no chances.

One morning when his father felt well enough to leave the house, Tinsley asked a Golfsmith employee to drive his father across Westlake Drive and up to the club, where the young man helped Harvey from the car and guided him down the cart path he knew so well. They passed the familiar pro shop, the copse of oaks under which Harvey once waved to players and wished them good fortune for their rounds and reminded them to take dead aim, swing the bucket, chip under the bench, mind their grip, and rid their thoughts of anything beyond *hitting that ball*—to give luck a chance. The men stopped between the tenth and first tees.

Tinsley met them there. "Look," he told his father. "It's you." Harvey studied the rendering through failing eyes. *Yes,* he thought. *It is me.* In the sculpture, it looked to be about 1970, Harvey reasoned. He was wearing a short-sleeve shirt buttoned to the top, leaning on a middle-iron, and watching Kite, whose figure the artist had positioned in a flowing, balanced attitude of exquisite follow-through. Harvey noticed the face—his own face. He was smiling just a little. His timeless gaze out into the yawning canyons of the golf course seemed to suggest he had just detected a chorus of angels down by the holes on the lake. Davis, the sculptor, described it as "the look of satisfaction on Mr. Penick's face on seeing a famous golfer's swing."

In the precarious days before the ceremony, Harvey hoped to attend the gathering. He even chose the ensemble he wanted to wear. But he was listless, weak, spectral in his bedclothes, unable to rise, and barely strong enough to notice that someone trying to tidy his room had picked up a bundle of flowers in his bedroom. Harvey rose slightly. "You can't take those," he rasped. The flowers were important to him. The Crenshaws had brought them to Harvey before they left for New Orleans. The arrangement needed to stay where he could smell it.

In the kitchen, Harvey's daughter Kathryn fixed her father an egg. He barely nibbled it. He looked at Kathryn and said in his small voice, "I just can't do it."

The family decided that Kathryn's husband Bill would stay with Harvey, and the rest of them prepared for the short drive to Austin Country Club. Harvey remained in his bed, under a purple floral-print comforter, moving very little. "He was hanging on to life, giving us a last lesson about grace and fearlessness," Kite said. Soon everyone left the house, hoping Harvey would be alert enough to listen to their accounts of the ceremony when they returned. They stepped outside. The sky was crisp. A lazy breeze blew. It was a warm, buoyant, brilliant Sunday in Austin, the second afternoon of April 1995.

Some of those attending the ceremony wore wide-brimmed straw hats in the bright heat of the Central Texas sun. Many in the crowd appeared to have hastened over from church. There were charcoal suits, paisley ties, polka-dot dresses with wide, white collars and broad shoulder pads. The green tarp covering the statue rippled under a cloudless sky.

Club president Fred Davis stood at a wooden dais and said that he had been taking golf lessons from Harvey since March 1975. He added that when asked recently at another golf course about Harvey's approach, he answered: "He is simple but not simplistic, reserved without being passive, disciplined but not rigid, and confident without being presumptuous." Davis concluded: "Harvey Penick is effective without affectation."

Tinsley spoke next. He wore a double-breasted navy blazer and sand khakis, the kind of understated and neutral ensemble his father would have worn. He even looked like his father did when he was fifty-seven: chalk-white hair, narrow at the waist, and tanned from so many afternoons on the practice line at the country club. "Thank you all for coming out to honor my father today," Tinsley said in his airy voice. He looked up from his notes. "He is with us in spirit."

What he said next resembled an early but timely eulogy, a summary of and affectionate tribute to his dying father's ninety years of life, which would end in a matter of hours. Tinsley described how his parents met in the church. He reminded the gathering that Harvey often talked about his eighth birthday, because that was when he was deemed old enough to join his four brothers in the caddie yard at the new country club.

Tinsley mentioned 1923, when Harvey became the head professional, and he mentioned 1971, when his father retired. "He has always described himself as a lucky man who was privileged to be able to work outdoors, doing something he loved, with friends and people who shared his love for the game," Tinsley said. He added, in case there was any question, "I wish my father's health would have permitted him to be with us out here today."

When it was Kite's turn to speak, he asked everyone to imagine, when passing the statue they were about to see, a different image in the place of his own. He wanted everyone to feel a part of it. "Put your own face right there," Kite said, referring to his on the statue.

Published accounts from that afternoon suggest that Kite returned to Fawn Creek Path and was with Harvey when he died. Journalists used the touching anecdote in stories about Harvey's death. The scene has appeared in books and magazines and endured in oral histories; followers of Harvey tell the story because it beautifully and symmetrically closed an important circle established in 1963 when the Kite family moved from Dallas to Austin. But no such encounter happened.

Kite fetched a golf cart after the ceremony to play a round of golf. He had struck his drive on the third hole and was motoring down the cart path when an assistant professional caught up with him and told him Harvey was dead.

The false account that put Kite at Harvey's house that afternoon included another familiar, but untrue, detail. That day Davis Love III, the son of one of Harvey's fondly remembered players at Texas in the mid-1950s, had the final-round lead at the tournament in New Orleans, which Love had to win to qualify for the Masters the following week.

In the false account, Kite told Harvey that Love had indeed won. It was supposed to have been the last message Harvey heard before he died.

But in fact he never heard the news.

The events in New Orleans did, however, factor into the sentiment, symmetry, and closing of circles brought to Augusta in the week after Harvey's death. Love had bogeyed the seventeenth and eighteenth holes at English Turn, forcing a playoff with Mike Heinen. Both made par on the first hole. They processed to the tee of the 190-yard par-3 seventeenth, where Love had made that bogey minutes before. Heinen's shot landed in the fringe; Love's 6-iron never wandered from its line. His true birdie putt from three feet meant an invitation to the Augusta National the next week.

"I've collapsed a lot this year," a drained Love said after the playoff. "I feel like I've always stayed positive, but something always happens. I hit a bad shot. I just fail to execute. I like to think it was the pressure of trying to win and get into the Masters, and maybe now I can relax. I've been thinking too much about the Masters."

Harvey slipped away before he knew that. His daughter, Kathryn Powell, had appeared from the living room to check on her father. Harvey was fidgeting with his bedsheets, she said, and she tried to straighten them. "I'm so tired," Harvey whispered.

"Those were his last words," Kathryn recalled in December 2013, sitting on her sofa in Brady, where she sees her father's golf-cart placard—TAKE DEAD AIM!—each time she walks through her den. Her father's rolltop desk was there too, up against a bank of windows. Harvey's yellowed labels remained on the eighteen small drawers. PETTY CASH RECEIPTS. KEYS. BANK. TAXES. Kathryn had had many opportunities to remove them, but the precisely worded old labels were a warm reminder of her father. She stared outside, at the now-leafless trees of looming winter. She could see Harvey under the purple floral comforter, telling her on that Sunday afternoon in April on Fawn Creek Path that he knew.

"He put his head down," Kathryn remembered. "Then he just died."

Chapter Sixteen

TINSLEY WAS ON the practice range at the country club, giving a lesson arranged months before to a couple from Germany. A member approached, then stopped some distance away, which made Tinsley uneasy. Tinsley excused himself from the golf lesson. "Your father passed away," the member told him.

Back on Fawn Creek Path, friends streamed through the front door to console Helen, Kathryn, and Tinsley. Kite and Betty Ann Penick, Tinsley's wife, greeted Harvey's friends in the bedroom. "They just wanted to see him one more time," she said. They remained with Harvey until the funeral director appeared. Kite had come from the third hole at the country club.

No one talked a great deal. Kite and Betty Ann Penick watched the men and women who learned golf from Harvey pause at his bedside for a final, private moment in his presence. "He and I sat in that room for what seemed like hours," she said. Then, before he left, Kite slipped outside and stood on the wooden deck with the telephone in his hand.

Everyone agreed that he should make the call. It was nearing six o'clock when he dialed the number to Augusta National Golf Club, where the fifty-ninth Masters Tournament would begin in four days.

The maitre d' handed Julie Crenshaw a slip of paper. "Call Tom or Christy Kite," it read. Julie sensed immediately what had happened.

She went outside, leaving their guests, Masters chairman Jack Stephens and CBS broadcaster Pat Summerall, and dialed Kite. When she got the news, she motioned for her husband to join her on the porch, where she told him Harvey was dead. The two of them cried.

The couple returned to the house the family rented each April in Augusta. Later that evening Crenshaw called Kite, who suggested they play practice rounds Monday and Tuesday and charter a flight Wednesday from Georgia to Texas for the funeral. Crenshaw agreed.

Kite left for Augusta in the morning. By the time he coasted down Magnolia Lane on Monday, the first major championship of the season was already feeling less like a celebratory springtime reunion of the best golfers in the world and more like a wake for one of the better teachers the world had ever known, if only, for so many people, through his omnipresent books.

The *Austin American-Statesman* devoted its above-the-fold space on page 1 to Harvey's death. "Penick remained a hidden treasure until he gave author Bud Shrake the pages of a journal in a red notebook that he carried with him for 60 years," wrote sports reporter Mark Rosner. "With the exception of many No. 1 books by Austin transplant James Michener, Penick is believed to be the first person from this city to have a book top *The New York Times* best-sellers' list." The long story, accompanied by a color photograph of Harvey in his cart with Kite and Crenshaw, holding a golf club, noted that the publication of the red and green books had lifted Harvey's spirits late in life. "If you had seen him a couple of years ago, you would have thought he wouldn't be around in two or three months," Tinsley Penick told Rosner. "He was incoherent. I guess part of it was determination. But there is no doubt in my mind that it [the book] helped. What motivates him is the need to be needed."

Harvey's death was mentioned in the *New York Times* itself. The newspaper selected eight short passages from the *Little Red Book* to publish in a box next to the obituary: "Harvey Penick, 90, Golf's Top Author, Dies."

The *Times* also commissioned a tender tribute from Shrake, who opened with this line: "Heaven is a better place today. Harvey Penick is there." Shrake had long accepted that Harvey had little time to live, but he still struggled with what he wanted to say and how he wanted to say it. What would he want readers to know? What could he write that hadn't already been written?

"What is it about Harvey that the world fell in love with?" Shrake wrote. "I think it is his spirit. Always quietly powerful. Always positive. God is in the positive thoughts, the Devil in the negative. Also, I think, the world fell in love with Harvey's goodness, with his yearning to reach out and help, with his purity. Only the pure are strong enough to be simple. When Harvey spoke, in simple words, you listened, and sooner or later you understood." Shrake must have liked that passage from the essay he wrote, which appeared on page 23 of the *Times* sports section. He borrowed some of the same words to say at the funeral.

On the morning of the service, Kathryn and Tinsley met their mother at the house on Fawn Creek Path. Clouds threatened. Kathryn and her husband, Billy Powell, drove the short distance to Austin Country Club, where someone had left a brilliant spray of red roses at the foot of the statue of Harvey. Powell recorded a video as his wife walked slowly around the figure of her father. Thunder rumbled. "Trying to rain, the day of the funeral," Billy Powell said, narrating the moment.

The two-and-a-half-hour flight Wednesday morning from Bush Field in Augusta bounced Kite and Crenshaw through a thunderstorm. "It was surreal," Kite said. "We'd have stories and we'd talk about stuff. And then it would just be long, long moments of silence. Everybody's thinking." The Citation jet carrying the old friends and former teammates landed in a light rain.

One passenger had watched Crenshaw closely on the flight. "Harvey had always asked me to keep an eye on Ben," said Chuck Cook, the instructor, who was on the airplane with Kite and Crenshaw and their wives. "He was a total mess," Cook said. "He was distraught." Also on the flight was television executive Terry Jastrow, who had spent those two summers with Harvey in the 1960s.

Crenshaw first went home to find a muted navy suit to wear. He got to Amey Funeral Home a few minutes before the 11:00 A.M. service. As he approached the casket—it was open, surrounded by vivid flowers—his friends braced for his reaction. But Crenshaw betrayed little emotion that morning. He later explained to friends that his time with Harvey's body filled him with serenity.

Mourners arriving under black umbrellas were handed a one-page service program at the front of the funeral home. It included a passage from act V of Shakespeare's *Julius Caesar:* "His life was gentle, and the elements / So mix'd in him that Nature might stand up / And say to all the world, 'This was a man!'" On an easel nearby stood the original portrait that *Golf Digest* had published on its cover in 1993, the year of the green book. There he was, sitting in a canvas deck chair with his long legs crossed, his cane in his left hand, his right hand on his knee, wearing that bucket hat of his, a tie knotted under his sweater, tanned and eternal that morning, his face creased with quiet pride. Harvey smiled for all who came to mourn his death.

Neither Kite nor Crenshaw spoke at the service. That duty fell to Shrake, who told the room, now at capacity, about that recent Sunday afternoon when the Crenshaws visited Harvey after their brunch at Cisco's. "Harvey was having a bad day," Shrake said.

> For the first time in the years I've known him, I couldn't understand what he was saying. Then Ben and Julie Crenshaw came over with their two little girls. Ben talked golf, and Harvey said, "Go get a putter." Using Harvey's old wooden-shafted Sarazen putter, on the carpet beside what was to be his deathbed, one of the world's outstanding teachers was giving a lesson to one of the world's outstanding putters. Harvey's eyes were bright, the fog of his age and pain rolled away, and he was back in his own world again, doing what he loved best. Ben said, "I love you, Harvey," and Harvey said, "I love you, Ben. I'll always be watching you."

Shrake told the mourners that the Sarazen putter was in the casket with Harvey. Kite had given the club to John Amey, the funeral director who picked up Harvey's body. "Harvey can't go without having this," Kite told Amey.

It made for another lovely, tidy, fitting story and closed another circle. It seemed appropriate for the putter to be buried with Harvey's body, to spend eternity with a man who regarded golf clubs in the same manner a priest might regard a chalice. Shrake remarked that Harvey could employ the Sarazen putter in his heavenly lessons. The story sounded so perfect that morning at Harvey's funeral. But it wasn't true.

Tinsley discovered the Sarazen putter in the casket before the service. Mistakenly thinking the funeral home had placed it inside, Tinsley removed it, partly out of a sense of duty to Crenshaw. Tinsley wanted Crenshaw to have the Sarazen because he knew Crenshaw kept a collection of golf relics at his home in Tarrytown.

It belongs with Ben, Tinsley thought. He was closing the circle in a different way.

The cortege of dark cars left the funeral home for the short drive to Memorial Park Cemetery. The procession stopped in section 8 of lot 22, where Kite, Crenshaw, and six other pallbearers wearing white carnations on their lapels — including Billy Munn, who played for Harvey at Texas and had brought his two friends from Midland to see Harvey a year before — placed Harvey's casket under a canopy on four posts.

No rain fell now. The sun emerged, drying the mud. The gravedigger placed Harvey's casket into the soft ground, under an old and spreading Texas live oak, next to his parents and his four brothers, near the graves of Morris Williams Sr. and his son Morris Jr., and close enough to the old Austin Country Club and the two-story house on Cedar Street that it seemed like he already was home. Harvey wore his favorite black alligator shoes.

Kite and Crenshaw departed the cemetery for the seven-seat Citation waiting to return them to Augusta and the Masters. Their route to Robert Mueller Municipal Airport took the city streets, away from

Davenport Ranch and Austin Country Club. Had Kite and Crenshaw seen the club grounds that day, they would have noticed something touching and poignant on the Pete Dye greens.

The flags on the greens were at half-stick.

The two players slept through most of the flight to Georgia. "They said a few words about how nice the service was, but they were just worn out," said Crenshaw's friend Scotty Sayers, who was on the plane. They landed in Augusta late in the afternoon. There was enough time for Crenshaw to stop at his rental house on Aumond Street for a sweater. He drove to Augusta National, where he saw Love and exchanged sympathies. Love had learned of Harvey's death from his wife, Robin.

Sayers said Crenshaw's caddie, Carl Jackson, was waiting for him on the range, and Crenshaw went to find him. The two spent a few minutes there, loosening with some lazy, rhythmic iron shots. They moved to the practice green, where the current U.S. Amateur champion, a young Masters rookie named Tiger Woods, shook Crenshaw's hand on his way to the Amateur Dinner in the Augusta National clubhouse.

"There was nobody else on the course," Sayers said.

Crenshaw rolled solemn putts until the overcast skies turned charcoal. "He wanted to decompress," said Julie Crenshaw, who watched quietly from a white table near the green. Crenshaw later confided that he was simmering with a quiet but unmistakable confidence. He'd told his family after Harvey's service about an adjustment he'd made on the range at Augusta, where Jackson had suggested that he make a tighter shoulder turn and move the ball slightly toward his right heel at address. Crenshaw hit four balls, knew he had found something, and told Jackson that was the best practice session he had executed since his start to the season four months earlier.

"It just felt good," Julie Crenshaw recalled. "It just had this beautiful glow. It was calm. It was serene. He was just on his own. It was the perfect place to end his day."

Her husband's twenty-third year on the tour had begun that January with rare early-season sparkle. Crenshaw, now forty-three, tied for fifth in Hawaii. He shot 64 in the second round of the Phoenix Open at the end of the month. He finished with a share of third. He tied for thirteenth a week later at Pebble Beach, where he shot a final-round 66. It was his strongest start since his early years on the tour. He arrived that February at the Buick Invitational with no concerns about the way he was playing golf.

But then his game withered. His next six starts plunged him into another crushing slump. He tied for forty-first at Torrey Pines and sixty-first at Riviera. He left California for Florida, where he missed two cuts in three tournaments. Crenshaw failed to play the weekend in New Orleans, where he had won in 1994. Then Harvey died.

Crenshaw seemed ambivalent about golf early in the week of his teacher's funeral. When Love sought his counsel about whether to attend Harvey's service, Crenshaw encouraged him to stay in Augusta to practice because he thought Love had a chance to win. "The way I'm playing, it doesn't matter what I do," Crenshaw told him, Love later recalled.

The tip from his caddie Tuesday morning changed his bearing. The quiet moment at Harvey's casket the next day calmed his heaving emotions. In two days, much had changed.

Crenshaw shared his optimism with his father and brother before he returned to Georgia for his twenty-fourth start in the springtime invitational in the pines. "I really think I'm on to something," Crenshaw told them as he left.

Harvey's family returned to Fawn Creek Path after the burial at Memorial Park. The house was filled with flowers and friends, including Shrake and Kathy Whitworth. The mood lightened. More friends arrived. They grazed from a spread of fruit, vegetables, and sandwiches. Outside, on the wooden deck streaked with rain, Harvey's favorite plant, a potted hibiscus, began to dry in the sun.

Later, when almost everyone had gone, Helen sat in her husband's velour chair by the window. "Harvey's now at peace," she said. Helen cried, in sadness and relief. "He was suffering so much," she wailed in her funeral dress.

"He's not anymore," her son-in-law replied.

The Masters Tournament commenced Thursday morning, the sixth day of April, with rain falling from graphite skies. Colorful umbrellas speckled the grounds, dotting the green bleachers like flowers in a pot. Crenshaw and Jackson reported to the first tee for his 11:03 starting time to play with 1991 British Open Championship winner Ian Baker-Finch.

The round began sullenly. Crenshaw missed the green and made bogey on the first hole. He converted three birdies, however, and turned at 2-under 34. On the par-5 thirteenth, Crenshaw dropped from casual water, which took longer than it should have. The Master rules official put his pairing on the clock for slow play. Irritated, Crenshaw played the rest of the round without a birdie as others in the field passed him on the leaderboard.

He still shot 2-under 70, a gritty round on a dismal afternoon. Kite shot 72, and Love 69.

The first-round leaders — José María Olazábal, Phil Mickelson, and David Frost — ravaged Augusta National with rounds of 66. Crenshaw, Kite, and Love played through their lingering sadness, showing no signs of the drama to come. "I haven't had a good night's sleep since Sunday," Kite said after his round. Jackson said he was proud of Crenshaw's determination. "Ben's got a soft heart," Jackson said. "He did well today. A lot of guys came up to him before he teed off and talked to him. He understands Mr. Penick was old and lived a good life."

Woods opened with an even-par 72. He was a story. Fifty-five years old and nine years removed from his historic back-nine brilliance that led to his sixth Masters title, Jack Nicklaus shot 67. He was a story. Privately, Crenshaw was relieved that the attention was beginning to drift from him and Kite and Love to the players who finished high on the leaderboard. Crenshaw naturally missed Harvey and thought about him constantly. But he was ready to stop answering questions about his grief. He just wanted to get on with the tournament, to remind himself out there to turn a little more tightly over a ball a little farther back in his stance.

"Ben was in a complete mind of his own," said Colin Montgomerie, the Glaswegian, who shot 71.

The Crenshaws hosted a barbecue Thursday night at their rental house, then retired early. Crenshaw lunched on Friday at the Augusta National clubhouse, where he saw Dave Marr, Dan Jenkins, and Bob Drum, the former golf writer for the *Pittsburgh Press* who chronicled the career of Arnold Palmer. They shared salutations and a few welcome laughs. "I think it relaxed him to see people he knew," Sayers said.

Crenshaw played the second round on a cloud. He opened with a birdie, the first of seven. His shots puréed the air. His putts hugged their lines. He felt his hands lead his stroke through the ball, just as Harvey had reminded him on their last visit together. He felt Harvey in the shadows of the loblollies.

Crenshaw later spoke of the role of unexplained luck in the 1995 Masters. Luck was part of the game. Harvey regarded it as something to accept, just as he instructed his pupils to embrace misfortune as a part of the game. On the third hole Friday, Crenshaw shoved his tee shot under the limbs to the right of the par-4 fairway. The shot from there would require a certain amount of finesse merely to chase the ball up near the canted green. His shot, a low and carving cut, bounded toward a Masters volunteer positioned near the ropes, nearly striking him, and then, instead of settling in one of a million potentially impossible lies, the ball curled down the slope and stopped ten feet behind the hole. Crenshaw made the birdie putt.

He shot 67. He'd last shot 67 there in 1988, when he finished fourth.

"I was beginning to get a feeling," he wrote years later. "Everything felt seamless."

Kite missed the cut. Love paired a second-round 69 with his first, and Crenshaw started his third round two shots behind Jay Haas, whose uncle, Bob Goalby, won the Masters in 1968. The people around Crenshaw that week allowed themselves to imagine the extraordinary. Sayers even began taking notes out of view of his friend. "I thought something might be happening," Sayers said.

That third round unspooled on a crisp spring Georgia afternoon, presided over by one of the most compelling leaderboards in the fifty-nine-year history of the invitational. Crenshaw continued his graceful play with a 3-under 69, securing an appointment in the last group Sunday with Masters rookie Brian Henninger at minus 10. Haas, Mickelson, '92 Masters winner Fred Couples, Scott Hoch, and Steve Elkington finished a stroke behind them.

Two-time U.S. Open champion Curtis Strange and the South African David Frost were two shots out of the lead. Love and Greg Norman were behind by three. It was a tournament of many plots, all appealing, some potentially historic. And no one could ignore the most poignant one of all.

A reporter asked Crenshaw about the gravity of the final round, given the death of his teacher. Crenshaw replied that he preferred not to think about it. He told the reporter: "I'll carry Harvey in my heart until the day I die" — a sincere response that carried no risk of overthinking.

Nostalgia and something more than the usual anticipation reigned that Saturday evening on the club grounds. As the golf writers filed stories for their Sunday editions, they knew a meaningful narrative when they saw one. "Writers are not supposed to pull for teams or players," recalled Ron Green Jr., who wrote from the Masters that year for the *Charlotte Observer*. "But we all tend to pull for the story. That was the perfect script he [Crenshaw] gave us."

Crenshaw often described the Masters as the most emotionally charged major championship in golf. Nothing touched him like the refined arrangement of the surroundings, the antiquity of the interior spaces, the portraits on the walls and the artifacts on the tables, the explosions of color in the landscaping, the locker he shared with Jimmy

Demaret, the everlasting presence of Bobby Jones. Augusta National had appealed to Crenshaw the first time he saw it in 1972. It was everything he wanted out of golf. He revered it for what it was and what it had been and what it always would be. To Crenshaw, Augusta National was a course that wasn't merely seen or played, but a place that was felt.

However, as David Frost said, "Drama like that can let you take your focus away from your game." Crenshaw, too, wondered how he would govern his focus on Sunday afternoon. He had been at the Masters many times before, so he thought about what Harvey would tell him to do. *Trust your swing,* Harvey would say. *Trust your judgment. Play hard. Hope for the best.* Harvey would emphasize the elusive simplicity of great golf. He would remind Crenshaw to take dead aim. And even though Crenshaw had heard those three words so many times before, he knew they would sound different to him this time. This time they would have new meaning.

The phone rang often that Saturday night at the Crenshaws' rented brick house on Aumond Road. Ben's father called from Austin. His friends called from everywhere. Julie Crenshaw called Charlie, Ben's brother. "You need to get on a plane," she told him. "Your brother needs you."

The occupants of the house — Ben and Julie, Scotty and Julie Sayers, friends Pat and Julie Oles — scrambled for ways to fill the time, which seemed not to budge. They packed their suitcases. They watched the third-round highlights. They avoided the subjects of winning the Masters and winning it for Harvey. "We were doing everything we could to keep his mind off of the next day," Sayers said.

Charlie Crenshaw arranged a flight Sunday morning to Augusta. When he arrived at his brother's house around noon, he found Crenshaw in the yard, slapping at pinecones with a wedge. Ben had finished two breakfasts. "We were so bored," Julie Crenshaw said. Her husband paced. It was hard enough to lead the Masters, especially under these circumstances. It was harder still to wait for that final starting time, when the starter in the green jacket would raise his arms and say, "Fore, please. Now driving."

Nevertheless, Crenshaw seemed to his brother, wife, and friends far more collected than he had in 1987, '88, or '89. He took a walk down the driveway, stopped near the end, and stood by himself in studied repose.

He tried not to think but failed. He pictured Harvey. He pictured shots that would give him a chance to win. He said a short prayer. He petitioned only for the ability to accept what would happen that afternoon, nothing more. "That's where Harvey came into it," Sayers said. Harvey would have told Crenshaw to play the game he loved and to remember why he loved it.

After thirty minutes at the end of the driveway, Crenshaw returned and said, "Let's go."

He selected a periwinkle-blue Bobby Jones shirt, invoking sepia-toned memories of Jones from 1930, when he won the U.S. Amateur and Open championships and the British Amateur and Open. He wore pleated, bone-colored trousers and brown saddle shoes. On this crisp, windless, and charged afternoon in eastern Georgia, he eased down Magnolia Lane, parked, and looked for the familiar figure of Jackson, his white-suited caddie.

Crenshaw and Jackson marched to the range. On the other side of the clubhouse, crowds in linen and seersucker and broad, floppy hats swelled around the first tee to see if the man with so much on his mind that week could ignore the size of the job at hand.

Julie Crenshaw waited for her husband to finish on the putting green. She thought he looked settled. She did not worry. She knew he already had bargained with himself on the driveway, to accept the conclusion of this Masters Sunday before he took his first swing. "Harvey was with him every step of the way," Julie said.

Crenshaw holed his last practice putt and wheeled to find Jackson.

They walked through the corridor of spectators wishing for redemption.

They smiled for strangers hoping for miracles.

They stopped when Crenshaw saw his wife.

"Go have fun," she said.

He touched her hand. They kissed.

Crenshaw opened with a par on the long first hole, one of the most difficult at Augusta for its sheer length up the hill and also for what it meant. He made birdie on the par-5 second after a wedge to eight feet. He bogeyed the fifth. A partially blind hole with a green that moved like folded cake batter, the fifth was a hard par. Crenshaw recognized that. He pocketed his ball with neither anger nor remorse.

When he addressed his shot at the par-3 sixth, Crenshaw stared down the hill at the voluptuously contoured green. The slightest miss could result in a bitter struggle for par. He swung without fear. His ball rose. No one moved, and Crenshaw kept his eyes on its journey to the finish, five feet from the flagstick. A roar rose.

Hands ahead.

Birdie.

Crenshaw made another birdie on the ninth with a crisp sand wedge from one hundred steps. Back in Austin, Helen Penick watched the CBS broadcast with a close friend, Carrell Grigsby. An Austin photographer and Austin Country Club member, Grigsby often watched televised golf at the Penick household on Fawn Creek Path, regardless of who was winning. She felt like family there. But watching the tournament for the first time without Harvey seemed incomplete, if richly poignant, given Crenshaw's play that week. Helen sat in Harvey's chair by the glass door. She soon would migrate to the sofa, where she and Grigsby would have to hold hands and link arms to survive the next three hours of golf.

"Look at this!" they heard Ken Venturi blurt as Crenshaw's approach shot cozied up to a foot from the front-right hole at No. 9. "You need shots like that to win," Venturi said.

Henninger had vanished from contention in his first Masters Tournament. Crenshaw owned a one-stroke lead. He processed toward Augusta's famed back nine at 2-under for the round, at 12-under for the tournament, and on the cusp of the most sentimental Masters rally since Nicklaus's in 1986.

Helen and Grigsby heard the CBS announcer, Jim Nantz, say: "There you have it. The front nine is clear." Neither woman wanted to speculate out loud. Their imaginations whirled.

Ahead, Norman birdied the par-five thirteenth, and the excited commotion of the spectators could be heard through the pines. The Australian, who'd lost in a crushing playoff in 1987 to Augusta native Larry Mize, was a shot behind Crenshaw now. He and Love, playing together, marched to the fourteenth tee.

Crenshaw gathered himself. The back tee of the 485-yard tenth hole shared high ground with the clubhouse, the long first tee, the big oak tree, the lawn on which families and friends of players took their lunch and iced tea, Butler Cabin, and the practice putting green where Crenshaw had spent that meditative, healing Wednesday evening after Harvey's funeral. The vista swept out over the old orchard property like a panoramic still, drawing the eye from the fairway of the first hole bending to the right at the crest — empty now — to the wall of trees that guided players up to the eighteenth, to the hill between the tenth and eighteenth leading down to what waited for him in the lengthening shadows.

There was the par-4 seventeenth. Farther still, the fifteenth, the reachable and critical par-5. The thirteenth green. The sixteenth. It was impossible to discern through the pines, but down there lay Herbert Warren Wind's Amen Corner too.

Crenshaw made par at No. 10.

Three holes in front of him, Love, playing the par-4 fourteenth with Norman, nearly holed his second shot from 120 yards. The birdie tied Crenshaw's lead. Haas drove into the pine straw on the par-5 thirteenth. His chances ended there.

Back in Austin, Helen Penick watched the proceedings with her friend. "We have a huge battle," she heard Ben Wright, the British-born CBS broadcaster, intone gravely as Crenshaw bent to tee his ball at the eleventh tee.

Norman and Love attacked the par-5 fifteenth with brave second shots to the green, Love with a 9-iron from a mere 165 yards. Both shots finished near enough to the hole to inspire hopes of eagle.

Both missed.

Love took a fleeting lead at minus 13 with his two-putt birdie. Norman and Crenshaw now were tied for second. Crenshaw claimed pars at the eleventh and then the twelfth.

At the par-5 thirteenth, Crenshaw slung an exquisite tee shot around the right-to-left turn in the fairway. He stood over his 200-yard second shot to the green. In 1984 he had chosen to play to the back-nine par-5 holes in three studious shots, to not even risk a bold attempt over the creek. Caution had prevailed. So had he. Today, however, Crenshaw never doubted his choice. He aimed his 4-iron at the center of the green. "There he stands, destiny in front of him," a reporter declared on the CBS broadcast. In Austin, Helen and Grigsby waited, hands clasped. What might that destiny hold for Harvey's boy?

Crenshaw fired. The shot steered left. "God, don't pull it!" he admonished himself, momentarily in crisis, losing for an irretrievable second the composure he somehow had managed all afternoon. His ball skipped through the green and hung on the bank behind it, in the longer grass between two bunkers. Crenshaw studied his options.

He chipped — *under the bench, under the bench* — to twenty feet. He plumb-bobbed the swinging left-to-right putt for birdie. He took two practice strokes and let go. *Hands lead,* he thought. The ball scampered in.

He was relieved. A par there, Crenshaw knew, would equate to a shot lost on the field. He had no idea that Love had just taken three putts on the sixteenth, or that he now had a one-shot lead with five holes left to play in the Masters.

Helen Penick wept.

· · ·

The lead was brief.

Love birdied the seventeenth from two feet. Knowledgeable spectators wondered again if this would be like 1988, '89, or '98, when Crenshaw played in the final pairing on Sunday, shot nothing lower than 71, and finished no higher than in a tie for third. "What a couple of weeks this man is having," one of the CBS broadcasters pealed.

"I can imagine Harvey's clapping again," Helen heard him say.

Crenshaw heard the sound of the uprising from the seventeenth green as he addressed his drive on the fourteenth. He whipped through impact, ever slightly too soon. The ball drew hard, dove fast, and hopped toward the pine straw under the trees on the left.

But then something else happened: his ball steered right. When Crenshaw and Jackson got to it, they discovered a line to the green encumbered only by a low limb just ahead and the gathering tension of the occasion.

From 155 yards in the left rough, Crenshaw bore a hooded 8-iron under the branch to a dozen feet behind the hole. Norman bogeyed the seventeenth. The scoreboard at the eighteenth registered Love's birdie. The crowd there thrummed. Love and Crenshaw were tied again.

Crenshaw made his par at the fourteenth. Love drove wildly left on the final hole, near the abandoned ninth fairway. His 120-yard approach collected just short of the green and spun farther from the flagstick. "No good," Venturi said.

A breeze rippled the yellow flags at Augusta. "Just a gentle zephyr," Wright observed. Love gamely made par at the eighteenth, signed his scorecard, and waited for Crenshaw, who had driven ideally on the par-5 fifteenth, to play the final four holes. Love steeled — hoped — for a playoff.

"Right now it's Ben's tournament to win," Venturi told viewers.

Helen braced herself.

Throughout his career, Crenshaw had always sneaked a look at the Sunday leaderboard to see where matters stood in order to calibrate his planning. But through the front nine that Sunday he cast no glances in that direction. Something told him not to. He was, he re-

membered later, simply playing the golf course. He was Benny, the kid
Harvey sent out to the Austin Country Club course on Riverside Drive
with a sleeve of golf balls and instructions to embrace the pure libera-
tion of swinging freely. He was not thinking. He was not trying. Crenshaw was playing on instinct and intuition.

He was playing himself.

Crenshaw pounded his second shot from 220 yards through the fifteenth green. The ball stopped in shady, matted grass where spectators
had been standing since the gates opened very early that morning. He
allowed himself his first view of the scores as he examined his circumstances. Seeing that Love had shot 66 moments earlier to post a 13-un-
der-par 275, he knew what he had to do.

His third shot bumped short of the collar surrounding the green.
Worse, it stayed there. Crenshaw winced when he failed to birdie the
final par-5 on the course. He nonetheless strode freely through appre-
ciative applause to the sixteenth tee. He and Love remained tied. Norman and Haas shared third, two shots behind. Crenshaw wanted one
more birdie. Just one.

"The wind's freshening a little," Wright noted.

The tee of the par-3 sixteenth hole at Augusta can feel like a busy
train stop. Spectators sit on each side from the bleachers, near enough
that distracted players can hear the crinkle of cellophane if someone
unwraps a sandwich. Crenshaw was not distracted. He calculated the
183-yard distance to the hole, the slope he wanted his ball to catch, the
breeze summoning, the adrenaline coursing through him, the acceptance pending. He pulled the 6-iron from his bag.

Crenshaw later heralded those ten seconds of evaluating the conditions — the tension of his grip, the deliberation of his breathing, the execution of his move to the ball — as his finest calculation of the round.
The shot fell at just the right time, rolled just the right distance, tumbled left from the soft spine in the green at just the right place. Norman
and Love had missed that ridge, leaving dangerous putts from the high
shelf of the slope. But Crenshaw's ball commanded it perfectly, rolling

to the back-left flagstick as if directed by providence. "A lot of courage in that!" Wright exclaimed.

The five-foot birdie putt cascaded into the hole.

Some of the players who'd finished congregated around televisions in the Augusta National clubhouse. *Harvey's watching over him*, thought Peter Jacobsen as Crenshaw and Jackson reached the sixteenth green. Many years later, Jacobsen remembered feeling the properness of what happened that afternoon. "It just kind of had been lining up for Ben," Jacobsen said. "What happened there was the right thing that needed to happen."

Crenshaw had two holes to play and a one-shot lead. He tried again not to think. He tried again not to project. He tried not to try. His drive on the par-4 seventeenth afforded him an aggressive play to the hole, which he embraced with no hesitation. Venturi informed Helen, her friend Grigsby, and the rest of his viewers that afternoon that only one consideration mattered: "What club do I need to clear the bunker?"

Crenshaw chose his 9-iron. He assumed his stance and glanced at his target twice, then a third time. The club whooshed through the turf. The approach left Crenshaw thirteen feet for another birdie. He judged the left-to-right turn of the putt and kept his hands in front of the ball, just as Harvey had told him to.

Another birdie.

In Austin, cheers rose on Fawn Creek Path. "We definitely felt Harvey the whole time," Grigsby said. But they really felt him now. In Augusta, Crenshaw swiped the ball from the seventeenth hole and held the pose in a gesture of triumph, conviction, and tribute to his teacher. "I played it like a dream," Crenshaw said.

Verne Lundquist, meanwhile, had left his position at the twelfth hole to watch the finish at the CBS compound on the far side of the Par Three Course. His friendship with Crenshaw dated back to the 1960s, when Lundquist, a graduate of Austin High School and Texas Lutheran University in nearby Seguin, began broadcasting sports for Channel 7, the CBS affiliate in Austin.

He had known Crenshaw since his earliest days at the country club, back when he was Harvey's boy. With quiet pride, Lundquist watched Crenshaw and Jackson arrive at the eighteenth tee.

"It was mesmerizing," he said. "There wasn't a soul in there who didn't hope that Ben would win."

He saw Crenshaw rope a hustling 4-wood up the rising, calamitous fairway: the last march of the Masters.

The walk toward the green released the feelings Crenshaw had kept so carefully in check until now. He inventoried the events of the last seven days and wondered, briefly, about the significance of accomplishing something that had seemed impossible the night his wife told him Harvey had died. A CBS camera followed him, but Crenshaw ignored it. He inhaled deeply 145 yards from the flag and waggled an 8-iron.

"I don't know how it happened," he said later that evening. "When you're forty-three, you don't know how many more chances you are going to get again. You know how this tournament has gone. Fate is what decides it a lot of times. It was like someone put their hand on my shoulder and sort of guided me."

Guided. Harvey loved that word. He used it often when talking about his life's work.

Crenshaw made a bogey on the final hole — his fifth one in seventy-two holes. His blocked approach fell short, his chip onto the green steered away from the slopes with the most peril, and his first putt, from ten feet, slipped left. Crenshaw settled over his eighteen-inch putt to win. *God,* he told himself, *if you can get through this little foot-and-a-half putt, then you can go ahead and cry.* The putt fell.

Crenshaw slumped. His hat tumbled. He covered his face with his hands, and he could barely breathe. "That picture, I can still see it," remembered Nick Price, the popular South African, who missed the cut in '95. "That was pure emotion, determination, and guts."

Crenshaw heard Jackson's voice: "Are you all right?" He felt Jackson's big hands grip his heaving shoulders. He rose and put his arms around his caddie. They left the green together. "That picture speaks for itself," Venturi said.

You can go out there, a member told Julie.

"No," she replied. "It's their time."

Back in Austin, Helen Penick uncorked a special bottle of champagne, a 1983 magnum of Dom Pérignon. It was the one Simon & Schuster had sent for her husband's ninetieth birthday. There had never seemed a more appropriate occasion until Crenshaw holed that little putt to finish at 14 under par to win the Masters.

"Obviously we had our hopes up," Grigsby said. "But we were just as shocked as the rest of the world at how it happened." The two women drank until the bottle was dry.

Nantz's rich baritone narrated the sequence as the two-time champion shook Henninger's hand. "He'd been holding back the emotion, keeping it in check all week," Nantz said. "Until now." He added: "There is no greater tribute to the man he loved, Harvey Penick."

Officials escorted Crenshaw to Butler Cabin for the jacket ceremony. Someone from the media committee took Love to the press building alongside the fairway of the first hole. Inside, Love tried to explain what had just happened at the Masters. "It couldn't be a better end for Harvey Penick's life to have Ben win on the same week he passed away," Love said. "I don't think there was anything stopping Ben today."

In his televised interviews in the famous cabin, and later in the Masters press room, Crenshaw attempted to explain what had just happened outside. He mentioned his concentration. He discussed the tee shot on the sixteenth and the putt a hole later. He mused about fate. More than once, he just shook his head and said he was lucky—luckier than anyone else that afternoon.

What he really was saying was that he did not know how he won that day. But he was convinced that the spirit of his teacher had something very real to do with it.

"I had a fifteenth club in the bag," Crenshaw said, "and it was Harvey."

In the press building, the writers tapped away at their keyboards. They wrote about the weight Crenshaw had carried that week. They wrote about his fondness for the tournament and the course and its founder. They wrote about his critical putt on the thirteenth hole and the birdies on the sixteenth and seventeenth and the tears on the eighteenth green. They wrote about the "fifteenth club." "It did feel almost touched, the way it happened," said Green, the golf writer from Charlotte. That year's Masters would remain one of his favorites.

Crenshaw, his wife, and his friends changed for the Champion's Dinner in the Trophy Room, where the menu included pompano, lamb chops, and a New York strip. They had to hurry. Their flight was waiting. Then someone delivered a note to the table. No one pointed out the coincidence that exactly one week earlier the same maitre d' had brought a message from Austin to the same dining room.

The tone of this note was very different.

"Helen and Harvey Penick send congratulations and love on this special day," it read.

It was from Helen.

The Crenshaws left before midnight—before dessert—with a police escort to the Augusta airport. Someone brought a cake for the trip home, and Crenshaw called Helen Penick from the air. As the flight descended into Austin, the University of Texas Tower came into view outside the windows of the jet, just as it had in 1984. It glowed in orange light to commemorate what had already become known as "The Little Red Masters."

The week after the Masters, NBC broadcast the final round of the Senior PGA Championship at PGA National in Palm Beach Gardens, Florida. Harvey would have watched this tournament from his velour chair with great interest, given the men in contention. Raymond Floyd led, at minus 9, chased closely by Jim Colbert, DeWitt Weaver, Harvey's friend Jack Nicklaus, and fellow Texan Lee Trevino. The coverage broke for a reflection on Crenshaw's triumph seven days earlier.

Bob Costas narrated the segment, which included a photograph of Harvey with Morris Williams Jr. and the Texas Junior, Texas Amateur, and Texas PGA Championship trophies that Williams won in that magical 1950 season. "Here, now, are the thoughts of Crenshaw, and another Penick protégé, Tom Kite," Costas said.

The minute-long tribute, accompanied by gentle piano and cello music, opened with a scene of Harvey in a golf cart, flanked by Crenshaw and Kite. "Harvey meant all the good things in golf," came the voice of Crenshaw. The segment cut to Kite in a darkened studio. "He was a great man," he said. "You know, if you hang around good people, it's hard to mess up your life."

The piece pulled footage from Sunday at the Masters a week earlier. There was Crenshaw, arcing his pivotal tee shot on the par-3 sixteenth, watching his ball curl down the bank toward the hole. There he was again, stroking the left-to-right putt on the seventeenth, his hands ahead of the ball, trusting. And there he was once more, crumbling after the final putt on the eighteenth.

"I don't know," Crenshaw tried to explain. "I was as determined as I've ever been in my life. I let go. I did it for Harvey." The camera then returned to Kite, who sighed deeply. "Mr. Penick will be with my golf game for a long time," he said.

The piece concluded with Crenshaw reading a brief selection from *For All Who Love the Game,* the third book from Harvey and Shrake, the one written for women and scheduled for release that month. "It's a little passage called 'Home,'" Crenshaw said.

What a beautiful place a golf course is. From the meanest country pasture to the Pebble Beaches and St. Andrews of the world, a golf course is to me a holy ground. I feel God in the trees and grass and flowers, in the rabbits and the birds and the squirrels, in the sky and water. I feel that I am home.

• • •

The year of Harvey's death became a toast to his life.

On June 1, Shrake wrote his editor in New York a quick note: "Here's the beginning of the End."

It was a draft of the introduction to the book for seniors, an undertaking that had assumed an almost spiritual voice. Less a handy guide to life and the future, this last book was a somber rumination about faith and the hereafter. Shrake had prepared a list of twenty-five questions to ask Harvey for the last book. Many of them dealt with the nature of God and whether Harvey believed in heaven and the Devil. Shrake wanted to ask him what he remembered from the night before the statue ceremony at the country club, when Helen feared he might die. "Did you ever feel that your spirit crossed over and met with angels or beings from another place?" Shrake wanted to ask Harvey. "Do you think extranatural forces, such as the power of prayer, can have an effect on the flight of a golf ball?"

Under that, Shrake wrote: "Answer this question seriously."

Shrake never got his answers.

Simon & Schuster released the third book and continued to plan for the fourth. Holly Brubach, the style editor of the *New York Times,* liked *For All Who Love the Game.* "Penick has high hopes for women," she wrote in her review, published on June 11. "He looks us straight in the eye." Brubach found no fault in the message, but she chastised Shrake for occasionally parroting the hard-boiled delivery of Raymond Chandler, the detective novelist. "She was a classy-looking young woman, attractive, smart. She knew what she wanted, but I knew what she needed. She needed to get over her fear of sand traps." Brubach nonetheless cheered the new addition to the Penick anthology. "It's Penick's voice that stays with the reader, whispering in her ear."

The Texas House of Representatives approved a resolution that year to commemorate the Texan who taught golf for more than seven decades. "Harvey Penick was a man whose encyclopedic knowledge of the game of golf was surpassed only by his ability to communicate that information to others in a simple and instructive manner; although his warmth and wisdom are gone from us now, his unique spirit will surely live on in the hearts of the many people whose lives he touched during his time on this earth," the document read.

The measure passed with no dissent.

In August, Tinsley Penick sent club members a one-page letter announcing his retirement. He noted that he'd made the decision more than a year before, after twenty-five years in the position. Now, with his father's death, it was time to act on it.

"The members have always treated me and my family with respect, and more like a friend than an employee," Penick wrote. "How lucky can a person get, to be doing something he loves around friends that he cares for, and that care for him?"

The club gave Penick and his family a lifetime membership.

"They don't know how much it means to me," Penick said. "I was never a great player, so I'm looking forward to being strictly a member and playing lots of golf. The only advice I would have for a young person wanting to be a golf professional is to work hard, manage your money well and make all the right investments. If you do that, you can retire at age fifty-seven — especially if your dad writes a best seller."

For the first time since 1923, Austin Country Club would have a head professional not named Penick. The club in 1995 barely resembled the club of seven decades before, the era of sand putting surfaces and boy caddies from the neighborhood and championships known as handicaps. When Tinsley Penick retired, Austin Country Club had hundreds of golf members, annual revenues of $5.1 million, assets of $14.8 million, and one of the finest, and most punishing, golf courses in the state.

It would forever be known as the golf home of Harvey Penick.

Chapter Seventeen

AT THE RYDER CUP matches that late summer at Oak Hill in Rochester, New York, the PGA of America organized an evening banquet in Harvey's name. Many of the game's top teachers were on the invitation list. Tinsley prepared twelve pages of remarks, editing them by hand up to the moment it was his turn to speak. They spanned his father's career, from his early days at the original country club to his years as the University of Texas coach to his final lesson with the old putter and Crenshaw two weeks before the Masters.

"My dad always said that the day he stopped learning would be the day he stopped teaching," Tinsley told the gathering. "He must have been learning right up to the day he died, because he never stopped teaching. You may have heard the story about Ben Crenshaw visiting my father in his bedroom a few days before Ben was to leave for Augusta this year. Ben told my father he was having a little trouble with putting.

"My dad asked Ben, 'Have you been taking a couple of practice strokes before each putt, and imagining the ball going into the hole?'

"Ben said, 'You know, I don't think I have been.'

"My father said, 'Go get a putter and let me watch you take a few strokes on the carpet.'

"A little over a week later," Tinsley continued, "Ben won the Masters.

So if the question is, 'Would Harvey Penick's methods work today?' I guess the answer is, 'Yes, they do.'"

The Texas Sports Hall of Fame in Waco dedicated a room in Harvey's name on December 1, and the Penick family donated the original Scribbletex notebook to the hall. There the Harvey Penick Tribute Room joined exhibition spaces for former Baylor football coach Grant Teaff, former Texas coach Darrell Royal, and heavyweight boxer George Foreman. The ceremony on that December day included a golf outing at Ridgewood Country Club.

"He gave to all of us," Kathy Whitworth, who attended the ceremony, told the gathering. "He always made everyone feel special."

Harvey's name endured, and his academy at Golfsmith continued to flourish. At the end of 1995, Charles McGrath of the *New York Times* wrote a four-paragraph appreciation of Harvey, describing the hole he had left in golf. He noted the Calvinist nature of the *Little Red Book:* it taught that "golf is character, and the quality of your shots depends on the quality of your soul. That this was so in Penick's case is abundantly clear." McGrath suggested that Harvey "approached golf as a branch of the liberal arts."

About a year after Harvey died, Terry Jastrow found himself thinking again about 1965 and '66, the summers he had left Midland to be in Austin, picking up range balls for Harvey with canvas tubes. Now, three decades later, Jastrow still played golf often and was a member at tony Bel-Air Country Club in Los Angeles. He even had a single-digit handicap, but he had never attempted the PGA Tour, as Harvey had once thought he might. Instead, Jastrow embarked on what would be a very successful career in television, including eighteen years with ABC Sports. He had supervised coverage of the '92 U.S. Open at Pebble Beach, struggling to coordinate a dozen broadcasters and pick footage from forty television monitors as his old friend from those summers at the country club marched through the Pacific wind on that Sunday afternoon. Jastrow cried for thirty minutes after Tom Kite won.

He now was the Emmy-winning president of Jack Nicklaus Productions, a company in Santa Monica involved in televising golf. Jastrow had both the means and the desire to create something in his teacher's memory. He also thought he had the perfect idea: a Senior PGA Tour tournament in Austin. "I wanted to celebrate Harvey," Jastrow said.

He asked Kite and Crenshaw for their endorsement, which they gave. He contacted the PGA Tour, where he had many acquaintances, including the commissioner, Tim Finchem. Jastrow sought the blessing of Harvey's family.

On September 7, Tinsley wrote to Jastrow to express his "unqualified support" for the creation of a tournament in his father's name and suggested a venue: the Onion Creek Club, where Jimmie Connolly and Jimmy Demaret had invited their friends from the old days of the PGA Tour to gather in 1978 for the original Legends of Golf.

Jastrow discussed the possibility with Finchem, who liked the idea of returning the senior tour to its rightful home in Austin. The tournament schedule was already in place, however, and new tournaments were being planned for the future. There was simply no room for another one.

But Jastrow had another idea. On October 22, 1996, he wrote to Tinsley and Helen Penick about the possibility of having a women's tournament in Harvey's name: "As you both so well know, Harvey taught even more great women players than men. Given the tremendous growth of women's athletics in general and especially their new appetite for the sport of golf, the timing for such an event could be excellent as we make our way towards the 21st Century." Jastrow sent copies of the letter to Kite, Crenshaw, and Texas governor George W. Bush, and he also contacted LPGA commissioner Jim Ritts.

"It was only fitting," Jastrow remembered. "It was the confluence of a lot of great things."

Ritts and other officials at the LPGA liked the idea immediately. They appreciated Harvey's imprint on women's golf in the early years of the association, but they also recognized that his influence spanned generations. The LPGA even had a current player in Austin, Cindy Figg-Currier, who had sought Harvey as a teacher when she joined the

University of Texas women's team in 1978. Figg-Currier was the reigning Michigan state girls' high school champion when she enrolled at Texas that fall. She knew nothing about Austin, and she knew no one there, not even Harvey.

But her head coach at Texas, Pat Weis, lived two houses away from Harvey and Helen behind the country club on Penick Circle. Harvey often asked Weis if he could help any of her players, and while she knew he would accept all of them if she asked, she politely limited her recommendations. In this case, she knew Figg-Currier needed a friend in Austin.

The relationship lasted until his death. "He was always kind," Figg-Currier said. "It didn't matter to him whether you were Tom Kite, the ladies' club champion or a ten-year-old. Harvey was the closest thing to God that I can imagine."

The LPGA announced the new tournament in the fall of 1998. The Philips Invitational Honoring Harvey Penick was planned for the following May at the Onion Creek Club. The press conference included Ritts, Jastrow, and Tinsley and Helen Penick. "We will have no trouble getting top players," Ritts said. "This tournament will become one of the most important on the LPGA Tour from day one." The winner, Ritts added, would receive a Texas cowboy hat, a small brass bust of Harvey, and a dozen yellow roses. Ritts then presented Helen with a bouquet.

"Harvey would be so pleased about this," she said, "because he always did like the women."

A field of 144 players assembled the following spring of 1999 for the first tournament in Harvey's name, marking the first time since 1962, when Sandra Haynie beat Mickey Wright in the Civitan Open, that the LPGA had visited Austin. The participants included Juli Inkster, Meg Mallon, Laura Davis, and Michelle McGann, but organizers privately were disappointed. The top players in the LPGA — women such as Annika Sörenstam, Se-ri Pak, Karrie Webb, and Nancy Lopez — declined to enter, citing its proximity to the U.S. Women's Open, which was two weeks away.

Akiko Fukushima won that week. The tournament seemed to gain broader traction in 2000, when twenty-seven of the top thirty players on the LPGA money list traveled to Austin. Forty thousand spectators watched Laura Davies, the brash and long-driving Englishwoman, win with a 5-under 275. But the cheers were brief. The title sponsor, Philips Electronics, ended its support after two years.

California model Kathy Ireland sponsored the 2001 tournament, which continued to carry Harvey's name. Rosie Jones won in a thrilling, one-hole playoff over young Korean player Mi-Hyun Kim. Those cheers were even briefer. The tournament was left with no sponsor to finance the $1.3 million cost of staging the event.

Ritts was wrong. The tournament never became important, at least not to anyone with the financial means to support it. The invitational honoring Harvey lasted three years. There were no more yellow roses to give.

The fifth and final book was published in 1997. The original title of the anthology, *A Harvey Penick Reader,* later was changed to *The Wisdom of Harvey Penick.* Shrake selected 199 stories from the other four titles, including "Take Dead Aim" from the red, "Tommy Wins the Open" from the green, "Helen" from the white, and, fittingly, "Home" from the blue.

The epilogue was Tinsley Penick's address before the 1995 Ryder Cup matches at Oak Hill.

The PGA of America rewarded Crenshaw with the captaincy of the 1999 Ryder Cup team. The appointment thrilled Crenshaw, particularly because the matches would be played at The Country Club in Brookline, the course that had so broadened his perspective when he played the U.S. Junior there in 1968. His U.S. team that year fell four points behind Europe after the first two days of play. No team from either side had ever overcome a four-point deficit in Sunday singles play.

Crenshaw invited Governor George W. Bush to the team hotel on Saturday night. Bush recited William Barrett Travis's letter from the besieged Alamo in 1836. "I am determined to sustain myself as long as possible and die like a soldier who never forgets what is due his honor," Bush read. Crenshaw then asked each player on his team, a squad that included Harvey's friend Davis Love III, and their wives and girlfriends to speak.

Robin Love was last.

She conjured the spirit of Harvey. What would he say if he were here? she asked.

"Take dead aim."

The U.S. team won the next day.

It was nearly dark after the closing ceremony at The Country Club on that historic Sunday in New England. Scotty Sayers, Crenshaw's childhood friend and business manager, was walking near the practice range when he saw Helen Penick.

"You've got to come say hello to Ben," he told her.

He escorted Helen into the clubhouse.

"Ben, look who I found," Sayers said.

Crenshaw was delirious with joy and sticky with champagne. The two held a long embrace.

In 2002, Harvey was elected to the World Golf Hall of Fame.

Tinsley Penick received a letter in May from Jack Peter, the chief operating officer of the hall, notifying him that his father had "joined a very special group of individuals whose accomplishments and contributions to the game of golf will forever be remembered and respected."

The inductees that year included Tommy Bolt, Tony Jacklin, Bernhard Langer, Marlene Hagge, and, coincidentally, Ben Crenshaw. More than one thousand people attended the outdoor induction ceremony — televised nationally on the Golf Channel — that balmy November evening in St. Augustine, Florida, under a three-quarter moon. Harvey's was the fifth class enshrined since 1998, when the World Golf Village opened. He joined ninety-five other members, including his old friend and putting mentor Horton Smith; his inspirations in Francis Ouimet and Bobby Jones; his former pupils in Betty Jameson, Betsy

Rawls, Kathy Whitworth, and Mickey Wright; and his contemporaries in Demaret and Hagen and Hogan. He was among friends.

M. G. Orender, the president of the PGA of America, presented Harvey's candidacy that night to his son Tinsley. "He was America's gift to golf," Orender said. But Crenshaw wanted to say more. In his speech, emotional and halting, Crenshaw evoked Harvey at every one of his own rites of passage. He described their introduction, when Harvey placed Crenshaw's young fingers on the cut-down mashie and said, "Now, just leave your hands there." Although he played for a different coach in college, Crenshaw said, "Harvey was watching us, always." He cited the 1995 Masters, when he played with what he called the abandon of a child. "We buried our friend and, ladies and gentlemen, I don't know what happened." He scanned the crowd for the women who learned under Harvey. He gave them a knowing nod. "When you hear pupils talk about him, it's love," Crenshaw said. He read "Home," the essay from the third book, the one he recited the week after the '95 Masters. And then he looked at Tinsley.

"We're lucky we had you in our lives."

The First Tee of Greater Austin named its new facility for Harvey in the summer of 2003. The property in East Austin opened with a public nine-hole course and, fittingly, a succulent short-game practice area for players of all ages and ranges of talent. The ceremony on a warm July morning included tributes from Tinsley Penick, Cindy Figg-Currier, and LPGA Hall of Fame member Carol Mann.

"I believe there will be a beam of light that shines down on this place," Mann said.

Helen Penick died five days after Christmas in 2006, at the age of 101. She was buried next to Harvey.

Edwin "Bud" Shrake died from cancer in the spring of 2009. He was seventy-seven. The service included music from Ray Benson and Willie Nelson; Jerry Jeff Walker played at the gravesite at the Texas State

Cemetery and could barely get through the music without sobbing. Shrake was buried beside Ann Richards.

Shrake had spent the last good years of his life contented, in comfortable wealth, and with sustained sobriety. He sometimes opened the files and boxes he kept in his cabin in the woods, the repositories of his life in letters and film, to take stock of his contributions.

When he explored the boxes devoted to Harvey and their books, he might have seen the eulogy he delivered at Harvey's funeral in 1995: "What is it about Harvey that the world fell in love with? I think it was his spirit. He was always wisely powerful, always positive. Harvey spoke in simple words, and if you listened, sooner or later you understood."

Shrake might have read the rest of the eulogy. He might even have seen these words:

> Harvey Penick, who was known and loved all over the world, never really left home. Except for a few tournaments and teaching seminars, Harvey stayed at home in Austin, at his beloved Austin Country Club.
>
> The world came to Harvey.

Epilogue

BEN CRENSHAW NEVER won another professional golf tournament after the Masters in 1995. He made just three cuts on the PGA Tour after the sun-spackled afternoon in April when the spirit of Harvey carried him up that long, final hill to the seventy-second green.

He joined the Champions Tour in early 2002 and finished second once, in 2007. He continued to play the Masters. The lengthening of Augusta National by 510 yards after 1995, the demands of his successful golf-course architecture business with partner Bill Coore, and the steady deterioration of his own skills ensured that he never would contend again. But his annual spring return to Georgia meant more to him than a chance to be in contention. His indelible attachment to the Masters ran as deep as any other emotional bond in his life.

At the Masters tournament every year, Crenshaw would always remember and relive the week he played a difficult game on a difficult course through a difficult week in the spirit of the man who taught him to play. Crenshaw felt that when he left the Masters he would leave that too. Augusta National and the Masters had inhabited his golf soul the moment he arrived as a twenty-year-old amateur from Austin in 1972. His attachment to the place only intensified through the years, strengthening when he won in '84, bonding like a sacred resin in '95. It became his home of homes.

Crenshaw thought a lot about his final Masters before the second

Thursday of April in 2014, when he and Carl Jackson reported to the first tee for his forty-third start in the tournament that had meant so much to him. He had made the decision long before he signed his scorecard for an 83. The next day Crenshaw shot an 85. He made bogey on the last hole, just as he had in 1995, but the consequences were different. He finished last.

He returned to the club on Saturday morning, put on his green jacket, and sat down with Rich Lerner of the Golf Channel. The two-time champion, now sixty-two, his once-brown hair now a slate shade of gray, announced his intention to play his last Masters in 2015, on the twentieth anniversary of his second title. "It is hard, very hard," he told Lerner. "But I have been so fortunate. I have to pull over and watch. I'm resigned to being an encourager."

He explained that he had come to the decision that Thursday. He and Jackson were on the quietest part of the grounds, the place most buffered from the swells of spectators, in that fleeting period in every round at the Masters when a man and his caddie are alone with their present, future, and past. It's where white dogwoods become Golden Bells, which become azaleas. Players cross Rae's Creek on the Ben Hogan Bridge. Then they walk over the bridge named for Crenshaw's friend and fellow Texan from the caddie yard at Glen Garden, Byron Nelson. About there, Crenshaw turned to Jackson and said the words they knew were inevitable.

"Carl, I've been thinking about this for a long time," the player told his caddie. They were on the thirteenth hole. It was the end of Amen Corner.

A year later, Crenshaw arrived in Augusta for his forty-fourth and final start in the Masters. He accompanied Jackson, his longtime caddie, at a ceremony Monday in which officials of Augusta presented Jackson with a key to the city. Crenshaw played a practice round with Tom Watson, now sixty-five, the champion in 1977 and '81, and joked that it felt like the era of the gutta-percha ball. He adjourned his press conference on the Tuesday with an acknowledgment of the many mysteries of his triumphant week in 1995. "To have played that well is beyond my comprehension," he told reporters in the Augusta National press center. "But to have won my favorite tournament for his memory will always be my best moment." He opened the tournament on Thursday with a score of 91. Jackson wasn't feeling well, so his brother Bud carried Crenshaw's bag.

The next morning, Crenshaw put on a cornflower-blue shirt for his final walk in the Masters. By the time he made the turn from the ninth green to the tenth tee, Jordan Spieth, who attended the University of Texas for three semesters before turning professional in 2013, had already completed rounds of 64-66 to establish a Masters record for low score through thirty-six holes. (Spieth won the tournament. He was twenty-one years old. It was the farewell of one Texas Longhorn and the coronation of another.)

Crenshaw struck the last drive of his Masters career under a moody sky on that Friday afternoon in Georgia, through the rising tunnel of pines. He marched up the eighteenth fairway with a swirl of nostalgia and sentiment clouding his ability to concentrate. He thought about Harvey. He thought about fate. It was 1995 all over again when he reached his ball and the spectators ringing the green rose to applaud. Many of them removed their hats.

The CBS cameras found Carl Jackson, Crenshaw's caddie since 1976. He stood with Masters officials and Augusta members Billy Payne and Joe Ford, and he was waiting there for Crenshaw in his full-length, club-issued white caddie uniform. Lead announcer Jim Nantz reminded viewers that Jackson had given Crenshaw a tip on the range in 1995. "It led to one of the truly remarkable wins in the history of the Masters," Nantz said. The cameras panned to Crenshaw's wife and three daughters, then to Crenshaw, handing his ball to Bud Jackson, who wiped it clean. An airplane droned overhead.

"We're going to keep it here," Nantz said.

Jason Dufner and Bill Haas, who played with Crenshaw in the first and second rounds, holed their putts, even though Haas was closer to the hole. It was like the also-rans clearing the stage for the champion on the last hole, which has long been tradition and courtesy on the tour.

Crenshaw took one practice stroke, long and languid, hands pressed forward as Harvey had told him many times to do, before squaring his hips over his putt for par. It missed. Crenshaw later said it seemed like something else had happened on that stroke, "like I had won the Masters." His last shot — a sliding putt for bogey, about the same length as the one he made twenty years before — initiated a hearty and sustained cascade of applause. It wasn't a roar, not that sonic indication of an eagle or timely birdie at the Masters, and it wasn't the polite recognition of a disappointing round that wasn't quite good enough to win. It was the sound of a farewell.

Jackson met Crenshaw on the green. They embraced for eight seconds with their eyes closed tightly. It was '95. It was '84. It was a moment without regard for time. Crenshaw departed to kiss his family and find his wife's hand. He swept his hat to the people. Friends clapped his back on his walk away from the course. Then here came his daughters. Here came his brother. Here came the spectral assurance that Harvey Penick was forever a part of the lore of the Masters Tournament. "We're going to miss him," Nantz said of the man who had made sure of that.

And then he was gone.

Acknowledgments

The first fact I learned about both Harvey Penick and Bud Shrake was that they had many friends. Those friends found time to talk, plan interviews with others, open family scrapbooks, and share artifacts and relics, and they made their spare bedrooms available for me when I needed a place to spend the night. I thank them for their many contributions to this book. They looked out for Harvey and Bud with love and loyalty.

I am indebted to Kathryn Powell and Tinsley Penick, the daughter and son of Harvey and Helen Penick. Tinsley and I spent many pleasant hours in the living room of his Northwest Austin home, usually with his delightful wife Betty Ann sitting with us. Kathryn granted me a standing invitation to visit her home in Brady, in the bluebonnet-and-Indian-paintbrush-carpeted Texas Hill Country. I'm grateful I made that trip one summer afternoon with Tinsley in the seat next to me.

Cindy Slater, the extraordinary assistant director for library services at the Stark Center, assisted me in ways I'll never be able to reciprocate. She accommodated my research visits over the summer of 2013 with buoyant esprit de corps, no matter the hour. Terry and Jan Todd, the Stark Center director and codirector, trusted me with their extensive collection. Similarly, Steven Davis and the staff at the Wittliff

Collections, where Shrake's papers are archived, also have my lasting gratitude.

I'm indebted also to Frances Trimble, the premier golf historian in the state of Texas, whose husband John played for Harvey. No one knows more than Frances about who played when, who played where, who played what course, who beat whom, even whether rain fell. Furthermore, she knows the meaning of it all. Without her, I would have been doomed. Mark Button of the Texas Golf Association and Arthur "Sonny" Rhodes, a close friend of the Penick family, also contributed important material.

Sandra Haynie, Sandra Palmer, Betsy Rawls, and Kathy Whitworth granted extensive interviews whenever I needed them. Ben Crenshaw and Tom Kite, whose careers bloomed under Harvey's gentle stewardship, also provided new insights, building on the many observations they have shared about their beloved golf guide over the years. Their wives, Julie Crenshaw and Christy Kite (who died in January 2015), recalled meaningful moments. So did many of Harvey's former players at the University of Texas. Scotty Sayers, Crenshaw's lifelong friend, rose to many occasions for me, large and small.

I'm grateful for the players on the PGA Tour, past and present, who helped me better understand the important golf moments reconstructed in the book, notably the 1992 U.S. Open Championship and the 1995 Masters Tournament. The list includes Tommy Armour III, Fred Couples, Bob Estes, Brad Faxon, David Frost, Jay Haas, Hale Irwin, Peter Jacobsen, Don January, Colin Montgomerie, Nick Price, Jeff Sluman, and Hal Sutton. My thanks go to Colby Callaway, tournament director of the AT&T Championship, for his many courtesies. The media staff of the Masters Tournament and Augusta National Golf Club, where I spent a week for the 2013 tournament, also contributed greatly to this effort. Bob Denney, the historian for the PGA of America, read the early manuscript and clarified various historical facts in a way that no one else could have done. I'm indebted as well to the PGA of America golf professionals — Harvey's peers — who shared their keen insights, notably Lonny Alexander, Brent Buckman, Jack Burke Jr., Bryan Gathright, Ann Marie Gildersleeve, Jim Hopkins, Eddie Merrins, Dale Morgan, and Steve Termeer. Thanks also to the University of Texas golf coaches, former and current, who have carried on the spirit of Harvey: John Fields, George Hannon, Susan Watkins, and Pat Weis. I'm grateful for the time they spent with me.

My former colleagues at the *Austin American-Statesman,* especially Mark Rosner and Ralph Haurwitz, helped with important contributions to my reporting. I owe much to Debbie Hiott, the newspaper's editor, and the entire staff there. Also, I'm particularly grateful for early thoughts from John Bridges, a resolute and wholly collegial editor with whom I not only improved as a journalist but played many memorable rounds of golf in Texas and parts beyond. I hope for more.

I'm fortunate to be part of an incredible group of journalism practitioners and academics who motivate me always to think harder and better about our craft. My colleagues at the University of Texas at Austin School of Journalism, many of them authors far more accomplished than I will ever be, cheered me throughout the eighteen months I spent preparing this book. The dean of the Moody College of Communication, Roderick P. Hart, scaled back my teaching schedule in the spring semester of 2014 so I could devote the proper attention to Harvey's story. Three other colleagues deserve special thanks: Bill Minutaglio, a clinical professor who writes nonfiction books with effortless grace; Kate Dawson, a senior lecturer who encouraged me at every turn; and Glenn Frankel, a Pulitzer Prize–winning journalist, an accomplished author, and the former director of the journalism school, who buoyed my spirit when I privately needed the push. I also thank the school's new director, R. B. Brenner, whose example inspired me to finish with a flourish.

My students deserve my everlasting gratitude too. They were my earliest sounding boards. I hope they learned as much from me as I did from them.

Jim Hornfischer, my agent, always believed in me. Susan Canavan, my editor at Houghton Mifflin Harcourt, took a chance on a first-time biographer who will remember her fondly and always for that. Cindy Buck improved the story magnificently with an exhaustive and caring copyedit. I am also grateful for the work of Lisa Glover, the production editor, and Jenny Xu, who fielded my many questions at Houghton.

I finally and humbly thank the people I love and who loved me back, even when I had so little time to show or express it. My parents, Mary and Gary Robbins, cheered me from the Ozarks of Missouri, as did my brother Jeff, from nearby Columbia, and sister-in-law Kathy. My in-laws, Don and Donna Sharbutt, cheered me from Dallas. My friend the Rev. Tim Anderson, himself a writer and a former college golfer whose golf swing would have given Harvey goose pimples, nudged me whenever I needed a caring voice.

My wife and children cheered me every day, without fail. My wife, Suzanne, was my quiet and steadfast inspiration. This book would not have been remotely possible without her enduring faith — or the innocent question my son and daughter often asked before they went to sleep and I went to my desk: *Are you done yet?* They kept me accountable, both in that way and in many other more meaningful ways. Sweet Lila and dear Henry, this book is for you too. And the answer to your question is: *Yes.*

A Note on Sources

Portions of this book were written using primary source material obtained from the H.J. Lutcher Stark Center for Physical Culture and Sports at the University of Texas at Austin, the Wittliff Collections at Texas State University–San Marcos, the Dolph Briscoe Center for American History at the University of Texas at Austin, the Perry-Castaneda Library at the University of Texas at Austin, the Austin History Center, the Seagle Electronic Golf Library at the United States Golf Association, and the Buda Public Library, in the author's hometown of Buda, Texas. Material quoted from these collections is cited in the notes.

All other quoted material in this book was curated from more than two hundred personal interviews with Harvey Penick's and Bud Shrake's family members, their former colleagues in the PGA of America and at *Sports Illustrated,* former players for the University of Texas golf teams from 1938 through 1963, and many former golf pupils of Harvey's — all of them committed to ensuring a fair assessment of his life in golf, at Austin Country Club and beyond. Those interviews took place in person, by telephone, and by email from November 2012 to April 2015, in Austin, Dallas, Fort Worth, Houston, Midland, and San Antonio, Texas; Denver, Colorado; and Augusta, Georgia.

There are conflicting versions of the year Harvey first caddied at Austin Country Club. Harvey consistently said he began his life in golf when he was eight years old, which would establish that date sometime between October 1912 and October 1913. For consistency, this book uses 1912, the year most commonly cited by other accounts of Harvey's life, including Harvey's handwritten notes in his original Scribbletex notebook.

Notes

INTRODUCTION

page

xiv *"In death, Penick lives"*: Kevin Robbins, "Enduring Lessons from Golf's Great Coach," *Austin American-Statesman*, April 5, 2005.

xv *"Harvey knows as much"*: Jim Trinkle, "Why They Dig Harvey Penick," *Golf*, April 1971, p. 52.

"fine example": Herbert Warren Wind, *The Story of American Golf*, 3rd ed. (New York: Alfred A. Knopf, 1975), p. 524.

xvi *"One morning last spring"*: Harvey Penick and Bud Shrake, *Harvey Penick's Little Red Book* (New York: Simon & Schuster, 1992), pp. 22–23.

xvii *"I spend nights staring"*: Ibid., p. 23.

xviii *"I want to show"*: Ibid., p. 26.

CHAPTER ONE

8 *"support and maintain a"*: Frances G. Trimble, *One Hundred Years of Champions and Change: The History of Austin Country Club* (Austin, TX: Austin Country Club, 1999), p. 15.

9 *"just east of the University"*: "The Austin Golf Club: The Initial Meeting Held at the Driskill Hotel Yesterday Afternoon," *Austin Daily Statesman*, November 14, 1899.

"It is open and free": Trimble, *One Hundred Years of Champions and Change*, p. 12.

11 *"built on the style"*: "The New Golf Club House ... Was Formally Dedicated on Friday Night," *Austin Daily Statesman,* June 30, 1901.

17 *"Some players learn quicker"*: Jim Trinkle, "Why They Dig Harvey Penick," *Golf,* April 1971, p. 52.

18 *"An eighteen-hole golf course"*: *Austin Daily Statesman,* June 7, 1914.

19 *"Indecision spoils more shots"*: Trinkle, "Why They Dig Harvey Penick," p. 52.

20 *"It's all right to eat"*: Trimble, *One Hundred Years of Champions and Change,* p. 57.
"A golf pro is": Trinkle, "Why They Dig Harvey Penick," p. 52.

23 *"Psychologically"*: Ibid.

24 *"to see that all sports"*: 1923 *University of Texas Cactus* (yearbook), p. 201.

26 *"It is raining continuously"*: Joe Byrne, letter to Austin Country Club members, April 20, 1923, Harvey and Tinsley Penick Collection, H.J. Lutcher Stark Center for Physical Culture and Sports, University of Texas.

CHAPTER TWO

30 *"As the ball rolled"*: Frances G. Trimble, *One Hundred Years of Champions and Change: The History of Austin Country Club* (Austin, TX: Austin Country Club, 1999), p. 60.
"The growth and popularity": Ibid., p. 62.

31 *"Austin High School"*: 1924 *Austin High School Comet* (yearbook).

34 *"A man may teach"*: Jim Trinkle, "Why They Dig Harvey Penick," *Golf,* April 1971, p. 93.

35 *"and if the support"*: Ibid., p. 69.

36 *"You want a word"*: Harvey Penick and Bud Shrake, *And If You Play Golf, You're My Friend* (New York: Simon & Schuster, 1993), p. 148.

38 mother was a *"pillar"*: Trimble, *One Hundred Years of Champions and Change,* p. 76.
"hardwood floors": Ibid.

40 *"practically in downtown Houston"*: Harvey Penick and Bud Shrake, *The Game for a Lifetime: More Lessons and Teachings* (New York: Simon & Schuster, 1996), p. 188.

41 *"fine architect"*: Harvey Penick, letter to Francis Trimble, January 22, 1990, Francis Trimble personal archives.

42 *"Your short game will"*: Penick and Shrake, *The Game for a Lifetime*, p. 193.

"If there's one thing": Trinkle, "Why They Dig Harvey Penick," p. 93.

43 *"Bobby Jones did that"*: Ibid., p. 52.

CHAPTER THREE

46 *"Coach Harvey Penick"*: *1931 University of Texas Cactus* (yearbook).

49 *"Texas exhibited"*: *1932 University of Texas Cactus* (yearbook).

50 *"It had to be seven"*: *1933 University of Texas Cactus* (yearbook), p. 116.

52 *"When Ed lost"*: Harry Blanding, "Behind Fame of Texas Golfers Lies Coaching of Harvey Penick," *The Daily Texan*, May 21, 1936, Harvey and Tinsley Penick Collection, Stark Center.

53 *"I knew they'd have to"*: Harry Blanding, "Behind Fame of Texas Golfers Lies Coaching of Harvey Penick," *The Daily Texan*, May 21, 1936, Harvey and Tinsley Penick Collection, Stark Center.

"I guess I owe": Ibid.

59 *"She is an incredible"*: Don Van Natta Jr., *Wonder Girl: The Magnificent Sporting Life of Babe Didrikson Zaharias* (New York: Little, Brown and Co., 2011), p. 113.

"She is the longest": Ibid., p. 121.

62 *"The only justification for"*: George B. Kirsch, *Golf in America* (Urbana and Chicago: University of Illinois Press, 2009), pp. 122–23.

CHAPTER FOUR

66 *"That Harvey Penick be"*: Minutes of a special called meeting of the Board of Directors of River Oaks Country Club, April 22, 1943.

67 *"Some directors"*: Ed Turley, letter to the author (undated).

68 *"The world which emerges"*: *1945 University of Texas Cactus* (yearbook), p. 2.

"The powerful one-two": *1949 University of Texas Cactus* (yearbook).

71 *"his interest in students"*: *Professional Golfer,* April 1954, p. 7.

72 *"He wanted no credit"*: John Maher, "For Decades, Women Golfers of All Levels Listened to Harvey Penick . . . and He to Them," *Austin American-Statesman,* May 19, 1999, Harvey and Tinsley Penick Collection, Stark Center.

74 *"the old homestead"*: Frances G. Trimble, *One Hundred Years of Champions and Change: The History of Austin Country Club* (Austin, TX: Austin Country Club, 1999), p. 107.

75 *"will be one of"*: Morris Williams, "Nelson Still Great Golfer," *Sunday Austin American-Statesman,* March 19, 1950, Harvey and Tinsley Penick Collection, Stark Center.

77 *"Good ones, too"*: Morris Williams, "Hogan Shows Wizardry at Municipal, Fires 67," *Sunday American-Statesman,* May 14, 1950.
   "Okay, partner": Harvey Penick and Bud Shrake, *And If You Play Golf, You're My Friend* (New York: Simon & Schuster, 1993), pp. 165–66.

78 *"The Fort Worth ace"*: Williams, "Hogan Shows Wizardry at Municipal."
   "Few people remembered": Penick and Shrake, *And If You Play Golf,* p. 166.

CHAPTER FIVE

81 *"This was before"*: Taylor Glass oral history, May 23, 1974, Austin History Center.

86 *"couldn't match"*: Associated Press, "Williams Is Winner of State Junior Tourney," *Austin Statesman,* July 15, 1949.

88 *"Both played a sharp"*: Shorty Shelburne, "Gafford, Beford Take Lead," *Midland Reporter-Telegram,* June 2, 1950.
   "set off a lot": Shorty Shelburne, "Williams Low; Champ Leads Pros," *Midland Reporter-Telegram,* June 3, 1950.

89 *"torrid race"*: Shorty Shelburne, "Gafford, Nelson Tied at 206 to Top Professionals," *Midland Reporter-Telegram,* June 4, 1950.

90 *"The win by Williams"*: Shorty Shelburne, "Morris Williams Wins PGA Title, Nelson Cops Top Money for Pros," *Midland Reporter-Telegram,* June 5, 1950.
   "Byron Nelson still is": Shorty Shelburne, "Sport Slants by Shorty Shelburne," *Midland Reporter-Telegram,* June 5, 1950.

91 *"I was lucky"*: Ibid.

92 *"This boy had"*: Tom Davison, "Golfing Corner," *Houston Post,* October 21, 1956.

"Those who watched": Dan Jenkins, *Jenkins at the Majors: Sixty Years of the World's Best Golf Writing, from Hogan to Tiger* (New York: Doubleday, 2009), p. 4.

95 *"We've got to have"*: Fred Williams, "Top O' Morn," *Sunday Austin American-Statesman,* date unknown, Harvey and Tinsley Penick Collection, Stark Center.

"Things have changed": Ibid.

96 *The report suggested*: Frances G. Trimble, *One Hundred Years of Champions and Change: The History of Austin Country Club* (Austin, TX: Austin Country Club, 1999), pp. 129–30.

98 *"The expression"*: "Williams Trophy Ceremony Held," *Austin Statesman,* March 3, 1954.

99 *"Morris was a fine"*: "New City Golf Course Naming Gets Boost," *Austin American,* August 24, 1954.

CHAPTER SIX

102 *"Mr. Penick, my name"*: Harvey Penick and Bud Shrake, *The Wisdom of Harvey Penick* (New York: Simon & Schuster, 1997), p. 295.

"I hadn't seen Bobby": Ibid., p. 296.

108 *"listening to some bad"*: L. G. "Plug" Osborne, Wilson Sporting Goods Co., letter to Harvey Penick, June 24, 1955, Harvey and Tinsley Penick Collection, Stark Center.

109 *"pro who did the most"*: Morris Williams, "Fairways," *Sunday Austin American-Statesman,* October 28, 1956, Harvey and Tinsley Penick Collection, Stark Center.

"Wesley is another": Tom Davison, "Golfing Corner," *Houston Post,* October 21, 1956.

"Penick is one": Ibid.

110 *"Winning the Open is"*: Herbert Warren Wind, "The Tragic Fourth," *Sports Illustrated,* July 8, 1957.

111 *"Everyone in Texas knew"*: John Maher, "For Decades, Women Golfers of All Levels Listened to Harvey Penick . . . and He to Them,"

Austin American-Statesman, May 19, 1999, Harvey and Tinsley Penick Collection, Stark Center.

112 *"I've taken her as"*: Barry McDermott, "Wrong Image but the Right Touch," *Sports Illustrated,* July 25, 1983, p. 40.

CHAPTER SEVEN

119 *"Golf Digest just wrote"*: Betty Hicks, letter to Harvey Penick, July 22, 1958, Harvey and Tinsley Penick Collection, Stark Center.

120 *"The average player"*: Harvey Penick, "Proper Use of All Clubs," *Sports Illustrated,* May 19, 1958.

123 *"Since we have"*: Mary Lena Faulk, letter to Harvey Penick, March 28, 1960, Harvey and Tinsley Penick Collection, Stark Center.

124 *"If she didn't hit"*: Adam Schupak, "Winning 82 Pro Titles with Best Swing Ever," *New York Times,* May 19, 2012.

125 *"every Saturday"*: Beth Ann Nichols, "Catching Up with a Legend: Mickey Wright," *Golfweek,* November 16, 2011.

126 *"I treated hitting"*: Mickey Wright, "Hall of Famer Mickey Wright on Past of LPGA Tour," *Golf,* June 27, 2013.
"When Wright was over": Bill Fields, "The Wright Stuff," *Golf World,* November 24, 2000.
"I was always struck": Harvey Penick and Bud Shrake, *Harvey Penick's Little Red Book* (New York: Simon & Schuster, 1992), p. 17.

127 *"Why this should be"*: Harvey Penick, "Crispness in the Short Game," *Sports Illustrated,* September 12, 1960.

129 *"The association"*: Harvey Little, "Penick Ends UT Service," *Austin American-Statesman,* (date uncertain), 1964, Harvey and Tinsley Penick Collection, Stark Center.

131 *"You are indeed fortunate"*: Jackson Bradley, letter to Austin Country Club, May 18, 1963, Harvey and Tinsley Penick Collection, Stark Center.
"When I look back": Penrose B. Metcalfe, letter to Harvey Penick, May 22, 1963, Harvey and Tinsley Penick Collection, Stark Center.
"There are some rare": John Barclay, letter to Harvey Penick, May 24, 1963, Harvey and Tinsley Penick Collection, Stark Center.

"I carried him out": Dick Collins, "First Time Around," *Austin American*, July 5, 1968, Tom Kite Collection, Stark Center.

135 *"I spend most"*: *The Junior Golfer*, Spring 1967, Tom Kite Collection, Stark Center.

CHAPTER EIGHT

139 *"I had never seen"*: Herbert Warren Wind, "Austin and Augusta," *The New Yorker*, June 10, 1985.

140 *"Even though I didn't"*: Ben Crenshaw and Melanie Hauser, *A Feel for the Game: To Brookline and Back* (New York: Doubleday, 2001), p. 39.

142 *"It was about time"*: "Kite Captures Another Crown," *Austin American*, August 3, 1968, Tom Kite Collection, Stark Center.

"He's a tremendous putter": Dick Collins, "Crenshaw's 70 Wins City Title," *Austin American*, September 16, 1968, Tom Kite Collection, Stark Center.

143 *"Harvey taught me"*: Harvey Little, "Penick Ends UT Service," *Austin American-Statesman*, (date uncertain), 1964, Harvey and Tinsley Penick Collection, Stark Center.

"There is a certain": Ibid.

144 *"He has an almost"*: Ibid.

147 *"I thought at the time"*: "Favored Longhorns Just Hung Close," *Austin American-Statesman*, June 29, 1971, Harvey and Tinsley Penick Collection, Stark Center.

"The spark was Kite": Ibid.

148 *"It was one of"*: Doug Smith, "Remembering Texas' Remarkable Comeback for 1971 NCAA Title," *Austin American-Statesman*, June 8, 2006.

"Both are disappointed": "Longhorns Win NCAA Golf Title Again," *Austin American-Statesman*, June 25, 1972, Harvey and Tinsley Penick Collection, Stark Center.

"You've got to be": Ibid.

"I'm glad it's over": Ibid.

"I've met my first": Dan Couture, "Tom Kite Turns Pro," *Summer*

Texan, July 11, 1972, Harvey and Tinsley Penick Collection, Stark Center.

149 *"I think this is"*: Dick Collins, "First Time Around," *Austin American-Statesman,* July 24, 1970, Harvey and Tinsley Penick Collection, Stark Center.

"When I started playing": Doug Darroch, "Snead Made Penick a Better Teaching Pro," *Tulsa Tribune,* March 31, 1977, Harvey and Tinsley Penick Collection, Stark Center.

"Harvey has been speaking": Jack Gallagher, "Humble Penick Spices Seminar," *Houston Post,* February 25, 1976, Harvey and Tinsley Penick Collection, Stark Center.

150 *"Harvey tightens nuts"*: Jim Trinkle, "Why They Dig Harvey Penick," *Golf,* April 1971, p. 51.

"Harvey is the only": Ibid., p. 51.

"repeats under pressure": Ibid., p. 52.

151 *"I couldn't be happier"*: Joe Hornaday Jr., "ACC Names Penick's Son," *Austin American-Statesman,* January 1, 1971, Harvey and Tinsley Penick Collection, Stark Center.

"He said, 'You know'": "Jimmy Demaret at Onion Creek Club," 1974 video interview, Carolyn Jackson Collection, number 11, Texas Archive of the Moving Image.

154 *"I don't know why"*: Charles Richards, "Harvey Penick: A Lifetime at Golf," *The Surveyor,* July 21, 1974, Harvey and Tinsley Penick Collection, Stark Center.

156 *"A shrug of the hands"*: Ibid.

CHAPTER NINE

160 *"Writers adore instant heroes"*: Dan Jenkins, "Gentle Ben Is Very Tough," *Sports Illustrated,* February 11, 1974, p. 33, Harvey and Tinsley Penick Collection, Stark Center.

161 *"Ben beats you to"*: Ibid., p. 36.

"There is no golf": William A. Penn, letter to *Sports Illustrated,* February 13, 1974, Harvey and Tinsley Penick Collection, Stark Center.

164 *"I found out I"*: Sarah Pileggi, "That Palmer Is a Player," *Sports Illustrated,* November 24, 1975.

"I've always wondered": Ibid.

166 *"I stayed to myself"*: Ibid.

"Now that I've won": Ibid.

167 *"I was just fascinated"*: Kevin Robbins, "First Impressions: In 1978, Tom Kite and Ben Crenshaw Made a Run at the Claret Jug at St. Andrews," *Austin American-Statesman*, July 14, 2010.

168 *"My confidence was up"*: Ibid.

"At St. Andrews": Ibid.

170 *"We had a strong"*: Frances G. Trimble, *One Hundred Years of Champions and Change: The History of Austin Country Club* (Austin, TX: Austin Country Club, 1999), p. 159.

"There has never been": Charles E. Crenshaw, letter to Bill Gainer, February 19, 1982, Harvey and Tinsley Penick Collection, Stark Center.

171 *"Have a nice round"*: Mark Rosner, "Master Teacher: Penick Has Been Improving Golf Games for 61 Years, and His Success Is Legendary," *Austin American-Statesman*, July 29, 1984.

172 *"It was the worst"*: Sarah Pileggi, "This One Was for My Friends," *Sports Illustrated*, May 14, 1984, Harvey and Tinsley Penick Collection, Stark Center.

173 *"I told him to"*: Mickey Herskowitz, "The Wreck of the S.S. Crenshaw," *Golf Digest*, March 1983.

"What Harvey was saying": Pileggi, "This One Was for My Friends."

174 *"but that bunker shot"*: Ben Crenshaw and Melanie Hauser, *A Feel for the Game: To Brookline and Back* (New York: Doubleday, 2001), p. 85.

175 *"I wanted to win"*: Associated Press, April 16, 1984.

176 *"Mighty proud of you"*: Crenshaw and Hauser, *A Feel for the Game*, p. 90.

CHAPTER TEN

177 *"For seven decades"*: Joe Hornaday, letter to the Texas Sports Hall of Fame, May 22, 1984.

179 *"When you or Mickey"*: Barry McDermott, "Here's to the Good Ol' Times," *Sports Illustrated*, May 6, 1985.

"I'm just following Mickey": Ibid.

"You don't recapture": Ibid.

"Quitting a sport is": Ibid.

182 *"As you well can"*: Louis R. Brill, letter to Helen Penick, November 20, 1990, Harvey and Tinsley Penick Collection, Stark Center.

"Every day when I": Gary Cartwright, "The Old Man and the Tee," *Texas Monthly*, December 1993.

"My teaching methods": Harvey Penick, letter to Patrick J. Reilly, October 23, 1989, Harvey and Tinsley Penick Collection, Stark Center.

183 *"Golf needs a book"*: Harris Greenwood, letter to Tinsley Penick, March 21, 1990, Harvey and Tinsley Penick Collection, Stark Center.

185 *"This gift had not"*: Ibid., p. 26.

CHAPTER ELEVEN

187 *"My dad wasn't"*: Gary Cartwright, "The Old Man and the Tee," *Texas Monthly*, December 1993, p. 170.

189 *"I looked around at"*: Steven L. Davis, *Texas Literary Outlaws* (Fort Worth: Texas Christian University Press, 2004), p. 63.

"Everybody had this sense": Michael MacCambridge, *The Franchise* (New York: Hyperion, 1997), p. 54.

190 *"came to function as"*: Bud Shrake interview, November 8, 2008, Edwin "Bud" Shrake Papers, The Wittliff Collections, Texas State University–San Marcos.

"Sports pages are where": Davis, *Texas Literary Outlaws*, p. 81.

192 *"On any given night"*: Ibid., p. 114.

193 *"We had boundless energy"*: Shrake interview, November 8, 2008.

"I told [Terrell] that": Davis, *Texas Literary Outlaws*, p. 142.

194 *"There was no direct"*: Bud Shrake, *Land of the Permanent Wave: An Edwin "Bud" Shrake Reader*, edited by Steven L. Davis (Austin: University of Texas Press, 2007), p. 106.

"The Colorado River flows": Bud Shrake, "The Once-Forbidding Land," *Sports Illustrated*, May 10, 1965.

"This is a wonderful": Gary Cartwright, "Gone to New York," *Texas Monthly*, November 2009.

195 *"She is beautiful, twenty-three"*: Davis, *Texas Literary Outlaws*, p. 172.

196 *"He wanted to focus"*: Ibid., p. 222.

197 *"To me few finer"*: Ibid., p. 223.
     "I really liked going": Ibid., p. 251.

198 *"a very pleasant period"*: Shrake interview, November 8, 2008.
     "The longer we were": Davis, *Texas Literary Outlaws*, p. 257.

199 *"but commercial failure was"*: Ibid., p. 281.

201 *"I was going to"*: Louis Black, "Bud Shrake's Adventures in the Film Trade," *Austin Chronicle*, May 8, 2009.
     "The story involved": Davis, *Texas Literary Outlaws*, p. 368.
     "I notice it's been": Black, "Bud Shrake's Adventures in the Film Trade."

202 *"Even then, I actually"*: Davis, *Texas Literary Outlaws*, p. 441.
     "In a way I": Ibid.

203 *"I love the way"*: Cartwright, "The Old Man and the Tee," p. 172.

204 *"This is the only"*: Davis, *Texas Literary Outlaws*, p. 445.

CHAPTER TWELVE

207 *"I said, yeah, I"*: Bud Shrake interview, November 18, 2008, Edwin "Bud" Shrake Papers, The Wittliff Collections, Texas State University–San Marcos.

208 *"Maybe something got lost"*: Gary Cartwright, "The Old Man and the Tee," *Texas Monthly*, December 1993, p. 170.

210 *"Why is the grip"*: Tape 1, June 21, 1991, Edwin "Bud" Shrake Papers, The Wittliff Collections, Texas State University–San Marcos.

212 *"writing in another"*: Bud Shrake, email interview with the author, February 12, 2005.

216 *"be like eating peanuts"*: Cartwright, "The Old Man and the Tee," p. 170.

217 *"It scared me to"*: Shrake, email interview with the author, February 12, 2005.
     "What Harvey had to": Cartwright, "The Old Man and the Tee," p. 170.
     "It needed very": Jeff Neuman, email to the author, April 4, 2015.

218 *"This is simply the"*: Dan Jenkins, letter to George H. W. Bush, May 4, 1992, Harvey and Tinsley Penick Collection, Stark Center.

219 *"Dear Mr. President"*: Harvey Penick, letter to George H. W. Bush, June 2, 1992, Harvey and Tinsley Penick Collection, Stark Center.

220 *"the best and most"*: Ernest L. Ransome III, letter to Harvey Penick, July 29, 1992, Harvey and Tinsley Penick Collection, Stark Center.
"What a great thing": Byron Nelson, letter to Harvey Penick, September 26, 1992, Harvey and Tinsley Penick Collection, Stark Center.

221 *"I think of you"*: Billy Graham, letter to Harvey Penick, September 2, 1992, Harvey and Tinsley Penick Collection, Stark Center.
"The Little Red Book is": Betsy Rawls, letter to Harvey Penick, December 2, 1992, Harvey and Tinsley Penick Collection, Stark Center.
"Today I'm back": Charles Crenshaw, letter to Harvey Penick, September 15, 1992, Harvey and Tinsley Penick Collection, Stark Center.
"There are many books": Jeffrey Neuman, letter to Harvey Penick, April 9, 1992, Harvey and Tinsley Penick Collection, Stark Center.

222 *"I believe the Little"*: Bud Shrake, letter to Harvey Penick, undated, Harvey and Tinsley Penick Collection, Stark Center.

CHAPTER THIRTEEN

225 *"I began to wonder"*: Tom Kite and Mickey Herskowitz, *A Fairway to Heaven* (New York: William Morrow and Co., 1997), p. 86.

226 *"He was the 'other'"*: Jim Murray, "As Usual, Winner Didn't Throw Caution to Wind," *Los Angeles Times*, June 22, 1992, Harvey and Tinsley Penick Collection, Stark Center.
"Who won?": Bob Verdi, "The Day Golf Gave Something Back," *Golf World*, June 1992, Tom Kite Collection, Stark Center.

227 *"It was just awful"*: Mark Rosner, "Proud Papa Celebrates Son's Sense of Direction," *Austin American-Statesman*, June 25, 1992, Tom Kite Collection, Stark Center.
"It's a cruel game": Dave Anderson, "A Kite Steady in the Wind," *New York Times*, June 22, 1992, Harvey and Tinsley Penick Collection, Stark Center.

228 *"I think it's the best"*: United States Golf Association, "The 1992 U.S. Open: Kite Soars over Pebble Beach" (VHS tape).
"It's a great blend": Ibid.
"It's funny how": Ibid.

229 *"It looked like"*: Gary Van Sickle, "Kite Wins His First Major the Old-Fashioned Way," *Golf World,* June 21–28, 1992, Tom Kite Collection, Stark Center.
"We're all trying": USGA, "The 1992 U.S. Open."
"When you step": Ibid.
Like Kite in '89: "Kite Again Knocks at Open Door," *Austin American-Statesman,* June 21, 1992, Harvey and Tinsley Penick Collection, Stark Center.
"yucky": Ibid.

230 *"I prefer not to"*: Anderson, "A Kite Steady in the Wind."
"The wind has turned": "Kite Again Knocks at Open Door," *Austin American-Statesman,* June 21, 1992, Harvey and Tinsley Penick Collection, Stark Center.

231 *"I don't know if"*: Harvey Penick and Bud Shrake, *And If You Play Golf, You're My Friend* (New York: Simon & Schuster, 1993), p. 54.

232 *"It's going to be"*: USGA, "The 1992 U.S. Open."
"The course was out": Dwight Chapin, "Course 'Out of Control,'" *San Francisco Examiner,* June 22, 1992, Tom Kite Collection, Stark Center.

233 *"Right now"*: Thomas Boswell, "At Long Last, Kite Gets Just What He Deserves," *Washington Post,* June 22, 1992, Tom Kite Collection, Stark Center.

234 *"Congratulations on winning your"*: Tim Rosaforte, "Nicklaus Premature with Congrats," *Palm Beach Post,* June 22, 1992, Harvey and Tinsley Penick Collection, Stark Center.
"We'll just sit here": USGA, "The 1992 U.S. Open."

235 *"I feel very uplifted"*: Jayne Custred, "Kite's Win Thrills Longtime Coach," *Houston Chronicle,* June 22, 1992, Tom Kite Collection, Stark Center.
"How do you describe": Van Sickle, "Kite Wins His First Major the Old-Fashioned Way."

"I really relish those": John Maher, "Kite Finds Major Relief at Pebble," *Austin American-Statesman,* June 22, 1992, Tom Kite Collection, Stark Center.

236 *"I don't cry very"*: Associated Press, "Austin Swells with Pride, Tears After Kite's Victory," *Houston Post,* June 23, 1992, Harvey and Tinsley Penick Collection, Stark Center.

CHAPTER FOURTEEN

238 *"He's crippled"*: Frank Luska, *Dallas Morning News,* July 7, 1992, Harvey and Tinsley Penick Collection, Stark Center.

239 *"What it says about"*: "Lore of the Links," *People Weekly,* September 21, 1992, Harvey and Tinsley Penick Collection, Stark Center.

James Michener: Bud Shrake, "Harvey Penick and James Michener," unpublished manuscript, February 2000, The Wittliff Collections, Texas State University–San Marcos.

240 *"The book has given"*: Sam Blair, "Sam Blair's People," *Dallas Morning News,* October 23, 1992, Harvey and Tinsley Penick Collection, Stark Center.

"You just wouldn't believe": John Garrity, "The Little Red-Hot Book: At the Age of 87, Legendary Golf Teacher Has Become a Best-Selling Author," *Sports Illustrated,* August 10, 1992.

"If they read my": Gary Cartwright, "The Old Man and the Tee," *Texas Monthly,* December 1993, p. 174.

241 *"'There,' Neuman said,"*: Ibid.

"the best selling": Simon & Schuster news release, February 1, 1993.

"I'm glad to see": Harvey Penick, interview with Bud Shrake, January 26, 1993, audiotape, Harvey and Tinsley Penick Collection, Stark Center.

242 *The editor of* Golf Digest: Jerry Tarde, letter to Bud Shrake, September 29, 1993, Harvey and Tinsley Penick Collection, Stark Center.

250 *"I sense from hanging"*: Bud Shrake, letter to Esther Newberg, May 16, 1994, Edwin "Bud" Shrake Papers, The Wittliff Collections, Texas State University–San Marcos.

"At the age of ninety": Ibid.

"What a great feeling": Bud Shrake and Mickey Wright, Septem-

ber 16, 1994, interview transcript, Edwin "Bud" Shrake Papers, The Wittliff Collections, Texas State University–San Marcos.

CHAPTER FIFTEEN

256 "Joe Kirkwood was": Harvey Penick and Bud Shrake, *Harvey Penick's Little Red Book* (New York: Simon & Schuster, 1992), p. 168.

257 *"You're the only man"*: Herbert Warren Wind, *The Story of American Golf*, 3rd ed. (New York: Alfred A. Knopf, 1975), p. 525.
"Hitting trick shots": Penick and Shrake, *Harvey Penick's Little Red Book*, p. 167.

258 *"Helen [Penick] realized that"*: Tim Rosaforte, "Golf's Grand Old Man," *Sports Illustrated*, October 31, 1994, Harvey and Tinsley Penick Collection, Stark Center.
"There's not one person": Ibid.

259 *"I could never have imagined"*: Del Lemon, "Penick Took Joy in Success of a Student Until the End," *Austin American-Statesman*, April 6, 1995, Harvey and Tinsley Penick Collection, Stark Center.
"Harvey's purpose in making": Harvey Penick and Bud Shrake, *The Game for a Lifetime: More Lessons and Teachings* (New York: Simon & Schuster, 1996), p. 13.

260 *"I can't do it"*: Ibid., p. 15.
"Harvey is still hanging": Bud Shrake, letter to Jeff Neuman, March 27, 1995, Edwin "Bud" Shrake Papers, The Wittliff Collections, Texas State University–San Marcos.

261 *"You'd better hurry"*: Turk Pipkin, "A Final Lesson from Harvey Penick," original obituary prepared for the *Austin Chronicle*, undated.
"His game was all": Davis Love III, *Every Shot I Take: Lessons Learned About Golf, Life, and a Father's Love* (New York: Simon & Schuster, 1997), p. 166.

262 *"I can't die tonight"*: Mark Rosner, "Penick Buried with Tool of His Well-Loved Trade," *Austin American-Statesman*, April 5, 1995.
"Mr. Penick said": Mark Wangrin, "Smile of Satisfaction Lives Through Statue of Penick," *Austin American-Statesman*, April 5, 1995.

263 *"She walked up to"*: Ibid.

"*the look of satisfaction*": Ibid.

266 "*I've collapsed a lot*": Robinson Holloway, "That's the Ticket," *Golf World,* April 7, 1995, p. 22.

CHAPTER SIXTEEN

269 "*Penick remained a hidden*": Mark Rosner, "Penick Buried with Tool of His Well-Loved Trade," *Austin American-Statesman,* April 5, 1995.

270 "*Heaven is a better*": Bud Shrake, "Harvey Penick Gave a Lifetime to the Game," *New York Times,* April 9, 1995, p. 23.

274 "*The way I'm playing*": Davis Love III, *Every Shot I Take* (New York: Simon & Schuster, 1997), p. 170.

275 "*I haven't had a good*": Kirk Bohls, "Crenshaw, Kite: Bodies at Augusta, Not Their Souls," *Austin American-Statesman,* April 7, 1995. "*Ben's got a soft*": Ibid.

276 "*I was beginning to*": Ben Crenshaw and Melanie Hauser, *A Feel for the Game* (New York: Doubleday, 2001), p. 121.

277 "*I'll carry Harvey*": Ben Crenshaw and Carl Jackson, with Melanie Hauser, *Two Roads to Augusta* (Greenwich, CT: American Golfer, 2013), p. 175.

285 "I played it like": Thomas Bonk, "Crenshaw All Penick, No Panic," *Los Angeles Times,* April 10, 1995.

286 "*I don't know how*": Ibid.

287 "*It couldn't be a better*": Kirk Bohls, "In the Only Fitting Ending Possible, Crenshaw Follows Through on Dedication to Penick as He Dons a Second Green Jacket," *Austin American-Statesman,* April 10, 1995.

290 "*Answer this question seriously*": Bud Shrake, questionnaire for Harvey Penick, Edwin "Bud" Shrake Papers, The Wittliff Collections, Texas State University–San Marcos.
"*Penick has high hopes*": Holly Brubach, "Penick's Tips for Women," *New York Times,* June 11, 1995, Harvey and Tinsley Penick Collection, Stark Center.
"*Harvey Penick was a man*": House Resolution No. 698, House of Representatives of the 74th Texas Legislature, April 26, 1995.

291 "*The members have always*": Tinsley Penick, letter to the members of

Austin Country Club, August 24, 1995, Harvey and Tinsley Penick Collection, Stark Center.

"They don't know how": Del Lemon, "Penick Era Passing at Country Club," *Austin American-Statesman,* December 14, 1995.

CHAPTER SEVENTEEN

293 *"golf is character"*: Charles McGrath, "The Lives They Lived: Harvey Penick, Driving Force," *New York Times,* December 31, 1995.

294 *"As you both so"*: Terry Jastrow, letter to Tinsley and Helen Penick, October 22, 1996, Edwin "Bud" Shrake Papers, The Wittliff Collections, Texas State University–San Marcos.

295 *"He was always kind"*: John Maher, "For Decades, Women Golfers of All Levels Listened to Harvey Penick ... and He to Them," *Austin American-Statesman,* May 19, 1999, p. 1, Harvey and Tinsley Penick Collection, Stark Center.

"We will have no": Mark Rosner, "LPGA Honors Legend Penick with Austin Tour Event," *Austin American-Statesman,* October 6, 1998, p. C2, Harvey and Tinsley Penick Collection, Stark Center.

"Harvey would be so": Ibid.

EPILOGUE

301 *"To have played that"*: ASAP Sports, Masters Tournament press conference transcript, April 7, 2015.

Bibliography

Barkley, Mary Starr. *Travis County and Austin, 1839–1899.* Waco, TX: Texian Press, 1963.

Barkow, Al. *The History of the PGA Tour.* New York: Doubleday, 1989.

Berry, Margaret C. *UT History 101: Highlights of the History of the University of Texas.* Austin: Eakin Press, 1997.

Clavin, Tom. *Sir Walter: Walter Hagen and the Invention of Professional Golf.* New York: Simon & Schuster, 2005.

Companiotte, John. *Jimmy Demaret: The Swing's the Thing.* Ann Arbor, MI: Clock Tower Press, 2004.

Cornish, Geoffrey S., and Ronald E. Whitten. *The Architects of Golf.* New York: HarperCollins, 1993.

Crenshaw, Ben, and Melanie Hauser. *A Feel for the Game: To Brookline and Back.* New York: Doubleday, 2001.

Crenshaw, Ben, and Carl Jackson, with Melanie Hauser. *Two Roads to Augusta.* Greenwich, CT: The American Golfer, 2013.

Davis, Steven L. *Texas Literary Outlaws: Six Writers in the Sixties and Beyond.* Fort Worth: Texas Christian University Press, 2004.

———, ed. *Land of the Permanent Wave: An Edwin "Bud" Shrake Reader.* Austin: University of Texas Press, 2008.

Dodson, James. *Ben Hogan: An American Life.* New York: Doubleday, 2004.

———. *American Triumvirate: Sam Snead, Byron Nelson, Ben Hogan, and the Modern Age of Golf.* New York: Alfred A. Knopf, 2012.

Eubanks, Steve. *Augusta: Home of the Masters Tournament*. Nashville: Rutledge Hill Press, 1997.

Fehrenbach, T. R. *Lone Star: A History of Texas and Texans*. Boston: De Capo Press, 2000.

Frost, Mark. *The Grand Slam: Bobby Jones, America, and the Story of Golf*. New York: Hyperion, 2004.

———. *The Match: The Day the Game of Golf Changed Forever*. New York: Hyperion, 2007.

Giordano, Frank R., Jr. *A Chronicle of River Oaks Country Club*. Houston: Gulf Publishing Co., 1991.

Graffis, Herb. *The PGA: The Official History of the Professional Golfers' Association of America*. New York: Thomas Y. Crowell Co., 1975.

Hauser, Melanie, ed. *Under the Lone Star Flagstick: A Collection of Writings on Texas Golf and Golfers*. New York: Simon & Schuster, 1997.

Herskowitz, Mickey, and Tom Kite. *A Fairway to Heaven: My Lessons from Harvey Penick on Golf and Life*. New York: William Morrow and Co., 1997.

Hudson, David L., Jr. *Women in Golf: The Players, the History, and the Future of the Sport*. Westport, CT: Praeger, 2008.

Jenkins, Dan. *Jenkins at the Majors: Sixty Years of the World's Best Golf Writing, from Hogan to Tiger*. New York: Doubleday, 2009.

Kirsch, George B. *Golf in America*. Urbana and Chicago: University of Illinois Press, 2009.

Love, Davis, III. *Every Shot I Take: Lessons Learned About Golf, Life, and a Father's Love*. New York: Simon & Schuster, 1997.

MacCambridge, Michael. *The Franchise: A History of Sports Illustrated Magazine*. New York: Hyperion, 1997.

Merrins, Eddie, with Mike Purkey. *Playing a Round with the Little Pro: A Life in the Game*. New York: Atria, 2006.

Meyers, Reid E. *The Ghosts of Old Brack: A Pictorial History of the Brackenridge Park Golf Course*. San Antonio, TX: Reid E. Meyers, 2010.

Nelson, Byron. *The Little Black Book*. Arlington, TX: Summit Publishing Group, 1995.

Newberry, Kevin. *Texas Golf: The Best of the Lone Star State*. Houston: Gulf Publishing Co., 1998.

Penick, Harvey, with Bud Shrake. *Harvey Penick's Little Red Book: Lessons and Teachings from a Lifetime in Golf.* New York: Simon & Schuster, 1992.

———. *And If You Play Golf, You're My Friend: Further Reflections of a Grown Caddie.* New York: Simon & Schuster, 1993. Reprint edition published as *Harvey Penick's Little Green Book: Further Reflections of a Grown Caddie.* New York: HarperCollins, 1994.

———. *The Game for a Lifetime.* New York: Simon & Schuster, 1996.

———. *The Wisdom of Harvey Penick: Lessons and Thoughts from the Collected Writings of Golf's Best-Loved Teacher.* New York: Simon & Schuster, 1997.

———. *Harvey Penick's Little Red Book: Twentieth Anniversary Edition.* New York: Simon & Schuster, 2012.

Rapoport, Ron. *The Immortal Bobby: Bobby Jones and the Golden Age of Golf.* Hoboken, NJ: John Wiley & Sons, 1997.

Sampson, Curt. *Hogan.* New York: Broadway Books, 1997.

———. *The Slam: Bobby Jones and the Price of Glory.* Emmaus, PA: Rodale, Inc., 2005.

———. *Centennial: Texas Golf Association 110 Years.* Dallas: Brown Books, 2006.

Shelton, Emmett. *My Austin: Remembering the Teens and Twenties.* Boston: American Press, 1994.

Shrake, Bud. *Billy Boy.* New York: Simon & Schuster, 2001.

Strege, John. *When War Played Through: Golf During World War II.* New York: Gotham Books, 2005.

Texas Student Publications Inc. *The Cactus.* Gulf Publishing Co., 1931–1963.

Trimble, Frances G. *One Hundred Years of Champions and Change: The History of Austin Country Club.* Austin: Austin Country Club, 1999.

———. *Houston Country Club Centennial, 1908–2008.* Houston: Houston Country Club, 2008.

Van Natta, Don, Jr. *Wonder Girl: The Magnificent Sporting Life of Babe Didrikson Zaharias.* New York: Little, Brown, and Co., 2011.

Whitworth, Kathy, with Rhonda Glenn. *Golf for Women.* New York: St. Martin's Press, 1990.

Willoughby, Larry. *Austin: A Historical Portrait.* Norfolk, VA: Donning Co., 1981.

Wind, Herbert Warren. *The Story of American Golf.* New York: Alfred K. Knopf, 1975.

——— . *Following Through: Herbert Warren Wind on Golf.* New York: Ticknor & Fields, 1985.

———. *America's Gift to Golf: Herbert Warren Wind on the Masters.* Greenwich, CT: The American Golfer, 2011.

PHOTO CREDITS

Insert page 1, top left: Harvey and Tinsley Penick Collection, H.J. Lutcher Stark Center for Physical Culture and Sports, University of Texas at Austin

Insert page 1, top right: Harvey and Tinsley Penick Collection, H.J. Lutcher Stark Center for Physical Culture and Sports, University of Texas at Austin

Insert page 1, bottom: Crenshaw-Sayers Collection, H.J. Lutcher Stark Center for Physical Culture and Sports, University of Texas at Austin

Insert page 2, top: ND-50-269-02, Neal Douglass Collection, Austin History Center, Austin Public Library

Insert page 2, bottom: Harvey and Tinsley Penick Collection, H.J. Lutcher Stark Center for Physical Culture and Sports, University of Texas at Austin

Insert page 3, top: Harvey and Tinsley Penick Collection, H.J. Lutcher Stark Center for Physical Culture and Sports, University of Texas at Austin

Insert page 3, middle: Neal Douglass, *Austin American-Statesman*

Insert page 3, bottom: Associated Press

Insert page 4, top left: Harvey and Tinsley Penick Collection, H.J. Lutcher Stark Center for Physical Culture and Sports, University of Texas at Austin

Insert page 4, top right: Harvey and Tinsley Penick Collection, H.J. Lutcher Stark Center for Physical Culture and Sports, University of Texas at Austin

Insert page 4, bottom: Crenshaw-Sayers Collection, H.J. Lutcher Stark Center for Physical Culture and Sports, University of Texas at Austin

Insert page 5, top: Carrell Grigsby Photography

Insert page 5, middle: Tony Roberts/CORBIS

Insert page 5, bottom: Carrell Grigsby Photography

Insert page 6, top: Harvey and Tinsley Penick Collection, H.J. Lutcher Stark Center for Physical Culture and Sports, University of Texas at Austin

Insert page 6, middle: Carrell Grigsby Photography

Insert page 6, bottom: Bob Daemmrich

Insert page 7, top: Ralph Barrera, *Austin American-Statesman*

Insert page 7, bottom left: Ralph Barrera, *Austin American-Statesman*

Insert page 7, bottom right: Associated Press

Insert page 8, top: Drew Litton/drewlitton.com

Insert page 8, middle: Ralph Barrera, *Austin American-Statesman*

Insert page 8, bottom: Ralph Barrera, *Austin American-Statesman*

Index